# NO
# SYMPAThY
# FOR tHE
# DEVIL

# NO SYMPATHY FOR THE DEVIL

Christian Pop Music and the
Transformation of American Evangelicalism

David W. Stowe

UNIVERSITY OF NORTH CAROLINA PRESS   CHAPEL HILL

Library of Congress Cataloging-in-Publication Data
Stowe, David W. (David Ware)
No sympathy for the devil : Christian pop music and the transformation of American evangelicalism / David W. Stowe.
    p. cm.
Includes bibliographical references and index.
ISBN 978-0-8078-3458-9 (cloth : alk. paper)
1. Contemporary Christian music —
United States — History and criticism.
2. Popular music — United States — Religious aspects.
3. Evangelicalism — United States. I. Title.
ML3187.5.S78 2011
781.71′064 — dc22
2010041422

15 14 13 12 11  5 4 3 2 1

For Malcolm Magee

Introduction 1

# CONTENTS

# ILLUSTRATIONS

*For more images and video clips, go to*
*http://nosympathyforthedevil.wikispaces.com.*

# NO
# SYMPAtHY
# FOR tHE
# DEVIL

# INTRODUCTION

Sex, drugs, and . . . what else is there? The storied triumvirate of American youth culture since the Beatles. Three pillars that propped up much of the counterculture of the late sixties and that seem, despite the best efforts of moralists, politicians, and parents, to have fastened a kind of permanent grip on adolescents (and often postadolescents) coming of age in the leisurely fashion of recent decades.

Focused on one of the most powerful forms of American music, this book shows how that other famous trinity—Father, Son, and Holy Ghost—came to rub shoulders, hips, and thighs with rock 'n' roll. To some, the term "Christian rock" still rings oxymoronic, something like "Hindu abstract expressionism" or "Islamic comedy." But for many millions of Christians in the United States, Christian rock—more commonly known as contemporary Christian music, or CCM—is the default music of worship, sounding forth on Sunday mornings and evenings in thousands of churches across North America. The genre is familiar to anyone who has idly spun a radio dial, landing on a station that plays songs with a vaguely familiar sound but unexpected words dropped in—"Lord," "Jesus," "praise," and the like. CCM is now one of the fastest-growing genres of music, its records outselling those of classical, jazz, and New Age combined.

With roots stretching back to around 1970, the tail end of what most people consider the golden age of rock, Christian pop music has been around for forty years now. For the most part, these songs have existed in a kind parallel universe, off the radar screen of mainstream listeners and rock critics. But at some key junctures, they crossed into the world of mainstream pop music—or, perhaps, godless rock crashed into the tranquil subdivisions of young Christian listeners. This book tells the story of those crossings: what they reveal about rock 'n' roll music, American religion in the last generation or two, and the permanent changes occurring in American society during the seventies.

Popular music is often thought of as antireligious—look at the tension that long simmered between the blues and gospel—and this was especially so during the sixties and seventies, when rock 'n' roll was still relatively new and possessed of its in-your-face freshness. The Rolling Stones' "Sympathy for the Devil" captures this well, as do many other songs one could name: "Born to Be Wild," "Kick Out the Jams," "Paint It Black," "Why Don't We Do It in the Road?," and "Heroin."

But this impression is way off target. Popular music and religion have always been joined at the hip in America. I argue that the music of the late sixties and seventies, bookended by 1967's Summer of Love and the 1980 election of Ronald Reagan, helped create a space at the heart of America's commercial popular culture for talk of Jesus, God, and all things spiritual. Endorsed by several of the giants of American music, spiritually inflected pop offered an alternative to the nihilism and hedonism that accompanied the hangover from the sixties. The forms of music that emerged during the seventies can also, I believe, tell us a lot about the polarized, red-and-blue America of the twenty-first century, which is periodically addled by culture wars and paranoia. In short, I show that the spiritual emphasis of much of the decade's popular music helped baby boomers and their offspring form an image of religion that reinforced the messages delivered with increasing effectiveness by conservative evangelicals and the Religious Right.

Music did this in several ways. By getting the name of Jesus out into commercial culture through songs that rose high on the pop charts, music helped lessen the stigma of a religion that had seemed inextricably linked to square, Silent Majority culture. By inspiring new styles of worship, it made traditional religious beliefs seem relevant, even cool. The turn toward more-casual dress, less-formal liturgy, more-straightforward spiritual messages, and contemporary-sounding church music that everyone could sing without burying their nose in a hymnal—all this helped pack the evangelical Christian churches that sprung up after the seventies.

Once in church, the boomers and their kids imbibed a theology that emphasized traditional morality and gender roles—"family values" that helped conservative Republican politicians gain traction among voters. And the particular version of Christianity emphasized by much Jesus music focused on the imminent return of Jesus and the end of human history, a theology that emphasized personal transformation—saving souls for Jesus while there was still time—rather than attacking social inequalities or pursuing peace and justice.

This conservative turn among younger evangelicals has been well documented. A survey of members at influential megachurches to which many boomer evangelicals flocked found that only 6 percent identified themselves as liberal in 1992, while two-thirds labeled themselves conservative; their pastors leaned monolithically to the Right. By 2005 a survey of members at more than 400 megachurches found that the percentage of self-identified liberals remained at 6 percent, while 83 percent described themselves as somewhat or predominantly conservative. Even among the young people comprising the original Jesus Movement, many of whom began as political liberals, few remained liberal as they reached middle age, while the proportion of conservatives increased markedly. Studies that analyze voting patterns in terms of age and church attendance show that beginning in the 1970s, younger voters were becoming more conservative and Republican, while church-attending voters, including large numbers of baby boomers, were voting significantly more Republican. Evangelical Christians were also becoming increasingly well informed—and strategically mobilized—about political issues and elections at the local, state, and national levels.[1]

What role did music place in all of this? When we contemplate how music operates in people's lives, we face a conundrum: does music reflect the times, or does it shape them? The idea that popular music catches a particular tempo of the time or spirit of the age turns up in commentary about American music throughout the twentieth century but has its origins in the European Romantics of the early nineteenth century. But does music do more than reflect; does it actually alter the contours of history by working on people's conceptions of themselves, their communities, and their nation?

The answer is yes—of course it does. Our national life since the seventies simply would have unfolded differently in the absence of the musical developments that are described in the chapters that follow. To develop these arguments, I emphasize an understanding of music not as an artifact—a sound recording, sheet music, a set of song lyrics, or even a specific live performance—but as a social practice. Music draws on the contributions of artists and performers as well as audiences, listeners, and dancers. But music's meaning is also shaped by less obvious mediators: arrangers, producers, managers, agents, publishers, and critics. In the realm of religious music, ministers, worship leaders, and deacons also play crucial roles in determining which music gets heard and in what circumstances. This broader understanding of music less as a cultural object experienced individually through the sense of hearing than as a social activity produced by the complex interactions of people will guide my investigation of the emergence of Christian pop music as a pillar of evangelical culture.[2]

Likewise, my analysis depends on a more expansive definition of politics than is often assumed by people analyzing U.S. history. The seventies saw a major reorientation of U.S. politics as the nation was buffeted by traumas: the massive student strikes that followed the invasion of Cambodia in 1970, including the Kent State killings; the landslide election of Richard Nixon; recurring oil shocks and chronic inflation; Watergate; military defeat in Vietnam; and the protracted hostage crisis following the Iranian Revolution. But politics were being recast at the level of community, family, and the individual as well. People sought new answers to fundamental questions: How should one live a good life? What had become of the American Dream, or was that term obsolete? What did they owe their families, their communities, and their nation, and what was owed them?

Growing numbers of Americans were compelled to rethink basic assumptions about gender roles, about the proper arrangement and authority within families, about sexuality, and about the importance of ethnic or racial roots in determining one's personal allegiances. Increasingly, the personal was becoming the political. Well outside the domain of electoral politics, new forms of personal and group identity were being forged that would help reorient the political economy of the United States.

Popular music, along with many other cultural products like movies, television programs, journalism, and fiction, played a critical role in giving people a fund of resources for sorting out and positioning themselves in response to these challenges. In popular culture, people found narratives that helped make sense of their experiences and emotions; role models with which to identify; language to guide self-understanding and expression; and sound to move the body, lift the spirit, challenge the mind, and create bonds of community. Though ostensibly far removed from the world of institutional politics and generally experienced as entertainment or pleasure, music serves as a linchpin of this broad category often called cultural politics.

To map out these complex relations between society, art, politics, and religion, I draw on the notion of a "cultural front" developed by Michael Denning in his study of U.S. Popular Front culture in the 1930s and 1940s (which he in turn derives from the writings of Antonio Gramsci as interpreted and refined by Raymond Williams and Stuart Hall).[3] To borrow Denning's terms, my project involves seeing how American pop music converged with the social location known as the Jesus Movement to create a peculiar new cultural formation with unexpected consequences for the religious and political affiliations of large numbers of Americans. In broad terms, the music and movement were part of a larger groundswell that we call "the sixties": both shared what Raymond Williams called a "structure of feeling" with the hippie counterculture and, to a lesser degree, the politically charged New Left.

This theoretical model helps make sense of the cultural politics of the Jesus Movement and Christian pop music as flowing from both social affiliations and aesthetic ideologies — the politics of allegiances and the politics of musical form. It also offers a useful way of sorting out the various units of the "cultural apparatus" that inspired, produced, and distributed Christian pop: the spiritual and musical pioneers in the Bay Area and Southern California; the "movement culture" of the churches, intentional communities, and parachurch organizations that supported the Jesus Movement; and the interwoven culture industry of the record companies, radio stations, news media, Hollywood, and Broadway.

The roots of the late Cold War evangelical resurgence were diverse and complex. In the early sixties, many evangelicals cut their teeth on the presidential campaigns of Barry Goldwater. At the beginning of the seventies came the widely publicized appearance of the Jesus People — "Jesus Freaks," they were sometimes labeled — emerging from the drug-ravaged counterculture. These were kids who looked liked hippies but praised the Lord. For evangelical Christians, the twin national traumas of Watergate and the OPEC-led oil shock of 1974 were accompanied by a third catastrophic event: the decriminalization of abortion by the Supreme Court.

The Christian revival took on human form at mid-decade in the figure of Jimmy Carter, a born-again Baptist who taught Sunday school and made no bones about it. *Newsweek* declared Carter's election year, 1976, the "Year of the Evangelical," and Watergate convict Chuck Colson's *Born Again* became a best seller. More militant Christians were getting fed up and organized. Anita Bryant launched a crusade against gay rights in 1977. Two years later, Jerry

Falwell proclaimed the might of the Moral Majority and within a year had helped elect a president and depose several Senate liberals. By 1982 Phyllis Schlafly and her coreligionists had succeeded in derailing the Equal Rights Amendment, passed by wide margins in Congress and most state legislatures only a decade before.

These politics were often sharpened by an upsurge in Christian prophecy beliefs: the conviction that the end of human history is clearly foretold in the Bible, and that Cold War rivalries with the Soviet Union and shifting power balances in the Middle East signaled that the Second Coming of Christ — with its accompanying Armageddon — could be expected nearly any time. Thanks to best-selling books like Hal Lindsey's *The Late Great Planet Earth*, prophecy thinking penetrated the highest echelons of political and cultural power, from Ronald Reagan and George W. Bush to Bob Dylan.

The religious awakening was not only Christian and American; the seventies saw a dramatic rise in sectarian activity across the Muslim world, centered in the Middle East but stretching from North Africa in the west to Afghanistan and Pakistan in the east. In 1979 an Islamic revolution exploded in Iran, catching most of the world by surprise. And in a strange sort of synergy, Iran's Islamic revolutionaries joined forces with conservative Christians to drive a fellow evangelical from the White House. Much of our national life since then has involved an effort to understand and deal with the consequences of the worldwide revival of militant Islam and the fury and heat of politics in the Middle East, complicated further by the ascendancy of Christian revivalists in American politics.

My narrative thread begins in 1967 San Francisco during the Summer of Love, when a young couple from Iowa began witnessing for Jesus in Haight-Ashbury. Their most momentous catch was a young art student they met on the street, tripping on acid and ranting about flying saucers and Jesus Christ. Lonnie Frisbee would go on to become the emblematic Jesus Freak, a charismatic exhorter and healer who would ultimately die of AIDS. Chuck Smith, founder of Calvary Chapel on the coast in Orange County, invited Frisbee to join him as a youth pastor, and the congregation grew from 200 to 2,000 in six months. Teens gathered by the hundreds to be baptized in the surf, providing the iconic image of the Jesus Movement that burst into mass media consciousness in 1971. Pioneering Christian rocker Larry Norman enters the narrative at about the same time. Norman grew up attending a Baptist church in San Francisco but left because he hated the hymns. He started playing in rock 'n' roll bands and was offered a contract by Capitol Records at age eighteen. As a solo artist, Norman cut two of the founding albums of Christian rock, *Upon This Rock* (1970) and *Only Visiting This Planet* (1972), which contained the manifesto of the new music: "Why Should the Devil Have All the Good Music?"

The newly dubbed Jesus Movement was touched by the remarkable success of two Christian-based rock musicals of the early seventies: *Godspell* and *Jesus Christ Superstar*. Written by Brits, *Superstar* hit the United States first as a two-album record set released in 1970, selling 3 million copies in the first year and creating a media frenzy. *Godspell* and *Superstar* helped popularize a new image of Jesus Christ among the era's youth: a gentle rebel who reluctantly challenges the powers that be, lionized by his young acolytes but deeply ambivalent about the role he was expected to occupy. This resonated with the self-image of some of the decade's most famous musicians, including Dylan, who famously rejected the role of political/cultural messiah pinned on him by his worshipful fans.

Eventually, the evangelical Christian train emanating from Southern California picked up Dylan. To be sure, his interest in the Bible surfaced in some of his earliest songs. Through his friendship with Johnny Cash, Dylan helped link pop music to a musical scene that had long sanctified commercial entertainment with the Holy Spirit: country music. Cash had grown up in the hardscrabble Pentecostal religion of rural Arkansas, where he committed himself to Jesus at age twelve. After years of self-destructive behavior, Cash pulled himself together in 1968 with the help of June Carter, who steered him back to evangelical Christianity and married him. He included gospel songs in his famous concert albums recorded at Folsom and San Quentin prisons, yet he retained the irreverent outlaw image, clad in the black frock coat of the old-time Methodist evangelist.

Dylan had the ear of one prominent older evangelical, Jimmy Carter, who quoted the singer's lines frequently during his run for president in 1976. Beginning in 1979, Dylan announced that he was not just indebted to the Bible as a lyrical inspiration; he was a born-again Christian who took seriously the Second Coming and tried aggressively to win audiences over to the faith. Dylan's theology was shaped in the freewheeling evangelical culture of Southern California that Calvary Chapel and Larry Norman had helped create. Other notable converts from secular music included Barry McGuire, a star of the New Christy Minstrels and the Broadway production of *Hair*; middle-of-the-road star B. J. Thomas, famous for "Raindrops Keep Falling on My Head"; and Cat Stevens, who embraced Islam after nearly drowning off a Malibu beach.

Christian spirituality linked some of the dominant African Americans stars of the decade. Black music of the seventies was unmistakably shaped by the styles and messages of the church. Andraé Crouch became the soulful face and sound of the Jesus Movement. Billy Preston (who had sung with Crouch as a teenager), Aretha Franklin, and Marvin Gaye became superstars based on the singing style they had learned in church. Stevie Wonder's unsurpassed burst of musical creativity in the midseventies is shot through not just with the sonic signifiers of the black church but also with explicit prayers and supplications. Earth, Wind & Fire, perhaps the seventies' most successful black group, regularly laced their songs with lay sermons and prayers. Others turned to the spiritual from successful careers forged in secular music. Al Green was one, turning from a string of Top 40 hits in the early 1970s to buying his church and becoming an ordained minister in 1976.

Diverse as they are musically and otherwise, the individuals chronicled in the following pages are linked by one, certainly never more than two, degrees of separation. A few of them — Norman, McGuire, Cash, and Dylan — served, intentionally or not, as spiritual and musical connectors. These personal friends and connections help explain why I have chosen to discuss some musicians who may seem like far-fetched fellow travelers in either the musical or spiritual realms while ignoring others who by all rights belong in the narrative.

While many of the best-known musicians of the era were experimenting with evangelical Christianity in their lives and songs, born-again musicians were creating new music for use in churches. The impact of Jesus Movement popular music was not felt as much through album sales and radio playlists as through new styles of boomer-friendly worship music, which was invented in churches like Calvary Chapel and perfectly suited the larger theater-style churches that began to proliferate in the seventies. The first album of so-called praise music was issued in 1974. Nondenominational megachurches like Willow Creek Community Church, founded outside Chicago in 1975, pioneered the use of sophisticated sound systems and video projection screens in order to make worship visually and aurally accessible to people worshipping in enormous spaces. Amplified praise bands who led congregations through easy-to-sing choruses projected on overhead screens became the musical default setting of evangelical worship among boomer Christians, Generation X believers, and their successors.

In the end, evangelical worship music was transformed, as was the commercial world of Christian music. A musical genre that had emerged from the gritty amateur grassroots became increasingly sophisticated and market oriented. For a time, Christian labels attracted the attention of major labels, which acquired them then often dumped them when they didn't show the expected commercial results. Postboomer Amy Grant became the long-awaited crossover artist to accomplish significant sales outside the specifically Christian radio market. Through the nineties and into the new century, contemporary Christian music increased its market share and listenership, but to many who had helped create the Christian rock of the seventies, it had lost its soul.

There are many ironies and curiosities in this telling of the seventies. One is that the decade so widely associated with lowbrow junk culture—clothing, hairstyles, automobiles, decor, and, above all, music—actually produced the most influential and acclaimed styles of the last quarter century: punk rock and hip-hop. These may not be the genres that spring to mind, but both are unmistakable products of the day. The seventies is also regarded as a moral nadir, the decade of cocaine and casual pickups. It was the decade when the permissive attitudes of the sixties reached a mass audience before AIDS and the mainstream media began to push unruly Americans back into line. But it was also the decade that saw the founding of the Moral Majority. And there was this final irony: music that had been created to break down boundaries between Christians and non-Christians, to offer new sonic wineskins for the teaching of a new countercultural Jesus that would allow his message to reach thirsty nonbelievers, ended up hermetically sealed in its own new niche, the parallel universe of Christian popular culture.

My book shows how Christian pop music helped graduates of the Jesus Movement lay the groundwork for the reorientation of American society, politics, and religious culture that began in the seventies. Americans have felt these effects at the level of family and congregational life and in the development of a distinctive evangelical popular culture, but also at the level of local, state, and national politics. By helping elect Ronald Reagan as president in 1980, boomer evangelicals helped create a political style and voting coalition that has shaped national ideology and public policy in fundamental ways, even into the era of Obama.

Chapter 1

# JESUS ON THE BEACH

Hundreds of long-haired kids cluster around a public beach, perching on rocks overlooking Pirate's Cove, a small inlet off Corona del Mar near Costa Mesa, California. Cars jam the parking lot, full of blissful teens and twenty-somethings singing gospel songs they've just learned. People emerge from cars and find spots on the beach, singing, greeting strangers, and encouraging them to know Jesus. The sound of young voices and guitars mixes with the rolling surf and breezes streaming off the Pacific. People of all ages are there: surfers; kids in cutoffs, bikinis, tie-dyed shirts, or long granny dresses; vacationing families; relatives on hand to witness the occasion; and curious onlookers. People are hugging and crying.

Out in the water, a balding, football-coach-looking guy is performing baptisms, speaking a few words to each teenager before plunging him or her back into the Pacific. He tells each what baptism means: a chance to begin life afresh, to bury one's frailties and bad choices in the ocean and emerge from the water with new life in Jesus Christ. Near him, a long-haired, biblical-looking freak is doing the same thing—praying and dunking. Several hundred young people might be baptized in the course of an afternoon, sometimes upwards of a thousand. These beach baptisms happen about once a month.

The older guy is Chuck Smith, who built a tiny church in Costa Mesa, Orange County, into a congregation of thousands. His young sidekick is Lonnie Frisbee, who became the public face of the Jesus Movement of the early seventies. They make an unlikely pair, this square and this hippie, but their words and actions synchronize perfectly.

What attracts these kids to Pirate's Cove? Some are drug burnouts, runaways, pregnant teens, survivors of the harsher directions taken by the California counterculture. A writer named Brian Vachon reported his conversation with a girl named René who had just been baptized. Weeks earlier, she had turned up "stoned and scared" at one of the Christian crisis centers that were proliferating in Southern California and the Bay Area. "But on that day, I asked Jesus to come into my heart, and he's been with me ever since," she told Vachon.

> "But how long is it going to last?" I asked.
> "It's going to last forever. There isn't anything else."
> "You look very beautiful."
> "You see the Lord in me."
> "You also look very cold."
> "I'm not at all. I'm just filled with the Holy Spirit."
> "And you also look a little stoned."
> "I am stoned. I'm stoned on Jesus. Only it's far better than being stoned. Drugs are a down. This is the most incredible up in the world. I feel like I'm floating all the time, with Jesus."

Deciding he "didn't at all want to leave this shivering, frail, absolutely lovely and radiant young lady," Vachon got René to explain the Rapture to him.[1]

The media loved the Renés of the Jesus Movement, and there were plenty of them. But many were basically straight, rule-following teens looking for an identity, a spiritual difference. Thom Granger, who became active at Calvary Chapel and played in a Christian rock band, was no acid-dropping Frisbee but rebelled in his own way.

> I was pretty much a good kid. I wasn't involved in any hard drugs. Lonnie had a much more colorful preconversion experience. In my own suburban, baby boomer way, this was my big rebellion. Because I wasn't from a Christian home. My dad, he wasn't an atheist, but he was an agnostic and wasn't interested in going to church or organized religion. So in a way it was the perfect rebellion. Because I was not only able at seventeen—which is when you are probably the biggest

brat you can ever be to your parents — not only was I able to stand up to him, but I had the authority of God, supposedly. So, the ultimate name dropping. Now it's not just me disagreeing with you, Dad. It's "God disagrees with you, Dad. You're wrong and God said so." It worked really well and made him just absolutely livid. So I accomplished a great deal of good adolescent rebellion with these very clean means. It was amazing.

Granger described his own beach baptism as a momentous event in his young life.

I was invited by this group of Christians at my high school who had embraced this and were meeting with Lonnie once a week. And they were saying to me, "You gotta come down to the beach." Well, I was seventeen years old. I didn't have a car. And this was at Newport Harbor High School. Corona del Mar is not right around the corner. It's quite a ways away. I walked from high school, right after school I took off on foot, and walked all the way to Corona Beach, which was probably about a two-hour walk. I got down there completely alone, completely by myself, not really sure what I was doing but pretty sure I wanted to do it.

When I got there, there was a group of kids on the beach who had made a circle. Pirate's Cove was where it happened, a small little inlet off the main beach, off a jetty. There was a small group of people that were there early. Somebody had written in the sand, on a very large scale, "Jesus Loves You." And I saw that from up on the rocks. It was like, okay, this must be the place. It was a little like, "You Are Here." And I went down there and just started meeting a bunch of strangers, who of course welcomed me in that lovely hippie love, sort of flower-child manner that was happening at that time. And immediately I had a family. Immediately I was embraced. Immediately it was very warm and fuzzy. It really, really was. There were songs, and holding, and embracing. At the end of it I was in wet blue jeans and had to walk two hours home to frightened parents who wondered where the hell I had been. (We didn't have cell phones then. I'm sure I would have turned it off anyway.)

This was definitely my little rebellion, in a funny kind of way. Despite the positivity of all that, there was for certain of us a sense of rebellion about it. And it was personal. "This is not going to be about mom and dad, this is not going to be about anybody. This is my choice, my life." This was probably the biggest decision on my own in my life at that time.[2]

Jesus People, sometimes known as Street Christians, came in multiple varieties. The most colorful bunch, beloved by the media, were the hippie-styled Jesus Freaks who favored long hair, bare feet, and blissful smiles and gravitated easily to communal living arrangements. Some Christian ex-hippies intentionally dropped the outward signs of counterculture grooviness as unsuited to their new lives. A majority had never adopted those trappings. They came out of ordinary evangelical church backgrounds and had been organized by groups like Campus Crusade for Christ, InterVarsity Christian Fellowship, Young Life, and Youth for Christ, so-called parachurches that had little use for denominations and their fine-tuned differences and jealousies. *Time* described them as "Middle America, campus types: neatly coiffed hair and Sears, Roebuck clothes styles." A third cohort were charismatic Catholics, loyal to the church but given to ecstatic and unconventional practices like speaking in tongues.[3]

"Many of the Jesus Freaks are from broken or unhappy homes," observed Lowell D. Streiker, who wrote a book titled *Jesus Trip*. "Some are from the major urban ghettoes. Some are from very wealthy families. But for the most part the parents of the Jesus people are 'middle Americans'—hardworking, average income, 'one home in the suburbs, two cars in the driveway, summer at the seashore' Americans. They believe in God, send their children to Sunday school, occasionally attend church themselves, worry about property values, taxes, and layoffs at the plant." Most of all, they share a belief in "the American way of life": hard work, family, and the pursuit of happiness.[4]

Marsha Stevens—who would go on to great popularity among Jesus People as a member of the singing group Children of the Day—was sixteen when she accompanied her older brother to a gathering of youth from Calvary Chapel. Their home was a troubled one; their father was a minister with a history of molesting kids in the congregation, and their mother was an alcoholic. "It was the first time I'd heard people talking about Jesus as though he were alive," Stevens recalled. "And I thought, these guys are nuts—that's whacked! So I figured I'd go home and forget about it. But as I listened to them, they chitchatted about Jesus: 'Jesus told me this and said that.' How can they believe that stuff? But all week long I thought about how cool it would be to think Jesus really cared about your life."[5]

The next week, Stevens returned to worship in the unfinished Calvary

Street Christian evangelizing in Southern California (Image © Jack and Betty Cheetham; courtesy of Special Collections, Michigan State University Libraries)

Chapel and uttered her first genuine prayer. "I knew that my life had changed forever," she said. "I knew that nothing from that moment forward would ever be the same. And that's been true." A couple of weeks later, she packed an extra pair of jeans for Bible study and went down on Monday night at 11:00 P.M. to the 19th Street bay in Newport. She had written a short song, "For Those Tears I Died," to share her new faith to her friends and younger sister, and they had sung it once together at Calvary. As a surprise, everyone on the beach had learned it and joined in the singing as Stevens emerged newly baptized from the Pacific. Word got around; a few weeks later, Pat Boone called to ask Stevens if he could sing her song.[6]

Nearly all Jesus People fit into the loose category of evangelical—born again, focused on a personal relationship with Jesus, reverential toward the Bible as inerrant, and determined to spread their faith. Most engaged in public witnessing, seeking converts with greatly varying degrees of skill on city streets, public beaches, and other places that young people gathered. The majority of Jesus People stressed the imminence of the end times when Jesus would return to claim his faithful followers and leave the rest to their scripturally ordained, unpleasant fates. They extended and accepted generosity, opening rooms and houses to strangers in need. Some communities modeled themselves on the early church, with healing and speaking in tongues and other gifts and signs.

*Look* magazine produced one of the first articles to fan public interest in the movement.

> The Jesus movement seems to be springing up simultaneously in a miscellany of places, and often in the last places you would think to look. But maybe, because this is California, this should be the first place to look. In Orange County, an entire motorcycle gang converted. In Anaheim, a huge entertainment complex called Melodyland has been taken over by a nondenominational, solidly middle-class religious group. Dozens of go-go clubs throughout the state have been turned into religious coffeehouses, where kids go to sing and pray. Fundamentalist religious clubs are forming on the campuses of California—Stanford, Berkeley, and UCLA. Businessmen are turning their $40,000 homes into communes to give temporary shelter to runaways. Hundreds of ministers are joining this nondenominational movement, which has been swelled by tens of thousands of new converts. Young volunteers from all over are being invited to high school assemblies, singing rock/religious songs and giving testimony.[7]

On the other side of the continent, a Boston discotheque called the Boston Tea Party hosted "An Evening with God" for young spiritual seekers. "The ushers in beads and 20 wonderful girls in miniskirts passed out the wine and the home-baked bread," recalled Harvard theologian Harvey Cox, who organized the event with a woman named Sister Mary Corita. "Dan Berrigan read his poems and Judy Collins sang. Corita had a rock band and strobe lights going, and pretty soon everybody was dancing in the aisles." Cox explained: "Post-industrial man is rediscovering festivity. In churches all over the country there's been this eruption of multimedia masses, jazz rituals, folk and rock worship services, new art and dance liturgies. You know, there's always a John Wesley around to wonder why the Devil should have all the good things. Judson Memorial in New York and a few other churches have had 'revelations,' the nude dancers in psychedelic lights at the altar."[8]

Southern California may have been the epicenter — the "Burned-Over District" — of the Jesus Movement, but multiple networks linked young Christians across the country, from major cities to small towns in the heartland. In the Pacific Northwest, an evangelist named Linda Meissner in 1967 began recruiting young converts to what would be called the Jesus People's Army. Raised a Methodist in Iowa, Meissner honed her missionary skills through stints in New York City, the West Indies, Mexico, and Hong Kong before being called to Seattle, where she concentrated on reaching street people. An enterprising *Detroit News* reporter named Hiley H. Ward crisscrossed the country interviewing, and sometimes impersonating, Jesus People. Aside from multiple visits around California and Michigan, he found activity in Seattle, Vancouver, and Portland, Oregon; Chicago, Milwaukee, Detroit, Ann Arbor, and Toronto; and Worcester, Massachusetts, and Washington, D.C. So did Glenn D. Kittler, an editor for *Guideposts* magazine who visited dozens of communities and interviewed hundreds of young Christians over the course of a 10,000-mile trek.[9]

Jerry Bryant, one of the early figures in Jesus music radio, grew up in Carbondale, Illinois. The son of a Methodist minister, he was turned off by mainline Christianity, in whose churches long hair and blue jeans were not welcome.

> I remember being in my hippie Volkswagen van . . . and I was headed out to California. I got so busy having a great time I didn't pay any attention to the engine light. And my engine seized because of a lack of oil. And outside of Albuquerque, New Mexico, there I am in the middle of nowhere, stranded. And within just moments, some

Jesus Freaks showed up, asked me what was wrong, and I told them. Within an hour or so, I was sitting around a table, having dinner, had a place to stay, and they had hauled my Volkswagen back to a friend's garage to work on. (It was gone, unfortunately; I had to leave it in Albuquerque.)

But so many times, Jesus houses along the way, Jesus communities, were springing up everywhere. And people were doing things as you would have imagined it in the second chapter of Acts. For love, not for denomination or organization. Just simplicity, love. I don't know how we networked without e-mail and cell phones, but somebody knew somebody who knew somebody who knew somebody. And it wasn't long before you arrived in a city that you could probably find a Jesus house for a meal and a place to sleep if you wanted to. We had in Carbondale a brother's house and a sister's house that I raised up along with my coffeehouse. . . . We could take in people. And then of course we had the coffeehouse as a connecting place. And that's where my first church started, out of a coffeehouse. . . .

So we were right square dab in the middle of it. And a lot of it was the power of it just catching. It's much better caught than taught, John Wimber [founder of the Vineyard] used to say. . . . It was caught like a virus in the air, you know. We didn't have much to say about it except yield or be totally miserable. The guy I started the coffeehouse with told us all — this was after he was with us and as a Christian — he said, "I hitchhiked from California and back seven times to get away from God and inevitably on every trip I'd get picked up by a Christian hitchhiking and they would preach to me." And he just said: "All right, I got it. I'm not going to resist this any longer."[10]

Nearly all of these Jesus communes and coffeehouses were ephemeral, but a few survived. Nearly forty years after its founding, Jesus People U.S.A. (JPUSA) continues to operate an intentional living community in Chicago with hundreds of members and several businesses and social-service agencies. JPUSA dates back to 1971, when Jim and Sue Palosaari, charismatic Street Christians from Seattle with connections to the Jesus People Army, migrated to Milwaukee in the hope of starting an outpost among the disaffected youth of the Great Lakes. "I think the future strength of the Movement is here in the Midwest," Palosaari told Kittler. "California is full of transients. It always has been and it always will be. I know; I've lived there. Here in the Midwest, the current crop of transients is already in California. What we have left are more stable people. They're going to hang around. What they build will live."[11]

Over the course of the year, Milwaukee's Jesus People grew to more than 150 adherents, including a talented hard-rock guitar player named Glenn Kaiser. They then amicably broke up into smaller cohorts. One, led by the Palosaaris, formed a group called the Sheep and headed off to evangelize Europe. Another fragment, featuring Kaiser on lead guitar, his wife Wendy on vocals, and Wendy's brother John on drums, crowded onto a psychedelic school bus and headed south, playing music and preaching the Gospel. After a disappointing stand at the University of Florida in Gainesville, the entourage headed north and decamped, for no particular reason, in Chicago. Now known as the Resurrection Band, the musicians became the nucleus of JPUSA and still guide the community.[12]

If one ingredient held this human stew together, it was music. "The ability of Jesus rock and gospel melodies to generate rich, powerful feelings in a mood- and emotion-oriented age has brought and held the movement together," wrote sociologist Robert Ellwood in a perceptive 1973 study. "It is largely music that has made the movement a part of pop culture, and it is the Jesus movement as pop culture that distinguishes it from what is going on in the churches."[13] Acoustic guitars were ubiquitous in the communes, coffeehouses, and worship services where Jesus people congregated, and everybody sang along. Predictably, rock 'n' roll was regarded with some suspicion by the over-thirty people who often provided a modicum of guidance to the living spaces and worship services. Bethel Tabernacle, a rough-and-ready church in North Redondo Beach near Los Angeles that attracted numerous Jesus People, collected a huge pile of discarded secular rock albums in a corner of the sanctuary, a sign of abandoning the sinful blandishments of the world.

But virtually anything went when congregations gathered to worship, as Streiker observed at a gathering of a commune called the Christian Foundation in a barren canyon north of Los Angeles.

All the doors and windows were closed, and the body heat of two hundred wildly gyrating bodies raised the room temperature to well over one hundred degrees. Here was an old-fashioned revival service, with the beloved gospel songs ("What a Friend We Have in Jesus," "Amazing Grace," etc.), a ceaseless stream of personal testimonies (I counted forty), instrumental and vocal solos ("And now Sister Mary Jane will sing 'In the Garden'"), duets, trios, and a frenzied "Hallelujah Chorus" sung by the forty testimony givers (thus revealing that the spontaneity of the service was more apparent than real). Never have I seen such energy, such fervor, such body-and-soul enthusiasm spent on religious worship. They were on the edge of hysteria the entire time. Arms lifted heavenward, feet stamping, all stops pulled, they screeched song lyrics unto God, moaned and groaned, shuddered and had fits.[14]

Like its secular counterpart, Jesus music was often earsplitting. Despite the genre's repertoire of old-time camp-meeting songs (and general suspicion of commercial rock), electronic enhancement was okay. "Though the natural amplification verges on the threshold of pain," wrote another observer, "microphones bracketed to beams in the ceiling pick up and magnify the uproar. The effect is that of a spiral, each voice gaining intensity in an effort to be heard over an ever-increasing level of sound."[15]

"Music is the language of this generation, and we speak it," insisted David "Moses" Berg, who founded the Children of God, the most infamous of the Jesus Movement sects. "Our music is the miracle that attracts so many to our message about the Man. It's the magic that heals their souls and wounded spirits and proves our messiahship, that we are their saviors." Observers were struck by the group's Friday and Saturday "celebrations," when members would dance "in the Spirit" to the accompaniment of electric guitars and drums: "To see the Children in one of these uninhibited songfests is to see them at their very best. Spotlights are turned on the musicians; the lights are turned low in the rest of the room; and an eerie green light gleams in a corner. The loud music crashes through the room, overwhelming the senses. The Children clap with the music, sing enthusiastically, and dance the Hebrew folk dances, either in couples or in circles."

The group created prickly house music of their own: the Beatles' "Lucy in the Sky with Diamonds" became "Jesus in the Sky with Angels." Another song expressed grim satisfaction over America's many late-sixties travails: "Three cheers for the red, white, and blue / You've turned your back on God / Now he's turned his back on you."[16] The Children scored one of the earliest defections from secular music with the conversion of Fleetwood Mac guitarist and vocalist Jeremy Spencer. Distrusted by most other Jesus People, Berg's followers would become infamous as the seventies wore on.

Even for young Christians who intentionally distanced themselves from mainstream rock, the draw of loud ecstatic music was always present. And many found it easier to give up (or never try) free love and drugs than to give

up rock music. It was especially hard in California, with its booming music scenes both in San Francisco and Los Angeles. The Jesus Movement spanned the peak years of musical creativity in the Bay Area, when venues like Fillmore West and artists like Janis Joplin, the Jefferson Airplane, and the Grateful Dead were claiming a national audience. In Los Angeles, bands like the Doors, the Byrds, and the Mamas and the Papas ruled the clubs on Sunset Strip. It was no coincidence that Haight-Ashbury, Hollywood Boulevard, and Sunset Strip were hotspots for street witnessing and coffeehouses run by Jesus People.

"Music was so damn important to the baby boomers," insisted Granger. "To this day, it still is. And I see how . . . even though there's plenty of music in my kids' lives, it doesn't play the same role. I would even use the word 'prophetic' role, and I use that in a theological sense. Even for the nonreligious of us, music played that prophetic role. When the Beatles made a new recording, when Dylan made a new recording, people went out and bought it *immediately* and sat down and listened to it like he was an avatar. *What do you have to say to us, O Mighty Bob?* People don't get that now." A few elders grasped the power of this music. "Here I began to feel the full weight of the cultural revolution," wrote Don Williams, a sympathetic Presbyterian pastor from Hollywood, about the music of the counterculture. "And here I found a great secret: music is the key to this generation because music is the one place in the mass media where kids editorialize to kids." This wasn't necessarily a good thing. "Look at the mob that went to Woodstock," Williams told Kittler. "Jesus wasn't there. The kids spent a week getting stoned and smashed and pregnant. I feel that love died at Woodstock for the kids who were there. I doubt that rock could ever pull off another Woodstock. But rock-gospel could. And Jesus would be there."[17]

Most Christian kids faced a dilemma: their parents, pastors, and youth ministers told them that rock was unfaithful, the work of the devil, or at best irrelevant to their spiritual lives. John Styll grew up attending a Presbyterian church in Newport Beach, a few miles from Calvary Chapel. But he traveled in Calvary circles. He attended the same middle school as Lonnie Frisbee and knew Chuck Smith Jr. from high school. (He would go on to work at Calvary, be married by the elder Chuck Smith, and found *Contemporary Christian Music* magazine.) Styll remembered clearly being at church with the Presbyterian youth group, practicing one of the Christian youth musicals much beloved by tuned-in youth ministers. "And it was a good one, we were all into it and enjoyed doing it. But culturally it didn't connect to us," he said. "I remember I would get in the car and leave the church and turn on the local

rock station and listen to the Doors or the Stones, Hendrix—stuff I was into. Life was compartmentalized."[18]

Sometime later, the teens first heard one of the early Maranatha! albums, probably a compilation called *The Everlastin' Living Jesus Music Concert.* "And I remember it being at someone's house, after our Sunday night youth group," Styll recalled. "We all got together and had ice cream or something. And we played that record over and over and over. It just played and played. We were so fascinated by what it was. It was a real record, but it was our music."

## Dirty Hippies

Historians date the beginning of the Jesus Movement to 1967, the year of San Francisco's famous Summer of Love. That winter, a thirty-year-old sailmaker from Sausalito named Ted Wise and his wife, Elizabeth, became Christians. "I was confronted with the fact that I was always putting down Jesus and saying that they probably had it all screwed up," Ted recalled. "But I never actually read the New Testament. So I did. And I really liked Jesus. But he was so different than I thought he was. It was a complete surprise to me. He was *so cool.* I would have thought from what I heard around Christian people that he was a sergeant in the Marine Corps, you know? Or at least a Republican." During the Summer of Love, the couple began witnessing in Haight-Ashbury. Among their converts were a couple of Ted's old friends from Iowa, a disc jockey named Steve Heefner and a cigarette salesman named Jim Doop. Both had migrated to San Francisco for the drug scene. (Heefner reported that he took acid, lay down for a couple of hours, and got up a Christian.)[19] Another friend, Danny Sands, was inspired to sell everything he owned and drive up and down California with his wife and children proselytizing from a beat-up station wagon. Sands and his family eventually moved in with the Wises in Sausalito. Other new Christian friends joined them.

Aware of the dire conditions facing flower children on the streets of San Francisco, the group opened a storefront coffeehouse in Haight-Ashbury called the Living Room, where people came in from the street to rap about Jesus. Some local pastors kicked in some financial support, and the Living Room lasted two years. The hippie bait was a delicious homemade soup. "We used to sit around a table every evening and make the soup," explained one of the women. "During the day we'd go around to the butcher shops and get scraps of meat and bones, and we'd go to the produce markets and get the stuff that was too old to sell. But it was too old because it had ripened—it was perfect.

"Every night the soup we made was different," she continued. "We'd prepare the meat and vegetables and put them into the bowl and then let it all simmer on the stove overnight. The men would take it to the mission the next morning."

You never knew who might turn up at the Living Room. "I talked to Charles Manson almost all day once," recalled Ted Wise. "He came into the mission with about four girls. He was a kind of normal-looking chap, but he was very cold. His attitude was cold. I thought he was a speed freak. He wasn't open at all to what we were trying to say." Some 20,000 young people were witnessed to at the Living Room, according to historian Larry Eskridge.[20]

For all the street-level activity that sparked the beginning of the Jesus Movement, it would be inaccurate to ignore the role of older, more orthodox Christian figures laying the groundwork of the San Francisco Jesus scene. One was John MacDonald, pastor of a Baptist church in nearby Marin County, which Elizabeth Wise had begun attending periodically in 1965. After a time her husband Ted began joining her, eventually going forward to announce his conversion. By late 1966 the Heefners, Doops, and Sandses, all hippie friends of the Wises, had been baptized by MacDonald, who helped organize financial support from established Bay Area Christians for their street ministry in the Haight. Another early nonhippie Christian supporter was Baptist seminarian Kent Philpott, who befriended and eventually converted a devout Hare Krishna follower named David Hoyt, who was living in a lesbian commune at the time. Philpott and Hoyt went on to evangelize tirelessly on the street, founding a Christian halfway house called the Soul Inn in 1968.[21]

Meanwhile, the Wises' house had filled up with new Christians, and they moved to an old farmhouse on a tract in Novato. Still witnessing in San Francisco, they encountered a teenager on the street whose LSD-inspired rant had Jesus Christ emerging from a flying saucer. He turned out to be a fellowship student at San Francisco Academy of Art named Lonnie Frisbee. Just seventeen, Frisbee had recently landed in San Francisco from Orange County, where his grand vision of spreading Christianity among the masses had alienated his friends and family.

Frisbee had grown up in a troubled, blended home. His father had run off with another woman; his mother tracked down the jilted husband and eventually married him. As a kid, Frisbee was a self-described "frustrated Mouseketeer." Frisbee had a penchant for cooking and the arts. He won awards for his paintings and was a featured dancer on a local version of American Bandstand called *Shebang*, which was hosted by the young Casey Kasem. Frisbee exhibited a premature bohemian streak, painting his face half white and half black for dances at Corona del Mar High School. He periodically ran away from home. He also gravitated to marijuana and LSD, which he, like many of his peers, integrated into a spiritual quest.[22]

When tripping, Frisbee would read the Bible. One time, he led a group of friends into Taqhuitz Canyon in Idylwild equipped with oil paints, togas, pot, and LSD. Frisbee proceeded to paint a life-sized image of Jesus on the rock before opening his Bible to read to his friends about John the Baptist and baptizing them in the falls. If it happened in the Bible, Frisbee wanted to experience it; if it took psychedelics to boost the verisimilitude, so be it. A later acid trip in Taqhuitz produced a vision of a vast sea of people crying out to the Lord for salvation, with Frisbee in front of them preaching the Gospel. This was more than his friends or family could take, and he decamped for art school in San Francisco, where he had won a fellowship. Soon thereafter, he met the Wises on the street and was invited to join the Christian commune in Novato known as the Big House. He returned to his hometown to retrieve a friend, Connie, to whom he witnessed hard before getting her to accept Jesus. The couple lived platonically in the Big House until April 1968, when they got married.

By chance, Frisbee met Chuck Smith, a little-known minister in Costa Mesa who was struggling to grow a small, conservative, nondenominational church called Calvary Chapel. Smith was big, blond, balding, and old enough to be Frisbee's father. One journalist described him as a cross between a football coach and an airline pilot; he exuded gentle avuncular authority. Coincidentally, Smith had recently read a cover story about the Novato Big House in a magazine called *Christian Life* and wondered, along with his wife Kay, whether there was any way to reach the "dirty hippies" who were becoming increasingly difficult to ignore in their beach town. Smith had already been working with a young evangelist named John Higgins, a former racketeer and Catholic-turned-atheist who began witnessing on the street in San Francisco in late 1967. Higgins was moved by footage on the TV news showing people burying a casket to show that "God is dead." That day, he "decided to grow a beard, grow long hair and to go and talk to the kids because I knew the drug language." Smith gave Higgins his blessing.[23]

Like Higgins and Smith in the Bay Area, a couple of slightly older, traditional pastors played a role as midwives for the Los Angeles Jesus scene. Best known was Arthur Blessit, yet another Southern Baptist street evangelist. In 1968 he opened a popular mission and psychedelic coffeehouse called His Place on Sunset Strip, where fresh young converts were escorted to the bathroom to flush down their dope and pills. In order to blend in better, Blessit grew his hair and sideburns and began wearing bell-bottoms and psychedelic clothing. Also important was Don Williams, the college pastor at the large and wealthy First Presbyterian Church of Hollywood, who was drawn into counterculture ministry shortly after being recruited to the church in 1967. With generous support from the church, Williams was able to open a coffeehouse in 1968 equipped with "the best sound system money could buy at the time." Called the Salt Company, it became hugely successful and a model for hundreds of other Christian coffeehouses that began to spring up across the country in the following years.[24]

But Calvary Chapel, in archconservative Orange County, was destined to become the most famous outpost of the Jesus Movement. One night in March 1968, the Smiths' doorbell rang, and Chuck opened his front door to find his daughter's boyfriend standing next to Frisbee. Here was a bona fide dirty hippie. But when Frisbee shook his hand, Smith experienced a powerful bond and spiritual charge. He sensed that this young freak had unique powers. As a Jesus Freak, Frisbee showed a particular talent for the sorts of miracles associated with Pentecostal worship: healing, prophecy, and speaking in tongues. He owned a deerskin on which he painted an image of Jesus and wore as a cape. He would drape it over people while praying with them, and occasionally people would speak in tongues. For him, scripture was not finalized 2,000 years ago; it was set in the present, happening before our eyes. Kay Smith confirmed it in a prophecy: Lonnie and Connie Frisbee would have a powerful mission, starting on the West Coast and spreading across the United States and around the world.

By May, Smith had rented a small house, dubbed "House of Miracles," for the Frisbees and John Higgins to run as a halfway house for runaways. About a month later, the first guitar sounded at worship in Calvary Chapel.[25] Shortly afterward, Frisbee was ordained by Smith at Calvary Chapel. And under their dual ministry, the church began to grow, swelling from 200 members to 2,000 in about six months. They opened a tent to accommodate the young people who flocked to Calvary. Frisbee's Wednesday night Bible studies became legendary. With Smith, he baptized thousands in Pirate's Cove. His image turned up in the national newsmagazines and on network documentaries. Frisbee became the most visible face of the Jesus Movement (though he was usually unnamed in media coverage). "And the church for so long has been expecting a certain mold of what a Christian should look like or what a Christian should be or what a Christian should say," he said on one program. "And God is blowing everybody's mind. Because he's saving the hippies. And nobody thought a hippie could be saved."[26]

Glenn Kittler, just back from a mission trip to Sweden, attended a Frisbee-led Bible study at Calvary. "He was wearing a two-piece, Chinese-type suit," Kittler described, "that was white but which picked up flashes of pink and amber from overhead lights as he moved about. The sight of him silenced the crowd." Frisbee stepped to the microphone, pointed his index finger heavenward in a "Jesus People salute," told his followers "I love every one of you" in "a thin, high, boyish voice," and invited them to praise Jesus.

> The singing went on for an hour and a half, and it was terrific. The only person who used a hymnal was Frisbee himself, and he seemed to be using one just to pick out the next song. Some of the songs were rousing, some beautifully plaintive. One hymn — "Arky, Arky" — having to do with Noah's Ark, was perky fun with the animals coming aboard in "twosies, twosies," and it involved a great deal of gesturing, all of which the kids knew by heart. . . . Another hymn — "We Are One in the Spirit" — had a haunting melody and contained a moving thought. The last line went something like: "And they'll know that we are Christians by our love, by our love, oh, they'll know that we are Christians by our love." The kids sang it with such quiet sincerity and warmth that each time I heard it — three times that night, and other nights in other places — I found myself thinking: "I believe you."[27]

To save hippies, inspiring music was needed. Even churches intent on reaching out to youthful worshippers were almost hopelessly out of it. "Their idea of hip was a guitar playing Peter Paul and Maryish folk, and that really was about ten years behind," said Thom Granger. "And they weren't terribly interested in catching up." Chuck Smith had a taste for old-time gospel songs of the sort that Jesus People often sung boisterously, but something even more "now" was needed. Again, under Frisbee's direction, Calvary Chapel stepped into the breach. Christian folk-rock groups started to sprout, the better ones organized into a small label and booking agency called Maranatha! Music. "What God was doing among us created an immediate demand for something to sing," said Frisbee. "Music was the center of our culture."[28]

The best known of the Calvary groups was called Love Song. Its leader, Chuck Girard, had by then been around the musical block a few times. He was an established nightclub musician and spiritual seeker who began studying the Bible with musician friends around 1967. Their quest led them to Eastern religion, and Girard and a friend named Jay Truax sold their belongings and moved to Hawaii. "I went to the out-island of Kauai and lived in tents, or anywhere else I could find," recalled Girard. "I became a sort of 'holy man.' I sat on a rock for five or six weeks, and gradually I began to feel a sense of doing nothing for anybody."[29] On returning to the mainland, he was arrested in Las Vegas for possession of LSD. Back in California, Girard heard tales of Calvary Chapel from hippies they picked up along the Pacific Coast Highway.

"That's how we found Calvary Chapel," Girard recalled in an interview for the film *First Love*. "We were having a Bible study one night. We got in an argument . . . about tongues. We had no idea that was controversial. And we knew that there were a bunch of hippies that took over a whole hotel complex called the Blue Top at Newport Beach and they made a commune out of it. . . . We knew they were more Christian than we were. So we said, 'Let's go talk about this stuff in the Bible.' And we were all stoned."

The group drove the fifteen miles to the Blue Top and knocked on a cabin door. "I can kind of imagine the scenario inside," Girard continued. "These freshly born-again hippie Christians are in there saying, 'Lord, send souls to us.' And we're there with a Bible in our hand, stoned, saying, you know, can you tell us what tongues is about? They loved on us that night and told us about Calvary and Chuck Smith and excited our interest and a bunch of us went up that night."[30]

Girard was moved by the "cozy and warm atmosphere" of Calvary. "When I came in that night, it was in the little sanctuary, before they had the big tent," he recalled. "The people were all singing praises to God. It was a real feeling of love. I was twenty-six or twenty-seven by this time, and I wasn't too much into the emotional carryings on, but I could perceive emotions of a true nature. I was mentally and emotionally affected. The whole thing just hit me. I really could feel a genuineness in those people. I felt they really *did* know God. All the other people I'd talked to were always talking about a God that they had to attain, instead of the more personal concept of having him right now."[31]

"That night at that little commune, they invited us to stay for dinner and go to church," said Tommy Coomes, another band member. "In the name of being open-minded, we don't expect to find anything there, but we're going to go. When we got there, it scared me in a really good kind of way. 'Cause these people were so whole and loving and if I remember, Chuck Smith was talking about the end of the world. He was teaching about Revelations with this big grin on his face, and I said, man, this guy knows something I don't know."[32]

"I'd heard about Lonnie Frisbee," Girard said. "He was the hippie preacher there, and I was a little disappointed when Chuck Smith came out to preach that night. Chuck was an older man, but I decided to hear him out. He came out with this big grin and the whole thing was barraging me with images. What is this guy's trip? He doesn't look like the usual guy—the sober thing happening, with a robe and everything! This was more like a mellowed, relaxed atmosphere. He just started rapping. It was different. It wasn't like reading a portion from the Bible and then saying a bunch of words. It was like he was sharing someone he knew—Jesus Christ."

Coomes was impressed by both the straightforward message and the music: "They didn't read me the Four Spiritual Laws, they didn't ask me a bunch of questions, they didn't make me jump through hoops. . . . And the other thing that got me was that when they sang these simple little worship choruses, I knew that they knew God and that God was there. We all got saved within a month of that." Coomes and others were scheduled to appear in court for sentencing on drug-possession charges the next day. Upon hearing this, Smith said, "Let's just pray."[33]

Inspired, Girard retooled the band to reflect their new spiritual convictions—not always a familiar path for nightclub musicians. "About half of the songs on the album were written before we were Christians," Girard admitted. "When were we born again, you know? I thought we were Christians before we went to Calvary. A bunch of us, we actually went and got baptized because that's what the Bible told us to do, at a little Assembly of God church in Santa Ana somewhere. Then we went out and got stoned afterwards to celebrate." Despite certain doctrinal issues, Smith and Frisbee liked the songs, suggested a few lyric changes, and invited the band, now named Love Song, to play at Calvary. "All the gunk went away, and we revamped the lyrics to make them minister," according to Girard.[34]

The group enjoyed phenomenal success among Jesus People. It became the de facto "house band" of Calvary Chapel. Love Song's debut album was the first to be released on the Good News label and went on to sell well around the world, including rising to number one in the Philippines. And within six months of being sentenced on drug charges, the band played for an antidrug rally sponsored by the Costa Mesa police department. "Love Song had more popular appeal than the folk-type music that was germane to most hippie Christians who could play three or four chords on a guitar and could strum or pick, but not hammer out a screaming riff," said Chuck Smith Jr., son of the Calvary icon. "I cannot overemphasize that people heard the Christian message in their own voice. The reaction of hundreds of thousands of young people—even if Love Song did not sell hundreds of thousands of albums—was, 'Wow! This is my music and my faith.' The two had always been separated—at least since the advent of rock 'n' roll."[35]

## Warm Pickles

Despite a few institutional beachheads, the Jesus Movement was perpetually in motion. For every Christian band that recorded and developed some fame beyond Southern California, there were several that toured without leaving a recorded trace. One was Faith Flight, which featured Thom Granger on drums, guitar, or piano, depending on the need. Though loosely coordinated by Maranatha!, Faith Flight existed for years without a formal manager or booking agent and without cutting a record. (They did cut a two-song demo.) They mostly toured, playing at any church they could get into. "We'd be playing a Lutheran church one night, a Presbyterian Church the next, an Assembly of God the next, a nondenominational charismatic the next," recalled Granger. "You never knew what you were gonna get. Not a lot of Southern Baptists, because they were pretty closed to it at that time. And that was probably my favorite part of it."[36]

Conditions were bare subsistence. In some four years of playing "the circuit," Granger claimed, the band stayed in a hotel exactly once; the rest of the time, it was couches and floors of pastors and youth directors. The band barely scraped enough funds to pay for gasoline to get to the next gig. They might be offered a certain sum over the phone or a "love offering," whichever was greater, but often they were handed $100 and told, sorry, that's all there is. Faith Flight had to be prepared for anything when they arrived at a church. Sometimes a pastor would take one look at the drum set and tell them, "Nope, those aren't coming in this church." The band prepared an "unplugged" version of the entire set for those occasions: "Oh, acoustic set tonight!"[37]

Still, Faith Flight toured "like crazy" for the better part of four years. Their last tour took them through nine states in eight weeks, but they came back in debt. They still hadn't been offered a contract or cut a record. After praying together, Faith Flight decided to disband. Half an hour later, according to Granger, a Maranatha! staffer named Tom Stipe (coincidentally, the same Calvary pastor who baptized Granger in the Pacific) offered them a chance to record. After praying some more, the band stuck to its original decision: it was the end time.

Faith Flight's experiences were not exceptional among Christian rockers.

Randy Matthews, who went on to achieve considerable success in Christian music, recalled paying the same sort of road dues. "I learned that materialistic things, they just all pass away," he said later. "They're of no value really at all. . . . Another lesson that I learned was that dill pickles can be a great comfort to you. You can buy a five-gallon jar of dill pickles really cheap, man. What you do is get it and put it in the trunk of your car, and when you get hungry you open up that five-gallon jar of dill pickles, stick your hand down in the pickle juice, and you take out one big, green, warm dill pickle. After you've eaten one of those, you don't want to eat for a couple of days, anyway."[38]

Rick Warren, founder of Saddleback Church and author of *The Purpose-Driven Life*, was profoundly shaped by this itinerant scene.

I was working as a lifeguard and director of the campfire services at Cazadero Christian Camp in Northern California during the summer of 1970 where a revival broke out all summer. Some of the campers came up from Orange County and brought "Come to the Waters" and other early Jesus People songs. It was "our kind of music"—written by us, not for us, in contrast to the many youth musicals that were circulating in churches those days. We began to use them all at the camp and then where I went to high school that fall. The next year, 1971, I was the worship leader (with the requisite Martin D-35 guitar, long hair, and sandals) for a four-person team of kids that led "youth revivals" across Northern and Southern California. One of the host churches was in Santa Ana. I took the team over to Calvary Chapel, where we bought the first two albums, *Everlastin' Living Jesus Concert* and the first Children of the Day album. We rushed to a record player, soaked in the music, started using all the songs, and writing our own as well.[39]

In many ways, the lucky bands were the ones that got to stay in Orange County. Calvary started hosting free Christian rock concerts on Friday nights, then moved them to Saturday nights. Because of its explosive growth, the church met for a time under a large tent. "A couple of thousand people could be seated in the tent," according to Stipe, "so we wanted to have the concerts as often as possible." Calvary also sponsored concerts in public schools. The church minutes from March 1970 included a report by Chuck Smith on witnessing he had done at Huntington Beach High School, along with Frisbee and Love Song. "God's spirit was moving mightily and many of the young people gave their hearts to Christ, and many more were impressed to find out more about God and expressed a desire to attend Calvary Chapel," Smith reported. "Some of the young people who accepted Christ as savior actually turned in their drugs and drug-administering equipment then and there and said, 'At last they had found the real answer to life.' The teachers were excited about the program, and even some of them said they were going to come to Calvary Chapel, to find out 'What goes on?'" Smith emphasized that music was key to getting across the message and having it accepted: "He explained that in song, no one objected."[40]

Other high schools opened their doors to Calvary's Maranatha! bands: Children of the Day, Country Faith, Selah, Blessed Hope, Debbie Kerner, and, of course, Love Song. A story from a Long Beach newspaper reported that in March 1971, "six Jesus-rock groups with an anti-dope message turned the unassuming campus into a revival ground. Audience response was overwhelming." An earlier concert at another high school had resulted in more than 1,000 spectators being turned away. As a result, Maranatha! staged simultaneous concerts in the auditorium and gymnasium, with performers switching locations after each set. Even so, the crowds could not be accommodated. "Steps outside the auditorium were covered with silent devotees listening for strains of amplified heraldry," the story continued. "Many of the 5,000 seated inside had arrived as early as 6:00 P.M., anticipating a large turnout for the 7:30 P.M. concert."[41]

Orange County theme parks began to sniff a new market. They would close the park and admit only those with tickets to the concert. "Knott's Berry Farm started it, largely using Maranatha! groups. And they were hugely successful," according to John Styll. "You go to Knott's Berry Farm and hear Love Song and the Way, all these groups." A Love Song festival featuring several Calvary bands drew 20,000 people to Knott's, reportedly the largest nighttime crowd in the amusement park's history. Other theme parks took notice, and before long Disneyland and Magic Mountain were also featuring these semiprivate Christian music nights.[42]

Southern California's enthusiasm for Jesus music was not unexpected, given the role of the region as a petri dish for grassroots right-wing politics since the sixties. Lisa McGirr has traced the mobilization of "suburban warriors" who combined bedrock conservative values with an embrace of innovation, consumerism, and high technology. Originally galvanized by the threat of communism, the grassroots activists of Orange County built the modern conservative movement around the values of patriotism, individual initiative, free-market capitalism, distrust of government, and traditional moral values regarding sexuality, family life, and gender roles. The Barry Goldwater and Ronald Reagan campaigns provided a practical outlet for their energy.[43]

Calvary Chapel, with its relaxed style and welcoming attitude toward youth culture yoked to an anxious theology of judgment and apocalypse, was just one of many regional churches helping members reconcile tensions between the traditional and the modern. Nearby Los Angeles had spawned modern Pentecostalism and Sister Aimee Semple McPherson's wildly popular Foursquare Gospel Church. Robert Schuller established the first drive-through church in 1958 and opened the massive Crystal Cathedral in 1980. An evangelist named Ralph Wilkerson bought a seedy theater complex in 1969 and converted Melodyland into a church whose faith healing and uncompromising sermons attracted upwards of 18,000 people per week. Orange County was also a center of Christian broadcasting, including Charles Fuller's influential *Old Fashioned Revival Hour*, Charles Taylor's *Today in Bible Prophecy*, and the Trinity Broadcasting Network, which offered round-the-clock programming. In various ways, these churches and organizations were cutting-edge marketers seeking to reconcile modern technology and consumer society with a need for community and experience that felt authentic. In that way, they had something in common with the rebellious counterculture they generally distrusted and reviled.[44]

One way to capture this sometimes counterintuitive and unexpected continuity of values and orientations is what Raymond Williams first named a "structure of feeling." In his sweeping study of Popular Front culture of the 1930s and 1940s, Michael Denning defines structure of feeling as "a political and social charter for a generation." The notion of a sixties structure of feeling helps make sense of the succession of social and political attitudes that shaped the baby boom generation and linked the countercultural left of the sixties to the Jesus Movement and evangelical mobilizations of the seventies into the Age of Reagan and beyond. These patterns were identified both at the time and by subsequent scholars. Writing in 1973, Robert Ellwood listed a number of affinities between the counterculture and the Jesus Movement: an embrace of subjectivity as key to reality; the goal of life as a "high," whether through drugs or Jesus; the importance of music and visual arts; a strong sense of generational identity and cultural separateness; a suspicion of science, technology, and history; the call for a "new politics" animated by a crusading focus on particular issues rather than control of government; and an urban setting that idealizes a lost rural past.[45]

More than thirty years later, historian Preston Shires extended this analysis through the Jesus Movement to conservative evangelical activists of the eighties and afterward. He argued that baby boomers picked and chose among the mainstream values and attitudes of their parents—liberal theology, scientism, golden-rule ethics, intellectualism, affluence, and personal freedom. Americans who came of age in the sixties generally rejected both the liberal theology of the mainline churches and a secular faith in science and technology while embracing the golden-rule ideal ("Do unto others as you would have them do unto you") and personal freedom.

For Shires, Religious Right voters since the 1980s "owed a debt to the counterculture inasmuch as they upheld, in their minds, the golden-rule ideal, expressive individualism, intellectual sophistication, and an all-season antitechnocratic spirituality." Unlike many previous evangelicals, they refused to compartmentalize their faith, to distance themselves from popular culture, and to remain bound to traditions. As a result, he concluded, boomer evangelicals "had rejected the old mainstream, broken loose of the shackles of modernism, and reclaimed themselves and their godly potential in biblically grounded Christianity."[46]

Not that biblically grounded Christianity was the only spiritual destination for baby boomers. In *Getting Saved from the Sixties*, an influential work based on fieldwork and interviews conducted over the seventies, Steven Tipton studied three California faith communities that helped sixties youth establish a sense a moral compass and meaning in the wake of the counterculture's discombobulating impact on shared values and beliefs. Though the communities he studied—a nondenominational Pentecostal church, the Pacific Zen Center, and Erhard Seminars Training (*est*)—attracted members of very different class and educational backgrounds and differed in the values and beliefs they conveyed, all helped members reconcile certain values absorbed from the counterculture with the demands of a bureaucratic and technocratic society animated by capitalism. Extending Tipton's analysis, Stephen A. Kent emphasized the migration of sixties radicals into new religious movements, including Hare Krishna, Transcendental Meditation, Divine Light Mission, Meher Baba, Scientology, and the Unification Church. Disillusioned with the failure of their political organizing, Kent argues, activists became convinced that inner spiritual transformation was the only means for creating a better world.[47]

But in terms of membership and political influence, the new evangelical churches created by or for Jesus People would far outpace their spiritual counterparts among the alternative religious movements. And the musical innovations of the Jesus Movement were a crucial reason for this.

## Chapter 2

# JESUS ON BROADWAY

The most important early Christian rocker emerged out of a different orbit than the Orange County crowd turned on by Lonnie Frisbee. In contrast to Jesus People formed in the dense social network of Calvary Chapel, Larry Norman was always a bit of a loner, an odd man out. He came from San Francisco, grew his pale-blond hair really long, and rode a motorcycle, but otherwise he was straight as a razor. No acid, no dope, no ardent hippie chicks. Born in Texas in 1947, Norman retained a slight southern twang in his voice despite moving to the Bay Area at age three. Two years later, he accepted Jesus, the first of several conversions he would have; he also began writing songs. At age nine, he was performing his own music in public.

The oldest of four children, Norman grew up in a black neighborhood a few blocks away from the famous intersection of Haight and Ashbury. His grandfather had been a vaudeville actor, often playing Shakespeare, and his aunt toured the nightclub circuit with her own baby grand piano. Norman's father taught high school history, but at age ten he had played harmonica on his own radio show, accompanying his guitar-playing father. At ten, Larry began delivering newspapers for his grandfather in the Pacific Railroad hospital, distributing 500 copies a day. He got to play his grandfather's old 78s, including classics by Bert Williams, an African American vaudeville singer who would remain Norman's favorite. He also listened to Ethel Waters, Mahalia Jackson, and jazz trumpeter Lee Morgan. "I don't actually sing rock and roll," Norman said. "I sing black music, but I'm white."[1]

In 1966 Norman helped found a band called People! By that time, he had eclectic musical tastes. A band questionnaire identified his three favorite albums as Lee Morgan's *Sidewinder*, a jazz album, as well as Mose Allison's *Wild Man on the Loose* and the Beatles' *Revolver*; his favorite musician was jazz guitarist Django Reinhardt, and his favorite composer was Claude Debussy. And the Rolling Stones were—and still are—Norman's favorite band.[2] People! was signed by Capitol, the label that recorded the pre-Apple Beatles as well as the Beach Boys. To have a contract with Capitol in the late sixties was a big deal. Like other contemporary San Francisco bands—Jefferson Airplane, the Grateful Dead—People! was artistically ambitious. The musicians used elements of jazz and avant-garde art music, as well as the occasional experimental overdubs. Like the Mothers of Invention, their songs included multiple tempo shifts and meter changes. And they played their instruments furiously, at times being almost overwhelming in their energy.

People! songs mostly took on the challenges of girls and love. One of Norman's contributions cast a baleful eye on groupies, essentially telling them to get lost. But two of the songs clearly reflected his Christian concerns. "One Thousand Years before Christ" tackled the challenge of the end-times prophecy beliefs dear to most in the Jesus Movement. Norman's other apparently Christian contribution—"We Need a Whole Lot More of Jesus"— makes an uneasy contrast. He liked to tell the story that he quit People! when Capitol switched the band's debut album title from *We Need a Whole Lot More of Jesus (And a Lot Less Rock and Roll)* to *I Love You*, a single that reached the *Billboard* pop charts and sold a million copies; band members insist that the plan had always been to name their album after the hit single. In any event, "We Need a Whole Lot More of Jesus" is less revivalist jeremiad than lighthearted ribaldry. The track begins, "Let us all stand for this," with the scraping of chairs. What follows is unmistakably tongue-in-cheek. "We need more old-fashioned preachers / Pouring out their hearts in prayer," Gene Mason intones in a sanctimonious voice. "Cause when you're in their presence / Why you know that the Lord is there."[3] The effect is of the sort of parody running through the Beatles' *White Album*.

While the group never established itself as a top act, People! was successful enough to tour widely and play as the opening act for the Grateful Dead, Jimi Hendrix, the Doors, the Byrds, and others. This gave Norman a window into the stress and emptiness that often haunted the bigger stars of the pop world. "One night I was singing on stage," Norman recalled in an interview, "and Janis Joplin was sitting behind the front curtain watching the concert with a bottle of Southern Comfort in one hand and she was sipping whiskey from a paper cup. She was drunk and really unhappy. And every now and then, she would start yelling at me." Norman claimed his song "Why Don't You Look into Jesus?" was inspired by Joplin. "She was like the happy drunk hippie who felt very ugly because of her terrible pockmarks. And so if you talked to her she'd go, Hey, baby, how's it doin? And if you talked to her serious, if you said something like Jesus — yeah, Jesus, he's cool, and Muhammad, and Buddha, and . . . you know? She was just nonstop. Insecure and on display and performing. You couldn't give to her 'cause she was too busy protecting herself and giving her image back to you."[4]

Norman had plenty of people to witness to, but they were too caught up in their newfound fame to hear his message. For one thing, Norman only talked Jesus one-on-one, never with groups. "I also wasn't on the level that they were, and they were all snobs," he admitted. "They're not going to associate with some weenie who's not a superstar. . . . So it was just very hard to get into their dressing room, and then it was very easy to get asked to leave. And they weren't going to talk to me because I was a different pay grade. 'You opened for us, you're not the star.' . . . So I had a whole string of famous people, but rock people? No. It was so brief, you know."

Despite being professionally subordinate to many of the musicians he toured with during that era, Norman pointed out that their fame was actually quite fleeting. "Most of these kids didn't become stars until 1967 and a half," he said. "Their careers didn't last very long. If they had a couple of hit records, they were on top, and when the third or fourth single bombed, the record company stopped taking their calls. . . . So I felt sorry for these people 'cause they were so sure that this was going to go on forever."[5]

According to Norman, he quit People! the day their album hit the record stores in 1968 partly because of Capitol's meddling and partly because of tensions with other band members, several of whom had embraced Scientology, which Norman said he tried but couldn't tolerate. His bandmates counter that Norman, whose religious beliefs struck them as inscrutable, was asked to leave the group because he was growing increasingly difficult and demanding.[6] At a Friday-night prayer service about this time, Norman had a powerful spiritual encounter that threw him into a frenzy of indecision about his life. For the first time in his life, he had received what he understood to be the Holy Spirit. He gave up his apartment and moved back home. Not surprisingly, Norman's father asked what his plans were. "My plans? Oh, I've got great plans," he announced. "I'm going to sit down in the middle of my life and I'm not moving until God comes and gets me." A few weeks later, the phone rang; Youth for Christ, a parachurch organization, offered him a job. But, according to Norman,

> God was silent. Then I got a call about a week later from Herb End-
> ler at Capitol Records. He wanted me to come to Los Angeles to write
> musicals for Capitol. . . . And I thought, isn't Hollywood called the
> Sin City? . . . Well obviously, God, I can't go there, can I? Well, how do
> I know I can't go there? . . . So I just prayed and prayed and prayed.
> And I had no peace about joining YFC. And I had a lot of peace about
> Hollywood. But God was silent. . . .
>
> When I got there, there were auditions for *Hair*. And I thought,
> I'm going to try out for *Hair* just to see if I have what it takes. Because
> maybe I'm just some lame person and I shouldn't be in music at all.
> So I tried out for *Hair*, and they gave me a callback and said, "You're
> it. Come down on Saturday, there's a contract waiting for you to sign."
> So I went down and I told them, "I'm sorry, I can't sign this." And they
> go, "Why not?" And I said, "Because I have other things to do." They
> said, "What could you possibly have to do that's more important than
> this? You're going to be on TV three times just in this first season. Be-
> cause the producer for the *Smothers Brothers* is a coproducer of this
> show. You're going to get a feature spot. You're going to probably get
> famous." I went, "I have other things that are more important." They
> went, "Okay, we're sorry to lose you."

Completely broke, Norman said he went home and cried. He had rented a studio apartment at Gower and Santa Monica, across the street from a cemetery and walking distance to Capitol. But he locked his guitar in a closet. Rather than writing musicals, Norman became a street evangelist among the street people, runaways, junkies, and transvestites he rubbed shoulders with on Hollywood Boulevard. He threw himself into street witnessing with abandon, and he was good at it. But Norman never considered himself part of the Jesus Movement.

"I was the same age as everybody but I'd been a Christian longer so I had that advantage," he said. "I wasn't inspired by some message that I heard at a hippie rally. I became a Christian at a Southern Baptist church so I had a really solid Bible-teaching upbringing. So I just knew a lot more about the theology than a lot of kids do."

He had begun witnessing to classmates in junior high.

And then, later on, [I witnessed] on the streets of whatever town I was giving concerts in. . . . I never told anyone my name was Larry Norman. . . . I just started talking to people who I felt God led me to. And God would usually reveal to me what their problem was. And it was never wrong. So I was very, very terrified of God because he's an awesome God. . . . I would witness to people and pray with them to become a Christian. . . . I never connected people to their local church because that's to me like sending an innocent little lamb into cultural slaughter. A lot of churches just destroy people. So I didn't know what to do except trust the Holy Spirit to take care of these people.

When God started letting me know what people's problems were, I thought that I was supposed to tell them what their problem was so that they'd realize there was a God. That's what it was for. Not to prove that He existed by revealing what they had done, but allowing them the opportunity to reveal and confess and be free, liberated from it. So I did all this work, I did it quietly. Then all of a sudden other people came to my street, my beat. I went up and down Holly- wood Boulevard, stopped at King George's All-You-Can-Eat, $1.99, filled up, cause I had no money. . . . And then I'd go up the street again, and by the time I finished witnessing, it was getting dark and I'd just go home. And that was an everyday thing. But I didn't wear goofy clothes or wear a button or anything. . . . After doing that for a couple years, there got to be a trickle of other people into the Boule- vard. . . . It just got to be a real magnet. Friday night the church bus would pull up. All the kids would hop out, laughing with tracts in their hands, and the youth leader would come out with a Nehru col- lar and a wooden cross on a beaded hippie chain. So to me, that's the Jesus Movement.

Norman eventually did start writing musicals for Capitol, completing four. Two of them — *Birthday for Shakespeare* and *Alison* — were mounted in Los Angeles, featuring Ted Neeley, a friend of Norman. (Two other musicals, *Haight Street* and *Lion's Breath*, never got staged.) Both shows explored the hippie life of San Francisco, satirizing rather than celebrating the psychedelic counterculture. They were successful enough to kindle Norman's ambitions.

"When I wrote musicals, I thought, well, they're going to Broadway," he said. "The producer for *Bye Bye Birdie* had picked up the options for the first musical, and the producers for *Man of La Mancha* picked up the option for the second musical. I'm gonna be on Broadway. So I started going to movies every day trying to learn how to act from movies."

Christian musicals aimed at young people were part of the backdrop to the Jesus Movement. Beginning in 1966, folk musicals like *Good News*, *Tell It Like It Is*, and *Natural High* began to pour out of Waco, Texas, where Word Records produced records and sheet music. The musicals were written by fortysomething guys who had cut their teeth on big-band jazz: Kurt Kaiser, a staff composer at Word; Billy Ray Hearn, who would become a pioneering CCM producer; and, most important, Ralph Carmichael, who had written music for *I Love Lucy*, had a huge success with the song "Born Free," and would found Light Records. All three wanted to create more rock-friendly music that would hold the attention of boomers.

"We discovered that there was a great gulf developing between the youth and the traditional church," Carmichael explained. "There were very few youth choirs. The church didn't like the kids' music, and the church didn't like the way the kids were dressing. They didn't like their hairstyles, and the gulf was growing wider and wider." The musicals worked, to a degree. "The Gospel was very plain, but the music was those even eighth notes," Carmichael explained. "Different choir directors started to see the potential, and youth choirs started growing. . . . I think we ultimately sold something over a half million of that $2.98 music folio, *Tell It Like It Is*." To anyone under age thirty, though, the musicals were closer to Lawrence Welk than the Rolling Stones. "They were light years from what the youth were really into musically," John Styll admitted, "but it was what you could play in church. And they were pretty popular, and church kids liked doing them 'cause it was as close as they could get to their real musical life in church."[7]

Norman had his doubts about the Christian musical venture. He had already been to New York City, and he'd done well playing a club called the Bitter End. "I did fourteen shows there, and then went out into the street and witnessed during the day," he recalled. "That was a really great time in Manhattan. I had so many people pray. And one of them was a girl named Susan Perelman, a Jewish girl, who helped found Jews for Jesus with Moishe Rosen." But making it on Broadway presented a different challenge. As he explained:

Here I am, writing a musical that had a lot of spiritual songs in it.
Not to be prejudiced, but when I get to New York, I'm going to have

to pass inspection with the Jews because they're the ones who first come to the theater. Jews and critics, to be very general. And it's not until weeks or months later that the out-of-towners come in because they've heard about the musical. And I realized I was working so hard for something that basically had no chance to survive on Broadway because Jesus is hated by the world. The Bible promises us this. . . . So I said, okay, I can either go on Broadway and wait for people to come into town and spend $45 on a ticket. And this is a limited audience that goes to a lot of musicals. Or I can just break up my musical and start creating albums that only cost $4.95 and go all over the world.

Not for the first or last time, Norman's timing was off. Jesus was poised to become a star of stage and screen. In 1971, the year the national media descended on California's Jesus People, Christian musicals were invading Broadway, generating their own sort of media frenzy. When *Jesus Christ Superstar* opened on Broadway in October 1971, it had the rapt attention of the theater world. But *Superstar*'s gentler cousin, *Godspell*, had already opened off Broadway in May. This kind of Jesus saturation of modern American entertainment was unprecedented. If Calvary Chapel provided crucial social connections for the pioneers of Jesus rock, the big-time commercial Jesus shows would provide an equally important professional launching pad for Christian musicians over the seventies.

## I Don't Know How to Love Him

At first glance, the creators of *Jesus Christ Superstar* had little in common with Norman, Lonnie Frisbee, Chuck Girard, and the other leading lights of the Jesus Movement. True, they were bell-bottomed, long-haired baby boomers. Composer Andrew Lloyd Webber was born in 1948, a year after Norman, while lyricist Tim Rice was four years older. But both were English, and despite an upbringing in the Church of England, neither was particularly religious. (They were drawn to Bible stories, however; their first collaboration, a fifteen-minute cantata commissioned for a boys prep school in 1968, later developed into *Joseph and the Amazing Technicolor Dreamcoat*.) More important, their intention was not to celebrate the glory of Jesus Christ but to borrow a compelling story to create a work of popular music that they hoped would be a commercial hit. They had no interest in witnessing and winning converts to Jesus.

Tim Rice and Andrew
Lloyd Webber (Image
© Bettmann/CORBIS)

Still, it's difficult not to see a common cultural impulse at work. Certainly the national media that covered the Jesus Movement did. Whatever their intentions, Rice and Webber translated the figure of Jesus and the crucial drama of the Christian religion into contemporary terms. Their version of the Passion story may have shied away from the divinity of Christ, but it certainly made his life and teachings worth taking seriously. Rice felt it was a matter of asking the sorts of questions that would occur to "any fairly intelligent man who analyzes the Christ thing." He had trouble accepting the view that Christ was God incarnate. "For me, Christ was just a super-prophet who, as a fantastic man, made a big mark on His time," he said. "We don't really know all that much about Him." Rice's goal was "to humanize Christ, because, for me, I find Jesus as portrayed in the Gospels as a God is a very unrealistic figure. He doesn't really get through to me. The same is true, on the other hand, for Judas, who is portrayed just as a sort of cardboard cut-out figure of evil. It seems to me there must be much more to these central characters of the story."[8]

The evangelical theology of the Jesus Movement was more about glorifying Christ as Lord and savior, not highlighting his human frailties. But the emphasis on Jesus as an approachable, personal savior was not so far removed from the sort of repositioning Rice sought to do. In fact, as Stephen Prothero has brilliantly demonstrated in *American Jesus*, ministers and writers had been carrying out this project, in various ways, for centuries. At one point, Rice echoes a core principle of evangelical Christianity going back to Martin Luther: *sola scriptura*. Each individual believer has the power to read and understand the Bible without the mediation of priest or other experts. "We had been well-coached in the mechanics of Christianity and its legends and beliefs," he said. "That was drummed into us at school. They treated the legends, so we decided to treat the bloke as a man. We read the Gospels very carefully and that was it. What we did not read was eighty-three other people's interpretations of Christ because we didn't want to be affected by their views. We stuck to the text and put in our interpretation of what we think *could* have happened."[9]

Rice's approach had the support of at least one noted theologian. "The figure of Christ is ubiquitous," Harvey Cox declared in 1970. "He is now beginning to appear as Christ the Harlequin: the personification of celebration and fantasy in an age that has lost both. It is a truer sense of Christ than the saccharine, bloodless face we see painted so often. He was part Yippie and part revolutionary, and part something else. On His day of earthly triumph, Palm Sunday, He rode to town on a jackass." At L'Abri, a Christian commune nestled in the Swiss Alps, maverick evangelical guru Francis Schaeffer hosted a procession of backpacking hippies and counterculture savants like Timothy Leary. Dylan, Mick Jagger, and Keith Richards were scheduled but canceled at the last minute. Schaeffer's son Frank recalled meeting Led Zeppelin guitarist Jimmy Page, who had a copy of Schaeffer's *Escape from Reason* in his back pocket, which he pronounced "very cool." Page said Eric Clapton had given him the book. "According to Dad," wrote Frank, "Samuel Becket, Jean Genet, the Beatles, Bob Dylan, et al., were doing God's work. They were preparing men's hearts, in 'pre-evangelism,' and 'tearing down the wall of middle-class empty bourgeois apathy.' Jimi Hendrix was right to scorn that plastic business, man! All we needed to do was provide the answer after the counterculture rebels opened the door by showing people that life without Jesus was empty."[10]

Only a few years earlier, John Lennon had dismissed Christianity as a relic. "Christianity will go," he told a London newspaper in 1966. "It will vanish and shrink. I needn't argue about that, I'm right and will be proved right. We're more popular than Jesus Christ right now. I don't know which will go first—

rock 'n' roll or Christianity. Jesus was all right but his disciples were thick and ordinary. It's them twisting it that ruins it for me."[11]

Cox and Lennon were speaking for many. The year before, *Time* had run a cover story titled "Is God Dead?" Three years later, as the Beatles were breaking up and Webber and Rice were assembling a cast for recording the *Superstar* album, rumors surfaced that Lennon was being sought to sing the part of Christ. "We feel Lennon would be ideal," Rice was quoted as saying. "We are bound to upset a few people, but we don't want to annoy anyone. He is sincere in his efforts for peace — at least he is trying to do something." Even more risibly, these same articles reported that the part of Mary Magdalene might go to Yoko Ono — or perhaps Marianne Faithfull, Mick Jagger's girlfriend at the time.[12]

Webber and Rice did hire a rock star to sing the part of Jesus: Ian Gillan, lead singer of Deep Purple. While Lennon and Gillan were world's apart from Calvary Chapel, a variety of subterranean links connected the world of Southern California Jesus People to the gospel of Broadway. The musical *Hair* was the most important link. Though *Hair* celebrated the very behaviors that many in the Jesus Movement were trying to escape from or at least seeking an alternative to — fornication, recreational drug use, nudity, profanity, alternative spirituality, and general irreverence to any and all traditional authority — the show directly engaged questions that animated the young California Christians, even if the answers were different.

As if laying out the spiritual alternatives available in the Age of Aquarius, the stage directions for *Hair* specified two permanent set pieces: "a large, authentic, beautiful American Indian totem pole" and a "Crucifix-Tree" with "a rather abstract Jesus on it . . . electrified with tiny twinkling lights in his eyes and on his body." Billed as "an American tribal love-rock musical," *Hair* did not celebrate its hippie tribe unambiguously. The characters are deeply flawed in one way or another, as individuals and as a collective. The most sympathetic character turns out to be Claude, who is ambivalent about both his hippie friends and the Establishment that calls him to make "lots of money." With flowing blond hair and a beard, Claude came across to some as a Christ figure. ("I am the son of God," he says at one point.) He dies at the end, as any Christlike character must; he is killed in Vietnam.[13]

*Hair* turned out to be an extremely effective vehicle for transmitting the images and values of hippie culture. The show had originally been produced by Joseph Papp for the New York Shakespeare Festival. It was later staged at a Broadway discotheque before making it to a bona fide theater in April 1968. From there, it achieved legendary success both in America and overseas, with performances on every continent of the globe, some eleven original cast albums in eleven different languages, and an eventual world gross of $80 million. And ten years later, a film version was directed by Milos Forman.[14]

In a practical sense, musicals like *Godspell*, *Jesus Christ Superstar*, and especially *Hair* provided a musical apprenticeship for some of the leading lights of the Jesus Movement. It was easy to float among the various shows. Murray Head, who sang the part of Judas on the *Superstar* album, had played in the London version of *Hair*. Tom O'Horgan—acclaimed for the loose, encounter-group style of direction he brought to *Hair*—was hired to direct what turned out to be a flawed, over-the-top but publicity-generating spectacle of *Superstar*. His cast included several *Hair* alumni. Jeff Fenholt (Jesus) and Ben Vereen (Judas) had both recently played in *Hair*. So had Fenholt's understudy, Ted Neeley, who played Jesus in the L.A. stage production and later film version. Norman himself had been offered a part in *Hair*. Barry McGuire, shortly to become a major figure in Christian rock, played in *Hair* on Broadway for a year. Donna Summer, who was born again later in the decade, began her career in European productions of *Hair* and *Godspell*.

The rock opera *Tommy* points to an even more direct connection between these different sides of Christian youth culture. The success of the Who's rock opera was much on the minds of Webber and Rice as they wrote *Superstar*. (*Tommy* had come out on Decca in 1969, the year they completed *Superstar*, also for Decca.) "We naturally considered rock with my background and opera with Andrew's knowledge of the classics," Rice said. "Then we had this idea. 'Why not combine the two?' The Who had caused quite a stir by calling their *Tommy* a rock opera. That's how it all came about."[15]

Traces of a Christian parable are not hard to find in the Who's classic album. Tommy becomes catatonic—a "deaf, dumb, and blind kid"—after witnessing his father murder his mother's lover. Later, the father sings:

And Tommy doesn't even know what day it is.
Doesn't know who Jesus was or what praying is.
How can he be saved
From the eternal grave?

Tommy's repeated plea—"See me, feel me, touch me, heal me"—weaves through several songs. After a series of hair-raising traumas, Tommy is miraculously healed, thanks in part to a revelation he receives while gazing in a mirror and in part to his genius as a "pinball wizard." He goes on to become a charismatic spiritual leader with many disciples. But when he preaches a

gospel of austerity, pointedly rejecting mind-expanding drugs, Tommy's followers bridle; the pinball messiah is rejected and overthrown.

The Who's manager, Kit Lambert, is credited with encouraging Pete
Townshend to borrow extended-form structures from classical music, and
Townshend himself acknowledged the life-changing influence of his Indian-
born guru, Meher Baba—considered by his followers to be the reincarnation
of Moses, Buddha, Christ, and Muhammad, among others. But Larry Norman
believed that "The Epic," an extended song he wrote for People!, helped inspire the Who's masterwork while the bands toured together.

> It was not just an opera, but it was performed instead of just sung by
> people standing there. And when we killed the dragon, there were
> a lot of lights and effects. We didn't have any special effects, so we
> just shook one of the cabinets. . . . So Pete was really fascinated by
> that. And People! were on something like a forty-two-city tour, and
> so there was a lot of opportunity to talk. And Townshend told Denny
> (my drummer who's still with me) that he got an idea, that he was
> gonna go home to the Isle of Wight where he lived and write a rock
> opera. *Tommy* came out the next year. And then about six months
> after that, Denny and he were sitting and talking, and Townshend
> said, "You know that opera you did? That's why I wrote *Tommy*, be-
> cause of that opera." He confirmed it, but he's never admitted it in
> interviews, 'cause again, our pay grade is too low.[16]

*Tommy* rose to number four in the pop charts.

More than *Hair*, *Tommy*, or even *Superstar*, *Godspell* came close to the sort
of musical that the Jesus Movement could accept. The show was conceived
in 1970 by John-Michael Tebelak, a twenty-two-year-old student writing a
master's thesis in drama at Carnegie Mellon University. Tebelak was raised
Episcopalian and considered becoming a priest. Attending an Easter sunrise
service at Pittsburgh's Anglican cathedral, he noticed that "the people in the
church seemed bored, and the clergymen seemed to be hurrying to get it over
with. I left with the feeling that, rather than rolling the rock away from the
Tomb, they were piling more on. I went home, took out my manuscript, and
worked it to completion in a non-stop frenzy." (According to one report, after
the service, Tebelak was hassled for his clothes and long hair and frisked for
drugs by a cop.) He used large chunks of the Gospel of Matthew verbatim, de-
picting Jesus and followers not as neurotic revolutionaries doomed to failure
but as effervescent flower children whose faith is ultimately vindicated. Jesus

himself is staged as a gentle, compassionate clown. The songs, composed by Stephen Schwartz, borrowed liberally from old Anglican hymns, including the show's biggest hit, "Day by Day."[17]

Tebelak denied that *Godspell* was part of the Jesus Movement. "*Godspell's* arrival at this particular time enables it to capitalize on the trend toward Jesus awareness, but neither the cast nor myself could be styled Jesus freaks, nor would we wish to be." For his part, Schwartz took even more pains to downplay the significance of Christianity: "*Godspell* is essentially a show about the formation of a community, not about religion, at least in my view, and it was always on that basis that we rehearsed it."[18] But artists' intentions often fail to match audience reactions.

Scott Ross, a rock 'n' roll disc jockey in New York City before becoming a Christian and pioneering Jesus rock radio, recalled a "secular record producer" inviting him and his wife to see *Godspell* in New York. (Since Ross's wife, Nedra, sang in the Ronettes, the producer may have been Phil Spector.) Ross described the experience to journalist Paul Baker.

> We got to the end of the show where the Lord is crucified on the chain link fence. All of a sudden, this producer, who knows nothing about the Lord to my knowledge, grabbed my hand. I turned and looked, and he had grabbed Nedra's hand on the other side. He had sunglasses on, but I saw the tears streaming down his face. I'm not overdramatizing the instance — the tears were literally streaming down his face. I could not believe it, because I knew something about this guy's life. He trembled. He shook from head to foot. I looked around in the audience, and I'd say half of them were Jews, people in show business. It was a new show; everybody in town was trying to see it. People all over the auditorium were crying. This friend we were with couldn't take it any longer. He jumped up and ran out the door. After the end, when the cast had come down the aisle saying, "God is not dead," we went outside and our friend was standing on the sidewalk. He said, "We've got to go eat something." He was still trembling. He said, "Tell me about Jesus."[19]

Part of the cultural impact of musicals comes from the way they migrate off professional stages into high school and community productions. The unstructured, improvisational quality of shows like *Hair* and *Godspell* lent themselves to amateur productions. *Godspell* was first staged by Tebelak's classmates at Carnegie Mellon before moving on to New York. But *Superstar* created the largest scene among amateurs, in part because its hype surpassed the other Gospel musicals. As the first Broadway show based on a hit album and a commercial sensation before the first rehearsal was held, *Superstar* signaled a paradigm shift on the Great White Way. The album had hit number one in the pop charts in February 1971, and it would hover at the top for the rest of the year on its way to selling 3 million copies. The first authorized touring production began in July, and the Broadway premier had to wait until October. This was too long for some to wait.

As early as February, unauthorized concerts of *Superstar* were spreading around the country. Lawsuits and legal threats proliferated as well. Webber and Rice had asked their publisher to allow churches to perform songs as long as they were offered in churches free of charge. The Madison Avenue Baptist Church in Manhattan put on one very successful production for several weeks at various venues, after which it was pressured to disband. A dinner theater in Maryland advertised their fully staged production as *Superstar*'s "world premiere." "In Peoria, Illinois," according to Ellis Nassour, "within the span of eleven days three different companies played the city—one billing itself as the authentic production, a second calling itself the authorized production, and a third terming itself the complete independent production."[20]

Even public schools opened their stages to *Superstar*. On Long Island, far from the Bible Belt, students at Southold High School staged a June production in the auditorium after learning all the parts—without sheet music and directly from the recording. The humanities teacher in charge lined up a local Methodist church to provide theological cover. The whole plan was nearly derailed when one of the students got an angry call from Andrew Lloyd Webber demanding the students desist. "I told him there was nothing on paper, so there were no rights to buy, and anyway it was a high school production," recalled Steve Kaczorowski, who played Jesus on alternate nights. "So he said he wanted payment in the form of performance rights. He had me there. But then we decided to put on the show for free, and that took care of that. Finally, he gave his blessing, and even came out to see the show."[21]

The most tenacious rival to Robert Stigwood's authorized productions was the Original American Touring Company, organized by a New York producer and agent named Betty Sperber. Because her troupe used a published score for which she paid royalties, added and subtracted song numbers, and eschewed sets and costumes, Sperber claimed she was well within her rights. "If songs from *Fiddler on the Roof* can be performed for a live audience, what is the difference here?" Still, the skirmishes went on in courtrooms across the land. It was tough going, with frequent cancellations, strandings, and subpoenas of cast members. At one point, lawyers accused Stigwood of "now claiming exclusive rights to Jesus Christ." These wildcat productions were not limited to the United States. Similar unauthorized productions were mounted in Belgium and Germany. Stigwood even threatened legal action against a group of Catholic nuns in Australia, his native country, who wanted to stage *Superstar* as a charity benefit.[22]

The wild popularity of these outlaw productions is a reminder that links to the cultural grassroots survives even in an era of commercialized mass entertainment. Rather than promoting passive audiences, these blockbuster musicals encouraged a proliferation of cultural activity at the local level. And they were not the only indication that *Superstar* was touching a cultural nerve. Depending on what theological ground a person stood upon, she might perceive a beautiful convergence or the work of Satan. Certainly, *Superstar* served as a lightning rod for criticism from sectors of nearly all Christian persuasions. Webber and Rice had braced for controversy from the beginning, and the trial-balloon version of the song "Superstar" that Decca released as a single in December 1969 carried a proactive message from Dean Martin Sullivan of London's St. Paul's Cathedral. "There are some people who may be shocked by this record," Sullivan wrote. "I ask them to listen to it and think again. It is a desperate cry. Who are you Jesus Christ? is the urgent enquiry, and a very proper one at that. The record probes some answers and makes some comparisons. The onus is on the listener to come up with his replies. If he is a Christian, let him answer for Christ. The singer [Judas] says he only wants to know. He is entitled to some response."[23]

Predictably, despite this effort to disarm, the single precipitated a firestorm of controversy, particularly in the U.S. South. Some clergy treated it as a kind of teachable moment, joining roundtable discussions or requesting copies of the song and lyrics for Sunday school classes. Others condemned it as sacrilege. "Jesus Christ is a Person," wrote an Arkansas minister to Decca. "We Christians are not going to sit on the sidelines and let His name be ridiculed in such fashion. My advice to kooks like those whose lives are patterned after everything that is vile, vulgar, and profane, is to use their brain, as hard as it may be, and turn from their evil ways before they wake up in hell." He then threatened a $10 million lawsuit.[24]

It was hard for religious leaders not to take a stand on *Jesus Christ Superstar*, either the album or the stage version that followed. The archbishop of Canterbury, who attended a performance in New York, gave it a qualified thumbs up. Billy Graham was less enthusiastic. Some Protestants complained that the musical failed to show the Resurrection of Jesus, the most important part of the whole story. Catholics objected to the implication that Jesus and

Mary Magdalene were lovers and that the Holy Eucharist and Blessed Virgin were traduced. Rabbi Marc Tannenbaum of the American Jewish Committee complained that the plot "is historically and scripturally inaccurate and the Jewish people have been maligned." And he worried that *Superstar* "is at the center of a creation of a set of cultural images in the counterculture of America." A Presbyterian lay minister agreed, worrying that the musical would hinder the new spirit of ecumenical comity. "There are some good Jews and some bad Jews," Rice shot back. Except for Pilate, every character was Jewish. "The priests represent the establishment," Webber explained. "They're establishment people, not Jewish people."[25]

Something even more subtle caught the attention of Christians who disliked the show for religious reasons: who was the hero of this gospel, Christ or Judas? Not only is the Betrayer given some of the best lines and songs, he often seems the only clear-thinking one in the bunch. Judas comes across as more politically astute than Jesus, who seems tied up in a knot of ambivalence. Judas's actions become altogether plausible. Rice complained that the biblical Gospels make Judas out to be "a sort of cardboard cut-out figure of evil," a one-dimensional depiction that he sought to deepen in the musical. "We made him a type of Everyman," Rice said. "Judas did not think of himself as a traitor. He did what he did, not because he was basically evil, but because he was intelligent. He could see Christ becoming something he considered harmful to the Jews. Judas felt they had been persecuted enough."[26]

Rice identified an unlikely source for his revisionist portrayal of Judas: Robert Zimmerman, better known as Bob Dylan. Specifically, Rice mentioned Dylan's seven-minute song from 1963, "With God on Our Side," an extended meditation on American nationalism that proceeds through a series of military adventures—the Indian wars, the Spanish-American War, the First and Second World Wars, and the Cold War—with each stanza ending with the reminder that "God's on our side." The eighth stanza departs from this, turning unexpectedly to the thought—which has been haunting the narrator—that Jesus was betrayed by a kiss. It will be up to the listener, Dylan sings, "to decide whether Judas Iscariot had God on his side." The next and final stanza ends with the narrator confessing to feeling confusion, being "weary as hell," but deciding that if God is in fact on "our side, He'll stop the next war."[27] Years later, Dylan would play a large and unexpected role in the metamorphosis of Christian rock music.

Heated disputes over the ultimate spiritual merit of *Superstar* made good press, especially when charges of blasphemy were backed by well-informed ministers or college professors. But *Superstar*-phobes comprised a minority, even among religious folk, whether they were Protestant, Catholic, or Jewish. People could see the show because they were curious, or they just liked the songs; they didn't have to accept whatever theological implications it seemed to raise. "My heart is beating," a Catholic housewife from Queens told a reporter about her reaction to the musical. "I am moved more than I am by a sermon in church. It enlightens the scriptures for me." Decca was pleasantly surprised by the lack of complaints. "A spokesman for the record company estimated that in the first six months of 1970, 90 percent of the 'Superstar' mail was in favor of the song," according to Nassour. "And after the release of the complete opera in October there were dozens of testimonials from clergymen of all faiths on the value of the record as a tool to bring young people back into the churches."[28]

Among Jesus People, opinions about the show ran the gamut. Bernie Sheahan, a Jesus person from the Bay Area who later became a Christian music journalist, found *Superstar* compelling despite its theological shortcomings.

> I remember my freshman summer [1971], painting an old farmhouse that belonged to the church with one of my best friends. And he and I listened to that album every day—*Jesus Christ Superstar*. And I remember talking with Young Life leaders or people in church about how it was off kilter theologically. That Mary Magdalene probably didn't really feel that way about Jesus. Did Jesus really have those kinds of doubts? It took some liberties with the Bible, for sure. But it was so passionate. The songs were great. . . . Here was a record about Jesus, and Jesus was singing. It makes a real personality of him. Also, because it was controversial. . . . I remember my Jewish friends not listening to it, not being interested in it except liking the hip songs like "I Don't Know How to Love Him."
>
> *Godspell* was a different story. It was so happy and it was so true to scriptures. . . . I think because it wasn't controversial and because it was kind of like the real deal, more people paid attention to it. I remember in Young Life singing "Day by Day." We sang that for years. Seeing kids who weren't necessarily committed Christians, like at camp who don't come to regular Young Life, and seeing kids sing it like they meant it: "To see thee more clearly, love thee more dearly, follow thee more nearly, day by day"—that song had an impact. It was such a huge hit.[29]

Norman agreed that *Godspell* was tolerable—"it's kind of a sweet little musical"—but he took a dim view of *Superstar*. "It's not only sacrilege and blasphemy, it's just stupidity," he opined. "And it was written so that nobody except Christians could possibly be offended because there's no message. There's no confrontation about sin." He allowed that the show might inspire someone to pick up a Bible or go to church. "That's fall-out, God uses what he wants. But the musical itself at every turn is sacrilegious." He confronted his friend Ted Neeley, the "burned-out" Southern Baptist from Texas who played the role of Jesus on both stage and screen. "I asked him, how can you do this part? You know better than that. All this stuff is just hideous. He says, 'It's just entertainment, it's just a musical. I don't take it serious. How can you, it's lame. The lyrics aren't very good, there's only a couple of good tunes. But it's a job, I needed a job.' He's done it for forty years off and on."[30]

Street Christians were wary of *Superstar*, both because it pointedly ignored the Resurrection and because Webber and Rice were known to be non-believers. But the musical could be interpreted as being moved by the same Spirit that had prompted the multitudes to attend tent services, beach baptisms, and Christian coffeehouses and communes. The Christian God was all-powerful and inscrutable. Scott Ross did a segment on *Superstar* for his Christian radio program and interviewed Webber and Rice. "Many people obviously had theological problems with it," Ross said, "but we approached it from the direction that his name is above every other name under heaven and earth: Jesus Christ. Period. You put it on the marquee, and they've got to deal with it, because that's his name."[31]

"There's no doubt that it was a secular group of people who came out with those productions," Jerry Bryant agreed. "But the Gospel, when it's preached, does not return void. God can use anything. At the time, we thought it to be impure and counterfeit to some degree, because we knew its foundation. But then others said, 'Well, hey, they're at least telling the Gospel message, you know. It's being preached, even if it's being preached by someone who doesn't know Jesus.' . . . But I don't think we ever felt like it was really anointed."[32] People around Calvary Chapel didn't have much regard for the musicals, according to John Styll. But "Calvary tended to be a little bit cloistered and suspicious of anything that came from without. If it wasn't invented here, it didn't exist, in a sense," he admitted. "My attitude was that *Superstar* at least got people to think about Jesus, and that can't be a bad thing." The dramatic format of youth group productions of Christian musicals like *Good News*, *Tell It Like It Is*, and *Natural High*, after all, was how many young believers experienced the potent combination of faith and fellowship. *Superstar* might have flirted with blasphemy, but the attempt to transfer the Gospel wine into more contemporary wineskins was certainly a recognizable move.[33]

The Jesus Movement did produce at least one rock musical of its own, however: a little-remembered production titled *Lonesome Stone*. Created in England by Americans, it might be considered a kind of transatlantic payback for *Superstar*. It was written by a group called the Sheep, which had branched out of the same Milwaukee Jesus scene that produced the Resurrection Band and JPUSA. Heading off in 1972 to evangelize Europe, members of the Sheep succeeded in internationalizing the Jesus Movement, helping found England's Greenbelt Christian music festival and touring Scandinavia, where they recorded an album called *Jeesus-Rock!* Then they created a musical. Subtitled "How the Jesus People Came to Life," *Lonesome Stone* chronicled the origins of the movement through the conversion of a hippie on the streets of Haight-Ashbury in a striking production featuring slide shows, pyrotechnics, and other special effects. The musical was impressive enough to attract crowds during a 1973 run at the Rainbow Theatre on London's West End; a cast member from the touring version of *Hair* reportedly was inspired to leave that musical to join *Lonesome Stone*. For whatever reason (perhaps *Superstar* and *Godspell* had exhausted the market), an American run lasted only two months before closing. By that time, Larry Norman's musicals were long forgotten.[34]

## My Sweet Lord

In August 1971, as O'Horgan's troupe was gearing up for the October opening of *Superstar* on Broadway, Madison Square Garden opened its doors to a historic musical event: the Concert for Bangladesh. The event was an epic benefit concert for war- and starvation-wracked former East Pakistan. The concert was organized by George Harrison, who recruited an all-star lineup that included Ringo Starr, Eric Clapton, Bob Dylan, Leon Russell, and Billy Preston. Ravi Shankar had approached Harrison to express his concern about events in his native land and to ask for ideas on how they could help. "With a little help from my friends," Harrison said, he got superstars to fly in from great distances to perform for free. The concert itself only raised $250,000, but album sales brought in millions and established a precedent for future benefit concerts.[35]

As the concert opened, Harrison and Shankar wanted to set an appropriately reverent tone. Harrison warned that "the Indian music's a little bit more serious than our music, and I'd appreciate if you can try and settle down and get into the Indian music section." Shankar asked the audience to refrain from smoking during the program. Resplendent in traditional raiment, four renowned Indian musicians playing sitar, sarod, tablas, and tambura took their places on a stage furnished with an Indian rug, flowers, and incense. The group tuned up, which generated applause. ("Thank you," Shankar quipped. "If you appreciate the tuning so much I hope you'll enjoy the playing more."). The ensemble then launched into a raga, "Bangla Dun." The fifteen-minute performance built to a virtuosic climax of solo trading between Shankar and Akbar Khan that couldn't fail to impress connoisseurs of the sort of guitar showmanship exemplified by, say, Eric Clapton.

After the headline rockers took the stage and played Harrison's catchy "Wah-Wah," three spiritually inflected songs followed: "My Sweet Lord," "Awaiting on You All," and "That's the Way God Planned It." The first, a number-one single from Harrison's 1970 album, *All Things Must Pass*, was a logical choice for a benefit concert for a catastrophe in South Asia. The song had an infectious hook. The bushy-bearded, white-suited Harrison looked somewhat ill at ease as he strummed his acoustic guitar. Behind him, Ringo Starr slapped his drums, while Eric Clapton added piquant fillips on guitar. The song addresses an unnamed "Lord" (although a chorus toward the end substitutes "Hallelujah" with "Krishna, Krishna," a Hindu deity). The particular Lord seems less important than the effort made to attain awakening. It's a prayer of supplication, a recognition of the effort involved in spiritual enlightenment. The singer wants to "see you," "be with you," "know you," "go with you" — "but it takes so long, my Lord." Alternating choruses, though, assure the deity "that it won't take long." At the end of the song, Harrison chants a roster of Hindu deities: "Brahma, Vishnu, Deva . . ."

Next was "Awaiting on You All," also from *All Things Must Pass*. The song is a call to freedom and awakening — to salvation from "the mess that you're in," our inherently "fallen" nature — through opening the heart. The trappings of culture and organized religion — passports, visas, horoscopes, church houses, temples, rosary beads, even holy books — are unnecessary. The pope himself comes in for special criticism. But cleansing from pollution and relief from cares, from "the mess that you're in," are available to all. One must only chant "the names of the Lord." (Something Harrison had just done in the chorus of the previous song.) Harrison implies the Lord is one, but with many names; the only one mentioned in this song happens to be Jesus. To "emigrate" in order to "see Jesus" is unnecessary because once "you open up your heart you'll see He's right there: always was and will be."

For an evangelical Christian, street or otherwise, this was dangerous stuff. Harrison's lyrics exemplified what many in the Jesus Movement considered a lure and snare of the devil. No doubt the song was spiritually resonant, even reverent, but it leaves the all-important object of veneration vague. To invoke and praise the wrong Lord, let alone Brahma or Vishnu, was as bad as not worshipping at all, and perhaps worse. Fortunately, the next song up was Billy Preston's hit single "That's the Way God Planned It," rounding out the concert's opening sequence and offering an oblique connection to the Jesus Movement.

Preston was then at the peak of the most extraordinary career of any sideman in the history of rock 'n' roll. Nicknamed "the fifth Beatle," Preston played on the Beatles' final album, *Let It Be*, and was up on that London rooftop for the band's farewell gig. He was credited as a collaborator on the number-one single "Get Back," the first last time this happened for a Beatles song. Closest to Harrison, he also backed him on *All Things Must Pass*. Remarkably, Preston also worked his way into the starting lineup of the Rolling Stones, touring and playing on classic albums like *Sticky Fingers* and *Exile on Main Street*. Preston also found time to contribute funky organ to a series of hits by Sly and the Family Stone.

How Preston made all these connections is equally remarkable. "I first met [the Beatles] in 1962 when I toured England with Sam Cooke and Little Richard," he told *Rolling Stone*. Preston was just fifteen at the time, and the Beatles were still paying their dues in Hamburg's Star Club. "We became good friends, and when they first came to America when they had made it big, we partied. Then when I was touring Europe with Ray Charles in 1968, they called me to ask me to record." Having left the London studio in a huff during the stormy *Let It Be* sessions, Harrison wandered into a Ray Charles concert, where he saw Preston (whom Charles touted as his heir apparent). Harrison invited him back to the studio, where Preston helped pacify the feuding superstars. "In bootleg *Let It Be* session tapes," Richard Harrington noted, "one can hear several heated arguments between John Lennon and Paul McCartney about making Preston a group member (Lennon was all for it)."[36]

On top of this, Preston's gospel credentials were unimpeachable. Moving to Los Angeles from Houston when he was two, Preston was reportedly playing piano at the family church, Victory Baptist, at age three and directing a 100-voice choir there at age six. (His mother was the organist.) His first gig as a sideman came at age ten, when he backed Mahalia Jackson. Along with Andraé and Sandra Crouch, he helped found a singing group called the COGICS, after the Church of God in Christ. He also toured with a young, presoul Aretha Franklin and recorded with gospel powerhouse James Cleveland. By age twenty, Preston had recorded his first solo albums, instrumental

Billy Preston with George Harrison and President Gerald Ford
(Image © Bettmann/CORBIS)

gospel efforts for Vee Jay called *The Wildest Organ Ever* and *The Most Exciting Organ Ever*. His solo career continued in the early seventies, initially with the support of Harrison, who signed him to Apple Records.

"That's the Way God Planned It," Preston's contribution to the Bangladesh benefit, had come out in 1969 on Apple. The record was backed by British rock royalty: Harrison and Eric Clapton on guitar and Keith Richards and Ginger Baker on bass and drums. At the Garden, Preston accompanied himself on organ as he sang, wearing a large blue cap over his huge volcanic Afro. Preston's lyrics, like Harrison's, remain fairly vague, universal, and innocuous. He calls on listeners to "be humble," to renounce "greedy" ways "when there's so much left," to "help one another and live in perfect peace"—in short, to embrace God's plan for a better world. The song offers solace as well: "Let not your heart be troubled, let mourning sobbing cease." After a bluesy organ solo, the visibly transported Preston stood and did a holy dance—legs churning and arms flailing, worthy of any Pentecostal tabernacle—to the front mic for a few lines, then he holy danced his way back to the organ to finish the song. The performance brought down the house and in a way sanctified the ambiguous spirituality of that portion of the concert. He won his first Grammy for his contribution to the Concert for Bangladesh.

BY 1971 EVEN THE most cloistered Jesus People were unable to ignore the way Jesus had spilled into Top 40 radio, his name dropped promiscuously by artists not known for Christian piety. The trend had begun in 1967 at about the same time as the first stirrings of the Jesus Movement. "When the one who left us here returns for us at last / we are but a moment's sunlight fading in the grass," sang the Youngbloods that year. "Here's to you, Mrs. Robinson / Jesus loves you more than you will know," sang Simon and Garfunkel in 1968. "Why can't we be humble like the good Lord say?" sang Billy Preston in 1969. "Gotta have a friend in Jesus so you know that when you die / He's gonna recommend you to the spirit in the sky," sang Norman Greenbaum in 1970. Also that year: "I don't care what they may say, Jesus is just alright" (the Byrds and later the Doobie Brothers); "Won't you look down upon me, Jesus? / You've got to help me make a stand" (James Taylor); "Are you ready to sit by His throne? / Are you ready not to be alone?" (Pacific Gas and Electric); and "When darkness comes and pain is all around / Like a bridge over troubled water I will lay me down" (Simon and Garfunkel).

More followed in 1971. "Oh, Holy Jesus, let your love seize us," sang B. J. Thomas. "Take My Hand," sang Kenny Rogers and the First Edition. "Sing his name (Jesus), don't be ashamed," sang Johnny Rivers. "Take a look at yourself and you can look at others differently / by putting your hand in the hand of the Man from Galilee," sang Ocean. "He is now to be among you at the calling of your heart," sang Noel Paul Stookey in 1971. Many of these Jesus name-dropping hits were originals, and some made only the most oblique reference to a spiritual message, but a few were covers of bona fide hymns. "Oh happy day, when Jesus washed my sins away," sang the Edwin Hawkins Singers in 1969. "Amazing Grace, how sweet the sound, that saved a wretch like me," sang Judy Collins in 1970. "Morning has broken," warbled Cat Stevens the following year.

Some Jesus People regarded these musicians as opportunists, jumping on the Jesus bandwagon in order to sell more records. Others were more accepting. "It was just pop music," said Thom Granger. "People didn't just immediately assume Paul Simon was an evangelist when he wrote 'Bridge over Troubled Water.' It was a song that he wrote, and it was out in the culture." As with *Jesus Christ Superstar* and *Godspell*, a more lasting impact couldn't be ruled out. "There were thousands of people that started thinking about Jesus," said Bryant. "Not just because of those productions, but things like 'Spirit and the Sky' and 'Amazing Grace' and some of those early songs got people thinking. And of course, Dylan's stuff turned people's heads. But *Superstar* was responsible for a number of people coming to Christ."

This spiritual infusion into mainstream commercial music was a clear sign that the Jesus Movement was a component of the larger cultural front of the sixties, a movement that impacted all areas of social life and shaped the baby boom generation. But the relationship to that mainstream was vexed. Most Jesus People were quite aware of the flood of what came to be called "new religious movements" swirling around youth culture in the late sixties and seventies; many had dabbled in those forms of spirituality before turning to Jesus. While they embraced much of American popular culture, especially music, many Jesus People accepted the necessity of policing the boundaries of a Christian lifestyle against the many rival forms of belief and activity that were circulating. This was a challenging filtering act for Jesus People, made even more difficult by their relative youth and lack of seasoned mentors. Spirituality is an intrinsically fluid social quality, never more so than in the counterculture, where so many assumptions seemed to have come unmoored.

While adepts of Eastern and alternative religious movements often held Jesus Christ in high esteem, as Stephen Prothero has shown, Jesus People found little of value in the beliefs of their spiritual rivals.[37] In the world of Christian pop, fellow travelers like Billy Preston were the ones who withheld judgment on an eclectic range of spiritualities. Often, as we will see, they embraced them. And frequently these eclectic artists were people of color. The reasons for this are complex, but at the core it had to do with a perception of African Americans as somehow inherently spiritual beings and therefore less subject to the rules of Christian orthodoxy. "Doing church" came naturally, in other words. This could be an uncomfortable, not to say dangerous, position to occupy. Anyone could see that Judas was played by a black actor in both the Broadway and film versions of *Superstar*. True, he comes across as the character with the most depth and gets some great songs, but he ends up hanging from a tree. Judas was in, but not of, the original church of the twelve disciples; likewise, as we will see, African Americans were in, but not always of, the Jesus Movement. But their liminal status also gave them great influence in the evolving cultural front of the sixties.

## Chapter 3

# GODSTOCK

On a stifling June Friday in Dallas, upwards of 200,000 spectators descended on a grassy right-of-way soon to be a freeway near the downtown to participate in the official coming-out day for Jesus rock. An enormous stage, half as wide as a football field, had been erected for what was billed as the Saturday Jesus Music Festival, the grand finale to Explo '72. Starting at 7:25 A.M., a procession of bands and performers ascended a three-tiered, thirty-five-foot-high set designed by the man who had just created the backdrop for the Grammy awards. Looking very Peter Max, the stage was festooned with Day-Glo stripes, stars, Jesus slogans, and a heavenward-pointing index finger signaling "One Way."

*Godspell* star Katie Hanley was on hand to sing "Day by Day." Barry McGuire, formerly of the New Christy Minstrels and *Hair*, sang his 1965 hit "Eve of Destruction" along with a new song called "Don't Blame God." Randy Matthews performed his stark hit "Didn't He," slapping his guitar to simulate the sound of Christ being nailed to the cross. Children of the Day offered "Jesus Lives." Love Song performed, as did the Maranatha Band and a group called the Armageddon Experience. A former Miss America sang "Mighty Clouds of Joy." An ensemble called Great Commission Company performed a number called "Anticipation." "Jesus is coming soon," they sang breathlessly. "No more mythology, ecology, astrology / No wars, just peace and truth."

Nashville was represented through Reba Rambo, Connie Smith, and Kris Kristofferson, who offered a testimonial about his recent conversion before joining soon-to-be wife Rita Coolidge for "In the Garden."[1]

The Man in Black was also there. Johnny Cash, along with June Carter Cash, began with "If I Had a Hammer." "I hope and pray you remember the light of God you've seen here today and that you carry it with you throughout your life," he told the crowd. "Nothing satisfies like the kingdom of heaven built inside you and growing." Cash and his entourage continued with "I See Men as Trees Walking," a song from *Gospel Road*, his forthcoming movie about Jesus, along with some narration from the film. At 2:00 P.M. Cash introduced the event's featured speaker, Billy Graham. The evangelist quoted one of the most familiar Top 40 Jesus songs, urging members of the crowd to put their hands in the hand of the man from Galilee: "When you do, you have a supernatural power to put your hand in the hand of a person of another race. You have a new love in your heart that will drive you to do something about poverty, the ecology question, the racial tension, the family problems and, most of all, to do something about your own life."[2]

The spectacle would not have been complete without Larry Norman strumming away on an acoustic guitar, singing "Wish We'd All Been Ready" and "Sweet, Sweet Song of Salvation." They were already Jesus classics, the two best-known songs from *Upon This Rock*, the album Capitol invited him to record after he quit People! Norman recalled:

> Every night in the Cotton Bowl, there was a concert. And right down in the middle was a group that would do a couple of songs. This was a typical Billy Graham format, the music and then the sermon. I was thinking, gee, I didn't get invited to do this. I think it's because I cause such problems. Well, that's fine. But I was invited to sing on Saturday, and it turned out I was top billed, right below Johnny Cash. It was 180,000 people. So I went backstage and I'm looking at Johnny and his wife. . . . He looked like an old man with no teeth. His cheeks would go in so far. And he was so exhausted, and it was hot. And he had all these clothes on, a jacket over a vest over a shirt. I didn't realize he was the Man in Black and he had to wear black. So I went up on stage, climbed up these tall steps, and went up on this wooden platform and did my concert and then I came back down.[3]

Norman waited until Cash went on and then moved around to the front, where he started taking photographs.

He [Cash] said, "I'd like to introduce you to a good friend of mine, Kris Kristofferson." And so Kris came out and he sang "Why me, Lord? What have I ever done to deserve . . ." That was a very gigantic hit. And then he sang another song. Well, he had such trouble with the microphones, they were feeding back and squealing. He was so frustrated. I don't know whether he had taken some pills for bravery, or what. He seemed a little out of phase. And then he finished his song, and he was getting ready to leave the stage, and he said as he turned: "Well, I guess the devil won that one." And he left the stage. And I started praying for him; I prayed for him for years.

Explo '72 was sometimes referred to as "the Christian Woodstock" or "Godstock" by its supporters, and it was geared to high school and college students. (Its official title was the International Student Conference on Evangelism.) But the prevailing vibe could not be confused with the groovy hippie style of Lonnie Frisbee and Maranatha! Music, or even *Jesus Christ Superstar*. The Dallas setting made some of the difference. Nightly gatherings packed the Cotton Bowl. There was also the planning. Explo '72 was the brainchild of Bill Bright, founder and president of the Campus Crusade for Christ, one of the most tightly run evangelical organizations in the United States. Budgeted at $2.4 million, the event's actual costs ran closer to $3 million.[4]

Hosting 75,000 registered delegates for a five-day conference in a major city was a logistical feat of mind-boggling proportions, and planning took a full two years for a staff that grew to 300 people. In all, 1,300 delegations arrived from 1,000 different cities, including 100-bus caravans from several cities. International delegates came from more than 100 countries. Workshops took place in sixty-three locations spread throughout Dallas, requiring 200 city buses, 750 chartered buses, and more than 11,000 automobiles for transportation. In addition to housing, one of the biggest challenges was making good on a pledge to feed 35,000 high school kids for the week. Dr. Pepper contributed enough syrup concentrate to fill an Olympic swimming pool. Downtown hotels were practically bursting with convention delegates. "We're bringing in rollaway beds from as far away as 700 miles to take care of these kids," claimed the manager of the ritzy Adolphus Hotel.[5]

Despite the intensive planning, logistical snafus were inevitable, most involving transportation or lodging. Among delegates, remarkable stoicism prevailed. "At one point there were between 10,000 and 15,000 people stranded in the parking lot at Market Hall because their bus drivers had worked their allotted hours and were in a six-hour rest period," recalled Explo's general

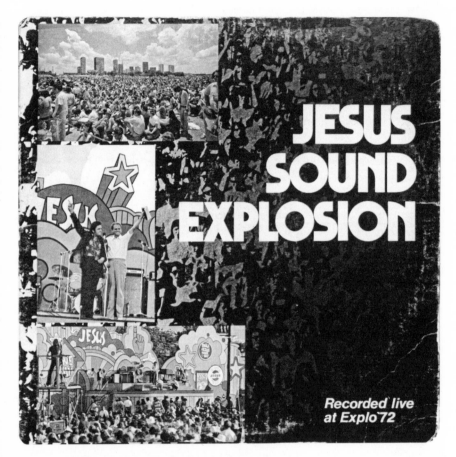

Live recording of Explo '72 (Author's collection)

director Paul Eshleman. "Those kids stood there patiently in the boiling sun until we could get shuttle buses and deliver them to their rooms. Their attitude amid the delays, heat, and inconveniences was tremendous! Many of them studied their Bibles and prayed during the long lines of waiting. Many said, 'You can't make it tough enough for me to complain.'" At the Cotton Bowl one night, emcee Bob Horner asked, "How many of you have had some kind of problem since you got to Explo?" Thousands of hands went up all over the stadium. Then he asked, "How many of you couldn't care less?" A resounding cheer shook the stadium.[6]

While Explo '72 is remembered chiefly for its Cotton Bowl rallies and all-star gathering of Christian musicians, the main focus was actually daytime seminars aimed at a range of constituencies: high school students, college students, college faculty members, military personnel, businesspeople, professionals, and government workers. Athletes (one speaker was Roger Staubach, quarterback of the NFL champion Dallas Cowboys), pastors, international delegates, women, blacks, and Spanish speakers were also targeted. All were directed at one overriding goal: teaching people how to witness effectively for Christ.

The instruction was practical as well as theoretical. "Each delegate's 15 hours of concentrated instruction in sharing the Good News had to be coupled with scheduled 'walk-and-witness' tours," wrote Eshleman. "No coaxing was necessary. Armed with the Four Spiritual Laws, thousands of delegates in all divisions eagerly combed great sections of Dallas, Fort Worth, and suburban cities in pre-planned assignments. They gathered the spiritual fruit that was ripe. Their battle cry: 'Hearts must be changed before problems can be solved.'" Door-to-door visits produced about 5,000 professions of faith, and hundreds claimed to accept Christ in the street, "including a policeman seen kneeling downtown with three youths praying over him."[7]

There were few recognizable Jesus hippies among the tens of thousands of young people. Residents and police had braced for yippielike disruptions, but few materialized. Even the delegates who looked like hippies were strikingly law-abiding, according to Eshleman.

On the green lawns of Lee Park along the shores of placid Turtle Creek where several hundreds of hippies had been arrested six months earlier in a narcotics raid, Explo delegates gathered some 500 strong to study, sing, and witness. In blue jeans and colorful skirts they sat sprawled on the velvet of green munching sandwiches, writing in their tablets, and listening to musical groups. Just as naturally as one talks about the weather, the young people discussed the humility and compassion of Jesus Christ. Buoyed up together they were unabashed. There was no embarrassment and no restraint. Officer B. S. Lovejoy, who had patrolled Lee Park through the severest hippie onslaught, had his ears washed out with "Praise the Lord!," "God bless you, officer," and "One Way!" "Great kids," he said.

A sergeant working the Cotton Bowl gushed, "They're the most enthusiastic crowd I've ever seen. But so orderly. They obey every announcement. Tell them to sit down and they do. It's really incredible."[8]

A few young protesters representing more radical positions did penetrate the aura of consensus and civility. "The People's Christian Coalition, an antiwar group composed mainly of Trinity college and seminary students from Deerfield, Illinois, kept Crusade officials hopping to head off leafleting and pint-sized demonstrations," wrote an observer. "Two dozen Coalition members and Mennonites one night in the Cotton Bowl held up a large banner reading 'Cross or flag, God or Country?' and chanted 'Stop the war' but were promptly shushed by the crowd."[9]

During a Flag Day ceremony at the Cotton Bowl, a group unfurled an antiwar banner and chanted slogans during an invocation by the navy chief of chaplains. The rabble-rousers, including a young seminarian named Jim Wallis, accosted him afterward, asking him if he still loved them. "Throwing his arms around several of them he replied, 'Yes, I love you,'" according to Eshleman, which "brought tears to many of the demonstrators' eyes." So-called radical groups planned to create further disturbances but were hampered by internal divisions. "A Christian group which had made plans to register protest for their social and humanitarian causes backed off when confronted with love and reason by our staff," Eshleman claimed. "'We cancelled our plans,' the protestors wrote, 'when you acknowledged our right freely to distribute our literature.' . . . People trying to create turmoil were greeted with love. The outsiders couldn't cope with that."[10]

Probably the closest Godstock came to the muddy squalor of Woodstock was its sodden Tent City. For fifty cents a night, about 2,000 delegates camped out on a field twenty miles west of Dallas. Two circus tents were erected for day-long training sessions. Delegates were alternately buffeted by broiling sun and unexpected thunderstorms that soaked many of their possessions and threatened to bring down the huge tents. Mosquitoes swarmed. Returning late from a rainy session in the Cotton Bowl, campers were met by police who told them they would have to stay elsewhere; some 500 were moved to private homes. Delegates generally took the plagues in stride. "A bedraggled camper spreading wet clothes over a car to dry saw a purpose in the twin rainstorms," Eshleman observed. "'I believe God dumped rain on us to bring us into a closer fellowship with Him,' he said. 'I believe He wanted total commitment in any situation—not just something that we liked.'" In addition to the rain, sweltering heat, and mosquitoes, the thirty-eight-acre site offered only fourteen sinks and twenty-nine showers for the assembled delegates.[11]

Jerry Bryant remembered the conditions vividly.

> Love Song's first album was released that very week. There were 100,000 people at Explo '72. I stayed out at Mud City, they called it. It was a trailer park out in the country. That's where we camped in a lot of tents and got rained on and it turned into a mass of mud and so we all still call it Mud City. Barry McGuire did one of his first Christian concerts there. I still remember him up on the stage in these cutoffs, flip-flops, and a T-shirt, and stomping his feet so hard he could have gone straight through that stage. He was just keeping that beat and singing songs about Jesus so pure that it just peeled the duplicity off of your heart. You knew you either had to sell out or stop playing the game. And he'd just be weeping like a baby, he was so full of the love of God.

All in all, Explo '72 presented a complicated map of cultural and generational politics. Clearly, the Jesus Movement had attracted the attention of powerful Christian evangelicals not generally associated with counterculture tendencies. One was Explo's honorary chairman, Billy Graham, who seemed to be everywhere in Dallas that week. He gave the final message for 180,000 at the music festival. He gave an impromptu sermon at the opening of Tent City when the scheduled speaker failed to show up. Graham even "set the pace for street witnessing by hitting the pavement himself with his 14-year-old son Ned," according to Eshleman. "Great crowds followed him as he strolled along, talking to people about the Lord Jesus Christ. He often signaled the "one-way" sign, and in reply to a long-haired youth with a beard and cutoffs who gave the evangelist a peace symbol, Graham returned the salute, flashing the "one-way" sign on the other hand. "'That means—peace, through Jesus Christ,' the evangelist told him."[12]

Graham explained to reporters that he had done his share of street preaching years ago in Tampa, Florida, "and it's just as effective today." Graham had likewise been involved in evangelizing youth since the early years of his career. The father of several baby boom children, Graham grew increasingly concerned about the political rebellion, drug use, and promiscuous sex of the late sixties. Rather than condemn, he tried to understand, listening methodically to piles of rock albums and donning disguises to engage young people in dialogue at demonstrations and rock concerts. As early as 1967, he glossed Timothy Leary's famous slogan, urging young people attending his crusade to "Tune in to God, then turn on . . . drop out—of the materialistic world. The experience of Jesus Christ is the greatest trip you can take."[13]

In 1970 Graham was allowed to speak at a Miami rock concert featuring the Grateful Dead, Procol Harum, and Santana; he praised the "terrific music" and urged the audience "to get high without hang-ups and hangovers" through Jesus. He became dramatically aware of the stirrings of the Jesus Movement on New Year's Day 1971 while riding in Pasadena's Tournament of Roses Parade. He noticed crowds of young people pointing their index fingers up toward the sky à la Larry Norman and shouting "One Way!" Graham felt himself in the presence of a new Christian revival, and he made sure his American crusades directly addressed these new believers. "Indeed," wrote Larry Eskridge, "Graham saw in the Jesus Movement a cadre of young prodigals who—rejecting the counterculture—had metaphorically come home to their parents' America via the bridge of an old American tradition: evangelical religion."[14] He quickly pulled together many of his sermons in a book titled The Jesus Generation, with flip chapter titles like "Bad Vibrations," "The Sex Hang-up," "Copping Out," "Hanging Loose," "We Wanna Revolution," "Turning On," and "Getting High."

Graham's high-profile presence and enthusiasm for Explo underscores the long-term activities of youth-oriented parachurch organizations like Inter-Varsity Christian Fellowship, Young Life, and the sponsor of the Dallas event, Campus Crusade for Christ, which began in 1951 with an outreach to students at UCLA. Its founder, Bill Bright, had moved from Oklahoma to Los Angeles to make a fortune in the fancy-food business before turning to evangelism. Bright's formidable energy, organizational and business ability, and contacts allowed Campus Crusade to expand rapidly during the 1950s and 1960s, acquiring an expansive headquarters in a warehoused resort complex in Arrowhead Springs in the foothills of the San Bernardino Mountains near Los Angeles. Campus ministry remained a priority. Bright's ambitions were nearly infinite. "Our target date for saturating the U.S. with the gospel of Jesus Christ is 1976—and the world by 1980," he told Time. "Of course, if the Lord wants to work a bit slower, that's O.K."[15]

Like Graham, Bright was alarmed at the rebellious turn of college students beginning in the midsixties. But his politics were considerably to the right of Graham's, who appeared to be drifting left. Bright was above all a staunch anticommunist. His politician friends included South Carolina senator Strom Thurmond; former Minnesota congressman Walter H. Judd; former Arizona congressman John Conlan; and conservative businessmen like Richard DeVos, president of Amway.[16] Campus Crusade had a presence on the campuses of the California state universities since the 1950s, but in 1967 it decided to take its message aggressively to ground zero of student rebellion. Early in that year, it launched a week of evangelizing that came to be known as the "Berkeley blitz." Hundreds of staff and students descended for Campus Crusade's national convention. The delegates heard speeches and testimony, attended workshops, witnessed and made phone calls to students, and held meetings in dorms, fraternities, and sororities. Three thousand people gathered at Sproul Hall to hear a speech titled "Jesus Christ, the World's Greatest Revolutionary." As at Explo, Billy Graham was the closer, addressing 300 faculty and administrators and 8,000 students on the final day.[17]

The Berkeley blitz was judged a success, but as the hippie counterculture expanded, Campus Crusade developed a new strategy that would tie it closer to the Jesus Movement. Bright decided to create a front group to directly challenge one of Berkeley's influential leftist organizations, the Third World Liberation Front. "Christian World Liberation Front [CWLF] was, in the beginning, a *front* organization for Campus Crusade," Bright explained. "We asked three of our choicest men to launch it, and most of our staff didn't even know about the plan. Only about half a dozen of us were aware of what was happening, and it was a test. There was a powerful radical movement among the students then, and we were trying to figure out which route to take, whether *we as a movement* should adopt a radical countercultural approach on campus in order to be all things to all people that we might win them for Christ. So these men founded CWLF, and I worked very closely with them."[18]

In order to blend in, the Crusade staffers went beyond Graham's disguises: they grew long hair, beards, and mustaches. "The formerly meticulous and suit-clad Jack," wrote one of them about his own transformation, "changed dress completely and grew a full beard." According to Jack Sparks, who had taught statistics at Penn State and became CWLF's leader, what might appear to be "superficial changes . . . were not undertaken in a lighthearted fashion or even in a coldly calculated manner. Here were people with a passionate desire to be God's men and women in a changing world, and these changes were their immediate adaptation. They were nothing alongside what was to come."[19]

The CWLF quickly established Christian communes and crash pads for runaways in the Berkeley area, hosted "Bible raps," founded an underground Christian newspaper called *Right On*, and flooded Sproul Plaza with leaflets, buttons, and T-shirts—and aggressive public witness. Within a few months, the CWLF had "gone native," cutting its formal connection to Campus Crusade in order to operate more flexibly in the challenging countercultural environment of Berkeley. Rather than infiltrating and witnessing to the Jesus Movement, the CWLF became the face of the Jesus People in Berkeley and was much covered by the national media frenzy over the Jesus Movement.

"I attended one of [Sparks's] Bible raps, and this one had at least two hundred participants, ages seventeen to seventy," reported Brian Vachon, the journalist who published a watershed article on the movement for *Look*. "The uniform was generally tie-dyed T-shirts and jeans, with a sprinkling of Afros and plenty of bare feet. I was struck with the remarkable ethnic balance in the room—like a sit-down strike at central casting—Chicanos, blacks, straights, hippies, orientals, Latins, young and old. . . . After several songs—standard hymns as well as re-styled folk tunes—Sparks spoke to the group, a soothing semi-sermon that combined street language with scripture." When it came time to collect the offering, Sparks invited those present to contribute if they could but take what they needed: "I don't expect to see any money in this hat when we're through passing it." Not everyone was impressed by Sparks. "I took him for another of these middle-aged teenagers I have met in so many Christian groups," wrote Lowell D. Streiker. "After all, here was a forty-one-year-old man with a Ph.D. in psychological statistics who dressed like a hippie and dropped the 'g' every time he used a word ending in 'ing.'"[20]

The efforts of Sparks and the CWLF significantly raised the metabolism of the Berkeley Jesus Movement, showing that an evangelical Christian message could be linked to a variety of street-level social-action causes that more orthodox groups like Campus Crusade avoided. They were also invited to Explo '72, where they gave training sessions on street evangelism at Tent City. "Of all the Jesus People groups I met," wrote Glenn Kittler, "Sparks's was the only one that took on public issues—the war, Pakistan, pollution, unemployment, civil rights, overpopulation, corruption, the whole scene. Surprisingly, the CWLF was usually on the same side with the radicals in terms of criticizing the Establishment, but the big difference was in the approach to the solutions." Kittler summarized their credo: "You can't change the System by destroying it. You've got to change people."[21]

Because of his academic background, Sparks was better equipped than most leaders to operate in an environment like Berkeley. Sproul Plaza could be a bit of a free-for-all, with novice street witnesses and potential converts talking right past one another. Proponents of different causes frequently argued face-to-face. A Street Christian known as Holy Hubert became legendary on the West Coast for being hospitalized twelve times after beatings by irate radicals. "Holy Hubert preached the Gospel so strong and so hard that he got every tooth knocked out of his face," Jerry Bryant said. "Multiple broken bones. Had people threaten him, come after him with knives." On at least two occasions he was said to have "turned the other cheek" by bailing his attackers out of jail.[22]

Cynics could be forgiven for questioning the motives of older, square evangelical leaders like Graham, Bright, and even Sparks. These were the years when the FBI was systematically infiltrating radical groups through its COINTELPRO (Counter Intelligence Program) effort, and it didn't seem a flight of conspiracy theory to see Explo '72 or the Christian World Liberation Front as fronts for parachurch organizations whose goals were to co-opt and defuse youth rebellion by replacing it with an evangelical Christianity more compatible with the social and economic status quo. The fact that the group in question labeled itself a "front," and that Campus Crusade founder Bill Bright baldly described it as such, made that impression even harder to avoid. But the full political impact of Campus Crusade came about through the publication of an unlikely book by one of its staff members in 1970. Apart from the Bible, no text had a greater impact on the Jesus Movement and the boomer evangelicals that followed than Hal Lindsey's *The Late Great Planet Earth*.

## Maranatha!

Though he rose to fame in Southern California, Lindsey was born and bred in Texas. He attended the University of Houston, fought in the Korean War, worked as a tugboat captain on the Mississippi, and endured a painful divorce. In 1958 he entered Dallas Theological Seminary, founded in 1924 to combat theological liberalism in the American churches and still one of the most important redoubts of fundamentalist orthodoxy. Cyrus Ingerson Scofield, editor of the Scofield Reference Bible and much beloved by Christians preoccupied with end-times prophecy, pastored a church in Dallas. His successor in that pulpit founded the seminary in 1924. Calling itself "the largest independent evangelical seminary in the world," Dallas puts its students through rigorous training in Greek and Hebrew.[23]

Lindsey graduated from Dallas after studying the New Testament and early Greek literature. He then began an eight-year stint with Campus Crusade, based mainly at UCLA, where he directed a successful campus ministry. He spoke at the Crusade's 1967 "Berkeley blitz." The following year, with the Jesus Movement stirring and himself a rising star, he left the Crusade to begin a new ministry at UCLA called the Jesus Christ Light and Power Company. "Hal has a particular ministry of prophecy and is a very gifted teacher," Bright acknowledged, stressing he still had "very warm affection" for Lindsey. "His emphasis at the time was so much on prophecy that we both felt he should have the freedom to teach outside the ministry of Campus Crusade for Christ. I didn't want us to become known as a prophetic movement, and I surely didn't want us to ride any particular theological hobbyhorse."[24]

Larry Norman recalled Lindsey, whom he considered a friend, as "the most bullheaded person I knew. You couldn't change his mind about anything. . . . See, he sought me out because of 'I Wish We'd All Been Ready.' He wanted to get to know me. He and I started having dinner together. He liked to pontificate. I'd sit and listen and think, is this the line from the Texas school he went to? Is this his original thinking? Is this guy really amazing, or is he just repeating stuff that he was taught?" The acerbic Streiker spent five days at the Light and Power House, an off-campus Christian dorm and training center that housed about forty students.

> I had picked Hal Lindsey out of the crowd. You can always tell who
> the leader is. He is ten years older than anybody else, and he wears
> the wildest shirt. So it was with Hal. He came on strong like a used-
> car salesman. He was excitedly waving a magazine. "How many of you
> have seen this week's *Time* magazine?" he asked. "Let's have a clap
> for Jesus. This *really* is a *really* fair coverage of what *really* is happen-
> ing." . . . Hal personifies the "Jesus is coming soon" fervor of the entire
> Jesus movement. Everything is seen as a fulfillment of prophecy—the
> Arab-Israeli conflict, air pollution, the recent California earthquake,
> X-rated movies. Even the fact that I am a Jewish-Christian was cited
> as evidence.[25]

At the time, Lindsey had recently completed *The Late Great Planet Earth*, destined to be the number-one best seller of the decade at 10 million copies (and as many as 28 million by 1998).[26] The first of many best sellers Lindsey would write explaining the intricacies of the end times, *The Late Great Planet Earth* popularized and condensed a body of thought about the end of the world that reached back over a century. What made Lindsey's approach so successful was the breezy, informal style with which he wrote and the way he drew very clear links between what his readers could see going on around them — the Six-Day War of 1967, the Cold War rivalry with the Soviet Union, the rising interest in astrology and alternative spiritualities in the United States, the move toward union of the various churches, the general social turmoil of the late sixties — and what the Bible predicted for the world as it neared the Second Coming of Christ.

As predicted, the Jewish nation had been reborn in Israel in 1948 and had repossessed Jerusalem in 1967. All that remained to complete prophecy was a rebuilding of the Temple on its original site in Jerusalem, where the Muslim Dome of the Rock currently stands. Other developments were necessary to set in motion the end of history, and all seemed imaginable in the late sixties: the rise of an Antichrist promising to bring world peace; the bodily ascent of Christians to heaven, called the Rapture; seven years of persecution and disaster — the tribulation — presided over by the Antichrist; and a final showdown between Israel and her enemies — Armageddon — in which Jesus would return to lead Israel to final victory. Then would come the millennium — a thousand years of peace.

Lindsey's book was colored by his experiences with the Jesus People, but it was also addressed to them. He organized it in short subsections with a catchy subtitle on nearly every page: "Tell It Like It Will Be," "What Do You Say, Isaiah?," "What's Your Game, Gog?," "How to Make Enemies and Influence People," "What Else Is New?," "Stay Tuned to the Facts," "Scarlet O'Harlot." Like Billy Graham, he chose chapter titles with a certain contemporary ring, such as "Russia Is a Gog" and "The Ultimate Trip." He referred to the Antichrist as "The Weirdo Beast."

Lindsey's experience with Campus Crusade and the Light and Power House put him in touch with what he considered disturbing tendencies of the counterculture. "The hippy [sic] musical, *Hair*, has its own staff astrologer to advise the cast on personal matters and make sure the circumstances are right for business," he confided. Lindsey recounted observing some California students "indulging in a primitive sort of sun-god worship on the lawn of their fraternity house. When they were questioned about their rather strange activities they said, 'There's a bunch of us up at Big Sur who worship idols and stuff.'" Another fraternity member was "an outstanding young man" interested in hearing about Jesus but unable to commit. "When I met him a few months later he looked completely different," Lindsey recounted. "He said, 'I'm really religious now — I feel sorry for you — I've been taking trips and I've really seen God. Only this God is the King of Darkness — this is the one we worship.'" Lindsey concluded that he had "completely blown his mind" and was "completely beyond reach. Satan uses these hallucinatory drugs to take man to a deeper level of approach with him. You talk to some people who have been on drugs for a long time and they will tell you, 'I know the devil is real—I've seen him.'"[27]

All of these trends, from geopolitics to youth culture, pointed to the fulfillment of biblical prophecy, the nearness of the end. *The Late Great Planet Earth* was attacked from many sides, both secular and Christian. It was dismissed as "science fiction fantasy" and "a farrago of nonsense." Lindsey himself was deemed "the Geraldo Rivera of the Christian world."[28] Former classmates accused Lindsey of simply dumbing down his Dallas seminary lecture notes. But the book sold many millions of copies, inspired many imitators and fellow travelers in prophecy, and shaped evangelical belief over the decade. Lindsey himself went on to write many sequels to his 1970 book: *Satan Is Alive and Well on Planet Earth*; *The 1980's: Countdown to Armageddon*; and *The Rapture: Truth or Consequences*, among others.

*The Late Great Planet Earth* ended with the word "Maranatha," translated as "The Lord is coming soon." It was also the final word in Billy Graham's *The Jesus Generation*, and Maranatha! Music was the name of the Jesus rockers who assembled around Lonnie Frisbee at Calvary Chapel. Calvary's pastor, Chuck Smith, was a die-hard proponent of end-times prophecy. Through the impact of Lindsey and Smith, among others, the theology of the Rapture and Armageddon would become one of the central threads in the music and belief of baby boom Christians, touching the music of everyone from Larry Norman and Keith Green to Bob Dylan.

End-times prophecy resonated with the Jesus People for several reasons. They were hearing it from people they trusted, people with credibility, like Smith, Lindsey, and even Graham. It was being reinforced in some of the most powerful music they listened to, as well as in films. And looking around at the state of things circa 1970, the world did seem poised on the brink. Martin Luther King Jr. and Robert F. Kennedy had been assassinated within a few months of each other. The inner cities were going up in flames, and college campuses became nearly ungovernable. Above all, there was the Vietnam War and the intense social divisions that it caused.

"Vietnam, communism, the nuclear bomb hanging over our heads, our entire generation," recalled Rick Tarrant. "I can remember as a young high school student sitting in the bedroom of a buddy of mine talking about the book of Revelation and nuclear bombs and all sorts of wild, bizarre scenarios. We didn't have a clue what we were talking about, but as young people you could talk about those things. I'm sure that if somebody was offering up some spiritual answer that seemed plausible, we might have embraced it, that might have solved a lot of questions for us at the time.

"We all thought Jesus was coming back in the next nanosecond," Tarrant continued, ruefully admitting that Lindsey's book played a major role in his own conversion at age twenty-one. "I'm not sure why it clicked with me. I think it really boiled down to it's kind of a scare tactic, really. The terminology back then was, you better get right or get left. A lot of people still hold to that view. Maybe it was the predominant view of the fundamentalists of the time, which helped. Maybe they embraced the youth culture more readily."[29]

In the Bay Area, Bernie Sheahan recalled, counting down to Judgment Day "was just sort of a given. There didn't even really seem to be that much argument. Because everybody read *Late Great Planet Earth* and it was totally convincing, as I recall. I don't remember arguing about it. But I remember I think I had a little skepticism about it. And at the time, I didn't know where [the theology] came from." Lindsey even came to Sheahan's church, the Peninsula Bible Church, to talk to the youth. "Which is kind of surprising," she said, "because, in terms of the church at large, I don't remember it being really emphasized. There were a lot of students from Berkeley and Stanford, a lot of professors from there, so it was a very intellectually stimulating church."

Sheahan also experienced the end times through another powerful medium.

> And then I saw one of those scary movies. I saw it with somebody from church. . . . Creeped me right out. *A Thief in the Night*. It's the New World Order. There are these vans like the U.N. actually driving around, and they're rounding up the Christians, jackbooted soldiers going into the churches and asking people to renounce their faith. Some of them leave and some of them don't and come out the back of the church. Very dramatic, and it scares the hell out of you when you're thirteen or fourteen. . . . It made me think, okay, if at some time in my life it gets like that, it's going to make me say, okay, do you renounce your faith? Uh-oh, could I do it? But that whole idea of people just flying up into the sky—I'd never heard that before. I thought that was pretty wild.

There was another reason for the success of end-times prophecy among Jesus People: Larry Norman. "I remember the first time I heard 'I Wish We'd All Been Ready,'" said Sheahan. "I think that's the first time I came face to face with that notion. So I was being fed that, and . . . what is that all about?" Norman's definitive statement on the topic, and probably his best-known song, "I Wish We'd All Been Ready" first appeared as a track on *Upon This Rock*. (A different version appeared on *Only Visiting This Planet*.) In the song, Norman paints a chilling picture of a world wracked by suffering, "guns and war," alternating with the mysterious disappearances of the Rapture. A couple are lying in bed together, and the husband vanishes; friends are walking together until one disappears. "Children died, the days grew cold / A piece of bread could buy a bag of gold / I wish we'd all been ready."[30]

Norman had written the song while living in Los Angeles, witnessing on the street and waiting for God's call.

> It was a beautiful time of my life because it was just me and Jesus. And I had to depend on him, which I wanted to, because nothing else was happening. I wasn't performing, I'd given up music. 'Cause I wanted to be pure. And I slept on the hard floor because I wanted to be like a Spartan. I was actually preparing myself for the end of the world. When that came, if I was still alive, I wanted to be tough enough to survive all the torture. I had to go to the dentist so I went and told him, "No novocaine." I just did everything I could to abuse my pain threshold, thinking that I had to prepare myself as a sacrifice—that I'm not gonna deny Christ.[31]

But songs kept coming to Norman in his sleep. He sang one of them into a tape recorder, forgot about it, wondered if he had just dreamed the song, and began to doubt whether God in fact wanted him to give up music. "It took me five, eight, ten minutes, maybe," he recalled. "And I thought, what a weird song! That's not really very normal. So I finally started singing in public, and by now I had a whole batch of new songs." He found he couldn't finish the song in front of an audience without breaking down or choking up. "So I decided I'm not supposed to sing that song. But meanwhile the song had gotten out because people had either tape-recorded it or just learned it, it's really simple. . . . Eventually it went all over the world, and also into different languages." Years later in Italy, Norman claimed, he was invited to a Bible study by "a Mafia chieftain's daughter" who'd seen her father murdered, and they played him the song in Italian. "How did you know that I wrote that song?" he asked her. "You didn't write that song," the girl replied. "That's a folk song. It's been around for centuries."

The end times haunted Norman from an early age. "When I was ten, I was praying that the communists would take over America because I didn't see much faith in anybody at my church, any of the kids," Norman said. "I just thought, we're a wicked generation, Lord. Please do something to us to make us decide to stay close to you. . . . Again, everything was so cut-and-dried when I was young: communists—evil; America—slothful. So have the communists come in and then we'll become really strong Christians. We'll be tortured for Christ." He tried to make sense of the subtle differences of doctrine between different varieties of millenialism. "I bought so many books and fold-out charts with drawings. And that's why I finally decided—you know what, Jesus is going to come when he comes, and I don't care when that is. . . . But I think with the kids," he said, referring to Jesus People, "they thought of the Rapture as the escape. They're gonna get out of here before the trouble begins. And then they don't even care what happens to the world."

Even Norman's first album with People! contains the song "One Thousand Years before Christ." The title refers to the peaceful millennium expected by many believers to follow Christ's Second Coming (which would itself follow seven years of tribulation). The lyrics offer a warning to young people faced with unhealthy choices, including the spiritual confusion wrought by Asian religions. The song ends with a tricky, layered flameout:

Not much time is left to go
Not much time is left to
Not much time is left
Not much time is
Not much time
Not much
Not.[32]

Norman's second solo album for a major label, *Only Visiting This Planet*, is considered to be his masterpiece and maybe the greatest work of Christian rock. Recorded at George Martin's A.I.R. Studio in London, where Norman moved in 1971, the album was released by MGM. It includes the shuffle-boogie anthem "Why Should the Devil Have All the Good Music," a manifesto for Christian rock. "I ain't knockin' the hymns," Norman sings, "just give me a song that moves my feet / I don't like none of them funeral marches." But most of the album vents the social discontent of the end times, sixties style.[33]

In "Why Don't You Look into Jesus," he blasts the empty hedonism of the rock stars he opened for: "Sipping whiskey from a paper cup," "Shooting junk until you're half insane," "Gonorrhea on Valentine's Day and you're still looking for the perfect lay." "I Am the Six O'Clock News" takes on the indifference of network news amid conditions of war. A journalist packages "color movies of misery" from Southeast Asia while living in "a suite at the Saigon Hilton," "drinking black market booze," and attending "cocktail parties with Premier Ky." "The Great American Novel" blasts a country that "poured its love out on the moon," "murdered law," "learned to make a lie sound just like the truth," and lynched black men "just for talking to your daughter," then took their wives as mistresses. "Reader's Digest" scorches the rock business: the Rolling Stones have become millionaires, the Beatles preached love but broke up bitterly, Hendrix and Joplin died of drug overdoses, Jesus has become a "superstar."

For Jesus People, Norman may have been the bard of end times, but he did not invent the apocalyptic pop song. The idea that the world was headed for an apocalypse cropped up in the roots music of the folk revival, most famously in the songs of Bob Dylan. The urgency and eloquence of his early music, the fiery cadences of songs like "A Hard Rain's A-Gonna Fall," conjured up images of an Old Testament prophet—Jeremiah railing against a fallen America. "Hard Rain" is remarkable for its eerie, Revelation-like images: a newborn baby surrounded by wild wolves; "a black branch with blood that kept drippin'"; "ten thousand talkers whose tongues were all broken."[34] The antiwar, antiracist messages of Dylan's early acoustic folk recordings anticipated the hard-edged social criticism that Larry Norman would produce a decade later.

Johnny Cash, a friend of Dylan in these years and a star attraction at Explo '72, drew more biblically on end-times theology in his song "Matthew 24 (Is Knocking at the Door)." Included on the album *Johnny Cash and His Woman* (the woman being June), the song refers to the chapter of the first Gospel in which Christ prophesies to the disciples about the coming end times and Rapture. Jesus predicts widespread wars, earthquakes, famines, persecutions, false prophets, and lawlessness, followed by a triumphant return of the Son of Man: "With a trumpet blast he will send out his angels, and they will gather his chosen from the four winds, from the farthest bounds of heaven on every side." Cash's song compresses all this into two stanzas and a chorus: rumors of war on the radio, people readying for battle, and an earthquake. The second verse practically channels Hal Lindsey: "A great bear from the Northland has risen from his sleep," while the Chinese Red Army mobilizes "near two hundred million deep." The singer dreams of "lightning in the east." The chorus drives the message home: "Matthew 24 is knocking at the door / And today or one day more could be the last."[35]

Not even superstars like Dylan and Cash had more commercial success with the apocalypse than Barry McGuire. Despite the early sixties' reputation for innocence and optimism, the apocalypse figured in a hit in 1965,

McGuire's "Eve of Destruction." Actually written by nineteen-year-old P. F. Sloan, the song takes aim at a range of current events, from the Vietnam War and nuclear terror to greed and waste. It casts a global view, noting the "eastern world" exploding and bodies floating in the Jordan River. Currents of hate run all the way from "Red China" to "Selma, Alabama." And America's political system is inadequate, judging from the impotence of senators, while civil rights marches seem to tilt at windmills. Naturally, there is concern about "the button"; while a space launch provides a temporary respite, nothing back on earth changes.

"I thought that 'Eve of Destruction' was the truth," McGuire explained. "It was just a bunch of newspaper headlines set to music. It had to be sung. It was the first song I'd heard that laid it down just as it was." Despite being widely banned from radio, it managed to become a number-one hit in the year of the Beatles' *Rubber Soul* and Dylan's great trio of electric rock albums. It was widely covered by other groups, and it inspired answer songs as well. A right-wing campus-based group called the Christian Anti-Communist Crusade attacked the song on political grounds, claiming it was part of a plot to instill "fear" and "hopelessness" and therefore to "induce the American public to surrender to atheistic international Communism."[36]

McGuire was one of the first celebrity converts to the Jesus Movement. Originally a pipe fitter, McGuire borrowed a friend's guitar in 1960 to teach himself some folk songs. His talent led to increasing moonlighting work, and within a couple of years McGuire had helped form the New Christy Minstrels along with Gene Clark of later Byrds fame. The group made him famous and kept him busy, singing upwards of 300 concerts a year. "I didn't think we were being dealt with fairly financially," he recalled. "And I got tired of singing 'Green, Green,'" which had risen to number 14 on the pop charts.

McGuire was also spiritually restless.

[I took] an excursion into Eastern mysticism that was taking place at the time. And I thought, maybe there's some answers, spiritual answers that I'm missing. Like there's something spiritual about us human beings. And a friend of mine in the Christys, we used to sit up at night and talk and read and wonder about reincarnation, and if it wasn't reality, what would happen to the human spirit when the body dies? Is there any afterlife? Just questions like that. So I left the Christys really in search of some answers. And I thought, well, the only way I'm going to find the truth is if I speak the truth.[37]

McGuire was in the Broadway production of *Hair* for about a year, finding in the show "a statement of spiritual expansion, understanding, awareness." But he decided he didn't want to become an actor and moved back to Los Angeles. He explained his decision in a filmed interview.

> I'd been a hippie so long. You know, as far as I know I had the first pair of flowered pants that was ever worn at a love-in. Made 'em myself. So I was Hippie One, you know. I gave everything away. I figured the only way to find truth—this was before I met Jesus—was to get rid of all the stuff out of my life so I could get down to reality. What's real. And I got hold of this little paperback book called *Good News for Modern Man*. And I didn't know what it was. I thought it was just some existential thing. Picked it up, opened it up and right there on the first page it says, "the New Testament in modern English." And I got really—oh look, the Jesus Freaks! They're disguising the Bible! Threw it on the floor. And then a few days went by and just out of a sarcastic curiosity—well, what is this Jesus trip all about anyhow? All these weird people out, saying Jesus loves you.
>
> So for the first time in my life, I stopped looking at Christians. I stopped looking at preachers and denominations, organizations, and I took a look at the man Jesus and what he had to say. And as I put it to the test against what I knew to be true, just through my own life experiences, everything Jesus says rang true. And I said, this is it—this is the answer I've been looking for all these years. This is the answer to "Eve of Destruction," this is the answer to all our political problems, all our racial discrimination. Everything wrong with society— here's the answer. So simple.[38]

Belief in the apocalypse tends to work against active politics: why bother changing the political or economic system when all human endeavor is to be wiped away at any moment? But this antipolitics easily becomes its own kind of politics, a stance of quiescence, of passive acceptance of the status quo. Evangelicals in the United States have oscillated on this issue, moving to the forefront of social reform at certain moments (abolition, women's suffrage, temperance, civil rights) and bowing out at others, most pointedly after the Scopes "monkey trial" public-relations debacle of 1925. As the seventies began, evangelicals were poised to make their presence felt in electoral politics. The Jesus Movement faced a choice in 1972: should they throw their support behind the incumbent Richard Nixon or join the majority of their fellow baby boomers in support of the challenger, George McGovern. But the political agenda and loyalties of the movement remained extremely murky.

On the very day that Explo '72 came to a climax with its Jesus Music Festival, Republican operatives were caught breaking into the Democratic Party headquarters at the Watergate complex in Washington, D.C. A month later, the Democratic National Convention convened in Miami Beach and nominated George McGovern. Jesus People were among the many groups to flood the convention, creating a presence they called "Demo 72." Jack Sparks and the Christian World Liberation Front flew in from Berkeley, handing out hundreds of tuna sandwiches and thousands of donuts. The young activist Jim Wallis was working the convention. At a park, 500 young evangelicals shared space with Students for a Democratic Society, Vietnam Vets against the War, the Southern Christian Leadership Conference, the yippies, the Welfare Rights Organization, and the Gay Liberation Front. "I don't believe in what they're saying," Jerry Rubin said of the Jesus Freaks. "None of them has talked with me, and I wouldn't talk with them even if they tried. Jesus was a junkie. I don't want to be bothered by . . . those . . . questions." But Sparks claimed that fifteen radicals a day accepted Jesus.[39]

A month later, the Republicans met, also in Miami Beach. Nixon had been a particularly canny wooer of evangelical voters. "Every president in American history had invoked the name and blessings of God during his inauguration address," wrote historian William Martin, "and many, including Billy Graham's friends Dwight Eisenhower and Lyndon Johnson, made some notable public display of their putative piety, but none ever made such a conscious, calculating use of religion as a political instrument as did Richard Nixon." After taking office, he had instituted regular White House church services, often with Graham as preacher. "I just thought it was a great idea that the President of the United States would have services in the White House," the evangelist explained. "I don't think there was any political connotation. There might have been, but I think Nixon was being very sincere. He wanted to set an example for the whole country."[40]

So which way would young Christians turn, many of whom were voting in their first presidential election? A Dallas Morning News survey found that Explo '72 delegates favored Nixon over McGovern by a ratio of more than five to one. Even if the Dallas cohort was not typical of Jesus People at large, this was a startling anomaly within the larger youth vote. On the other hand, after talking with residents of Hal Lindsey's Jesus Christ Light and Power Company near UCLA, Robert Ellwood found them rejecting the view that

Lindsey's prophecy beliefs strengthened the political Right: "They cited Hal as saying that the right wing is just as dangerous as the left, if not more so, as a potential source of the Antichrist's demonic one-world government." Based on his observations among a similar cohort, Lowell Streiker predicted massive indifference to politics among Jesus People: "For there is no room in the movement for the discussion of politics, international or local issues, the salvation of the environment, or the resurrection of the cities. . . . [T]he Jesus people will be too busy discussing the Bible, proclaiming the salvation of souls, the resurrection of Jesus, and the impending end of the world to care who is elected to the presidency or the Congress of the United States of America."[41]

No wonder the New Left considered the Jesus Movement a right-wing conspiracy, he pointed out: "There is always the possibility that an unscrupulous politician may inject religion into the forthcoming campaign, may attempt to package himself as a 'Bible-believing, born-again Christian,' may appeal to his friendship with Billy Graham, may even declare that his opponent does not believe in God, Jesus, or the American way." Only then would Jesus Freaks be motivated to vote, Streiker believed.[42]

Clearly, parachurch organizations like the Billy Graham Evangelistic Association, the Campus Crusade for Christ, and the Full Gospel Business Men's Fellowship had an interest in dulling the potential countercultural edge of the Jesus Movement, and as the decade wore on, a more conservative politics became increasingly evident among evangelicals. But there is no evidence that these groups were motivated in their outreach by political concerns, that they worked together to co-opt the Jesus Movement, or that they maintained much control over the youth they sought to evangelize.

Like the Popular Front cultural organizations of the thirties and forties, the countercultural front in which the Jesus Movement participated encompassed a proliferation of fluid, evolving political viewpoints and strategies. Comparable to the Communist Party USA of the earlier period, groups like Campus Crusade sought to align with and organize young people, which isn't to say that they sought or achieved control. And to a degree, people like Billy Graham and Jack Sparks became fellow travelers of the free-floating Jesus People they attempted to reach and mobilize. Graham, Sparks, and others were converted to certain countercultural values just as they sought to convert disillusioned youth to their Christian faith. "The counterculture and the Jesus Movement impacted Campus Crusade in the late 1960s and early 1970s, as the rhetoric and music of the organization changed dramatically, and the ministry evidenced much greater social awareness than it had in the early

1960s," concludes John G. Turner in a recent study. "These proved to be enduring changes for Campus Crusade, even though its embrace of the Jesus Movement was only partial and temporary."[43]

Moreover, prominent evangelicals like Graham and Bright, not to mention Jerry Falwell, Pat Robertson, and other leaders of the Religious Right who would gain prominence during the seventies, considered themselves the real cultural insurgents. They positioned themselves diametrically opposed to, not aligned with, the "Establishment"—meaning the news media, mainline churches, higher education, Hollywood, record companies, and most of the federal government. These evangelicals defined themselves against the mainstream of American culture. But they also admired the powerful hold this culture had over the young. Over the succeeding years and in a variety of ways, evangelicals challenged the preexisting culture in which they operated at the same time that they set about creating a parallel culture of their own, one in which music would play a major role.

## Chapter 4

# SOUL ON CHRIST

The same month that Jesus People of many shapes and sizes descended on Dallas for Godstock, Atlantic Records released *Amazing Grace*, a double album by Aretha Franklin. Recorded a few months earlier at two consecutive night services at the New Temple Missionary Baptist Church in Los Angeles, *Amazing Grace* was a kind of homecoming for the soul superstar. Aretha was backed by the Southern California Community Choir under the direction of gospel titan James Cleveland, whom she had known as a girl in Detroit; the young Cleveland had been the musical director at New Bethel Baptist Church, where Aretha's father, C. L. Franklin, was senior minister. Reverend Franklin was present in the Los Angeles church for his daughter's performances, as were Clara Ward, the gospel great who had been a close family friend and mentor to Aretha, and John Hammond, the producer who signed Aretha to her first recording contract at Columbia.

"I wanted this to be a live recording with a real congregation," Franklin said. "Gospel is a living music, and it comes most alive during an actual service." She chose a canny mixture of gospel chestnuts and contemporary songs that would resonate with a broader audience. Songs from her childhood included "Mary, Don't You Weep," a sprightly waltzing 6/8 double-timed "What a Friend We Have in Jesus," Clara Ward's "How I Got Over," "Never Grow Old," and a soaring ten-minute rubato version of "Amazing Grace" that pushed the worshippers into frenzy. "'Precious Memories' is what the service is all about," Franklin said, and she sang a deeply grooving 6/8 version of that gospel hymn with Cleveland. In contrast were her versions of two contemporary hits: Marvin Gaye's "Wholy Holy" and Carole King's "You've Got a Friend," which was interwoven with fragments of the venerable Thomas A. Dorsey gospel anthem "Precious Lord, Take My Hand." Along with Cleveland at the piano, Aretha was backed by crack studio musicians who'd played on her secular recordings: Cornel Dupree on guitar, Chuck Rainey on bass, and Bernard Purdie on drums.[1]

As the first session began, Cleveland welcomed the congregation to be part of the recording and encouraged them to make their presence audible. "I'd like for you to be mindful, though, that this is a church," he added. "We want you to give vent to the spirit. And those of you who are not hip to giving vent to the spirit, then you do the next best thing." Judging from the recording, the congregation at the New Temple Missionary Baptist Church was transfixed by the music. Hammond noticed Clara Ward and her mother "moaning" along with the choir, and producer Jerry Wexler noticed several in the congregation carried away by the spirit. "I mean, where they go into a gospel trance," he elaborated, "and the ladies with the white coats with the red cross on them lead them to the ambulance, and they go into rigor and they speak in tongues."[2]

"Anybody here know anything about the sanctified church?" Cleveland asked on the second night. "Over in the sanctified church, when they begin to feel like this, all the saints get together and they join in a little praise. I wonder, can I get you to say one time: Yeeaahhh . . . Yeeeaaahhhhhh." Reverend Franklin took to the pulpit to proclaim: "It took me all the way back to the living room at home when she was six and seven years of age. It took me back to about eleven when she started traveling with me on the road singing gospel. I saw you crying, and I saw you responding. But I was about to bust wide open. You talk about being moved! Not only because Aretha is my daughter. . . . Aretha is just a stone singer!" He related a conversation with a dry cleaner in Detroit who had seen Aretha on television and expressed hope that she would return to church singing. "If you want to know the truth," the reverend had replied, "she has never left the church!"

Aretha took pains to emphasize the same thing: she was not a worldly entertainer returning to her spiritual roots. "When I say 'took me back to church,'" she explained, "I mean recording in church. I never left church. And never will. Church is as much a part of me as the air I breathe. I have heard people say that one singer or another 'gave up gospel for pop.' That is not my case." In 1971 she had assured an interviewer the same thing. "I don't want to sound phony about this," she told *Ebony*, "for I feel a real *kinship* with God, and that's what has helped me pull out of the problems I've faced. . . . No matter how much success I achieved, I never lost my faith in God."[3]

But according to Wexler, who produced the great string of albums Franklin recorded for Atlantic after leaving Columbia, the singer had to be coaxed to record *Amazing Grace*. "She didn't want opprobrium from the church," he claimed. "After all, she's a deeply religious person, and she's been brought up in the ministry, and there's been all the gospel people around her, the Clara Wards and the James Clevelands. She had a lot of qualms about going in and doing church music, when here she'd been singing blues and jazz— 'profaning,' so to speak." Some of those attitudes were loosening, Aretha observed. "I really believe that people have become more and more broad-minded about entertainers," she said. "They've come to realize that you can be an entertainer and still be someone who is trying to do the right thing by everyone—which is what I always try to do."[4]

For a gospel double album, *Amazing Grace* did stunningly well. The first album to list Aretha as a coproducer, it went gold (a first for gospel), reached number seven on the pop charts, and won a Grammy for Best Soul Gospel. Aretha had reason to take pride in helping spread gospel to new audiences and in repaying her "great musical debt" to Cleveland by talking him up among television producers. "And after that, the Grammys presented artists like the Clark Sisters and Shirley Caesar to a vast mainstream audience," she noted. "Along with Edwin Hawkins's 'O Happy Day,' *Amazing Grace* proved to the record industry that gospel could sell."[5]

But the album, Aretha Franklin, and black musicians more generally inhabited a sort of parallel universe to the goings-on at Explo '72 or in California's Jesus Movement churches. The Jesus People "weren't sure if Franklin was *really* an on-fire-for Jesus Christian or just a soul singer drawing on her background to sing some Christian songs," explained Mark Allan Powell, an authority on Christian popular music. "If the latter, they didn't want anything to do with it—no matter how well done the songs might be. Jesus people didn't buy Judy Collins's version of 'Amazing Grace' either—a number fifteen hit in 1970. They would rather listen to kids from Calvary Chapel warble little ditties than listen to stellar performances of masterpieces by divas who might not really mean what they were singing."[6]

At age ten, Aretha had been baptized at her father's church and "accepted Jesus Christ as my Lord and personal savior," as she would claim, using the requisite evangelical language. But that wasn't always enough. Her life included the sorts of crosses that other high-profile Christian musicians had to bear: teenage pregnancy, arrests for drunk driving and disorderly conduct, an abusive marriage and divorce, her father's legal troubles and a shooting that put him in a coma, and the deaths of her mother and, later, her sister and brother. Still: Was Aretha one of the Jesus People? Was she too success-ful, too worldly? Or was the Jesus Movement subtly colored white? Follow-ing directly on the heels of the civil rights and Black Power movements of the sixties and, like them, enlisting young people, the Jesus Movement could be expected to welcome blacks. After all, earlier periods of evangelical revival-ism—the Great Awakening of the 1740s, the Second Great Awakening early in the nineteenth century, and the Pentecostalism that emerged in Los Ange-les a century later—had all challenged America's color line.[7]

Contemporaries who got their first glimpse of Jesus People through NBC's televised special on the Children of God would have seen a fairly integrated pocket of the movement. For starters, most of the program was filmed at the group's headquarters near Thurber, Texas, an abandoned Bible camp re-named the Texas Soul Clinic. Viewers meet a "former black militant" named Simon, who evangelizes in Cincinnati and declares bluntly:

> I hate religion. I don't believe these pictures you see of Jesus Christ
> with the white skin, the big baby-blue eyes, and the Breck-shampooed
> blonde hair. That's not Jesus, you see. Jesus, as I heard one brother put
> it, was a dirty, funky, degenerate hippie out of the slums of Galilee,
> and the cat was for real. You understand? He didn't put up with church
> buildings. If he came back today, they would string him up for the mere
> fact of what he laid down in here. He laid down things so heavy in the
> scriptures that your top revolutionaries that have ever been, Lenin,
> Karl Marx, they all got it from right here, the scriptures. Because what
> Jesus laid down was a revolution, a spiritual revolution, you see.[8]

Simon was an exception. The ideal of integration was honored among Jesus People, but in reality the movement remained predominantly white. Hiley H. Ward went undercover to investigate the Jesus Movement, criss-crossing the continent to stay incognito at Jesus houses and chat up young Christians in coffeehouses. He published his findings in a 1972 book titled *The Far-Out Saints of the Jesus Communes*. "The Jesus People do have their conflicts and difficulties over race," Ward concluded. "But the integrationists tend to win out." Up in West Toronto, he found an African American from Brooklyn named John Woods serving as an elder at the House of Smyrna. "It never occurred to me, my color," he said when asked about him and his wife being the only blacks in the community. "Jesus appeared to all. He died for me as he did for white people." One of Woods's housemates agreed. "It never occurred to me there is any difference between John and me," insisted Ken Hollington. "The spirit puts these differences away."[9]

Ward summarized what he discovered in his journeys among the Jesus People.

> At Renewal House in Los Angeles, a black sits in a stuffed chair, his white peers scattered around the room on a divan and on the floor. Black and white pray out loud, each several times. A white girl brings a black date to the Christian House for a Bible rap in Vacaville, Calif. A black fellow marries a white girl in the Children of God in Detroit. A black, Jesse Wise, walks with Arthur Blessitt in a 3,500-mile trek across the country from Los Angeles to Washington pushing a life-sized cross. Ann Walker, a black, heads a white commune (Fountain Chapel) in Vancouver, after splitting off from the Jesus People Army group. Blacks and whites discuss contemporary subjects in the Emmaus House, Toronto, and never think to mention race as a topic.[10]

The Sacramento-based, black-led Youth for Truth, whose staff came from a variety of church backgrounds, races, and regions, made a particular impression on Ward. The group's director, Harold Brinkley, who'd logged three years in the army, admitted Youth for Truth encountered prejudice from the white Pentecostals with whom they shared spiritual affinities. "We try to go into churches, but there is a real fear there," he said. "Maybe they feel some of our black fellows might date their white girls."[11] The fact that more than half of the staff were women, and most of the men were African American or wore long hair, undoubtedly raised hackles among more conservative evangelicals not accustomed to casual mixing of races.

Scott Ross was one of the pioneers of youth-oriented Christian radio and founder of a Christian commune in upstate New York. Before becoming born again in the midsixties, he had been a top deejay in New York City, hung out with the Beatles, partied with the Rolling Stones, and married one of the Ronettes. He then met and teamed up with Pat Robertson, then in the early stages of building his Christian media empire. Checking Ross's references, Robertson was astonished to learn that he was married to a woman of color. "My heart did a flip-flop," he wrote. "Here I was, dependent on the conservative Christians of the Tidewater area for our support, and getting ready to bring in a hippie-type disc jockey with a black wife." Robertson decided to go ahead with the invitation anyway. "It turned out she was a perfectly charming person with rather light-colored skin," he discovered, "something that was to stand in her favor in those early days in Portsmouth."[12] For a time, Nedra Ross was able to pass as a dark-skinned white, but when her darker relatives came to visit, the couple (who had a baby) was asked to leave their three-floor townhouse. They relocated to upstate New York, where they founded the Love Inn.

In addition to the deeply rooted American bugaboo about miscegenation, another assumption operated among some white Christians, whether mainline liberals or evangelical conservatives: the notion that at some level, blacks were more properly the object of missionary work than they were fellow laborers in the vineyard of the Holy Spirit. There were many exceptions to this attitude, of course, Billy Graham being the most prominent. In *The Jesus Generation*, he asserted that "*the most volatile situation threatening our annihilation is that of racial prejudice and hatred*. A famous clergyman has recently stated that we are likely to be exterminated by a racially incited war before the end of this century."

Contrary to country singer Ray Stevens's number-one hit "Everything Is Beautiful," which opened with second graders singing "Jesus Loves the Little Children," Graham worried that "little love seems to be lost between the races at this inflammatory moment of history. Go with one of my team members, with a reporter, or with a social worker to any American city and you will see the tension between black and white," Graham wrote. "I had thought a few years ago that our tensions were decreasing. I have changed my mind. Tensions may be increasing, especially in our great Northern cities where people are pressed together, rubbing elbow against elbow." But Graham was cutting against the grain of many Christians most receptive to his message.[13]

Some of these ambivalent attitudes were evident at Explo '72. Pointing out that approximately 3 percent of the total number of delegates were black, organizers took pride in the extent of integration. African Americans were wooed by Black Lay Seminars on topics such as "How to Walk in the Spirit" and lectures on Black Theology, and their exuberant worship style drew praise. "The black delegates were good for their white brothers and sisters," claimed Explo's planning chief Paul Eshleman. "In many cases they led the joyful expressions of praise, walking through the streets singing." There, they encountered their first candidates for conversion. "Our reception in the black community of Dallas has been tremendous," noted Chuck Singleton, a Campus Crusade staffer and coordinator of black ministries for Explo. Acknowledging the relatively small presence of African Americans, he still praised Explo as "the most technicolor I've seen compared to past Campus Crusade events and other revivals." Singleton predicted a major multiplier affect as zealous delegates returned to their communities fired with zeal for missionary work.[14]

One street encounter captures some of the dynamics at work. Sandi Rakou was returning from a rally at the Cotton Bowl when a stranger accosted the group she was walking with.

> "Hey, you cats, what makes you so happy?" he asked. "Let me see your credentials."
>
> "Jesus Christ is my credentials," Sandi replied.
>
> They continued to talk, the black man growing angry. Finally he held up both hands. "These are the hands of a criminal," he hissed. "Can your whitey God forgive me?"
>
> Sandi assured him that God would forgive him of everything.
>
> "I'll be selling out my people to believe in a white God," the stranger insisted. But slowly the light penetrated his heart. He prayed for twenty minutes there on the street, pouring out a stream of contrition. The man in the group prayed for him to be delivered from the grip of Satan. As they raised their heads the stranger's cruel look of hate had vanished. In its place was serenity and joy.[15]

An exchange like this, with its talk of a "whitey God," obscures the fact that evangelical Christianity had long been at the core of African American culture, and that, statistically speaking, blacks were the country's most highly Christianized ethnic group.

## Straight out of Compton

Though several NFL players were in Dallas as part of Campus Crusade's Athletes in Action program, the most visible African American at Explo '72 was a young singer and gospel group leader named Andraé Crouch. Backed by a group called the Disciples, Crouch's version of his song "Satisfied" nearly burned down the Cotton Bowl. "You know the joy of the Lord was so wonderful," Crouch sang,

> that I wanted a little bit more.
> So I got down on my knees, I lifted my hands,
> I began to praise the Lord.
> And something started moving and turning
> in the bottom of my soul, good God!

Right then and there you know that God
filled me with the Holy Ghost. . . .
I've got a satisfied feeling down in my soul.

Crouch set up an electrifying call-and-response with the Disciples:

No drugs!
  *Satisfied!*
No drinking!
  *Satisfied!*
No more searching!
  *Satisfied!*
No more running!
  *Satisfied!*

No more lonely!
  *Satisfied!*
Jesus!
  *Satisfied!*
Jesus!
  *Satisfied!*

I found out!
  *Satisfied!*
I found out!
  *Satisfied!*
I found out!
  *Satisfied!*

Black man!
  *Satisfied!*
White man!
  *Satisfied!*
Red man!
  *Satisfied!*

Brown man!
  *Satisfied!*
Jesus!
  *Satisfied!*
Jesus!
  *Satisfied!*

"Andraé Crouch is easily the most important gospel singer of the modern era, possibly of all time," asserted Powell. "With no disrespect to gospel giants like James Cleveland, it was Crouch who changed the sound of gospel music forever such that, a hundred years from now, all gospel recordings from the twentieth century will be classified as pre- or post-Andraé." Memphis deejay Rick Tarrant agreed when asked who had the biggest musical impact during the Jesus Movement. "The number one name that comes to mind is Andraé Crouch. . . . Andraé was embraced by the contemporary Christian culture probably not unlike the way Elvis embraced black music and brought it across the racial line. I think in many ways, Andraé Crouch played a crucial role in bringing some of the same musical flavors over from the black church to the white church."[16]

Born in Los Angeles in 1942, Crouch grew up drenched in the Church of God in Christ, for which his great-uncle served as a pastor and the California state overseer. (The church, located at 23rd and Central Avenue, was christened Crouch Temple in 1962.) Early on, music was a huge draw for Andraé. "During church, I remember sitting there enthralled when Sister Garnett would sing," Crouch recalled. "She had a deep, anointed soprano voice. She'd sing 'even me, let some drops now fall on me,' or a song like 'I'd Rather Have Jesus.' But when the jumpin' songs came on, I dug those too. Boy, how I dug them! I'd clap my hands until they were strawberry red. I had my own rhythm section; a group of boys my age, in short pants and high-top shoes."[17]

The family owned a dry-cleaning business, but Andraé's father Benjamin practiced some part-time ministry as a "bootleggin' street preacher" among drug addicts and alcoholics. After nearly being killed in a hit-and-run accident, Benjamin pledged more and more of his time to ministry, first in Val Verde and later in the San Fernando Valley. Andraé's musical career began in the miraculous way that seemed to characterize many events in his life (and the lives of fellow Pentecostals). "One day in the service Dad called me up front," he wrote. "He laid hands on me and prayed, 'Lord, I don't know what you want me to do. But if you want me to pastor full time here, will you give Andraé the gift of music?'"

Andraé got his chance two weeks later when, without any preparation, he was propped up by his father on a piano bench in front of the church. "The congregation had song books so I'd have to run up the scale to find out what key they were singing in, but I was soon playing for them. I remember one of the first songs I played, using both hands, was 'What a Friend We Have in Jesus.' Dad kept his promise and took the pastorate. I played for all the services and later started a choir."[18]

Crouch began to become aware of his spiritual gifts, like seeing visions and speaking in tongues, and he overcame his childhood stuttering. He was drawn to the church but ambivalent about the demands and hours involved in ministry. "All my friends at school went to parties, had stereos, and listened to Aretha Franklin and Nancy Wilson," he wrote. "I longed for the days I could have my own stereo equipment and an apartment of my own. But the Lord had other plans for me. When He called, He let me know that He was my source and I wasn't to rely on people."[19]

While attending San Fernando High School, Crouch joined with six other singers to form a group called the Church of God in Christ Singers. "The COGICS were a bunch of Spirit-filled kids," he wrote about the group, which included future "fifth Beatle" Billy Preston; Edna Wright, who would sing with the Honeycombs; Gloria Jones, who would write for Motown; and Crouch's twin sister, Sandra, who would later join Janis Joplin's Full Tilt Boogie Band. Next, Crouch assembled a vocal trio with a couple of young men he had witnessed to at his father's church. He encouraged them to perform at a church in Pasadena where Crouch knew the pastor and his family. "We sang four songs that night at the Nazarene church," he recalled. "The congregation kept applauding but we didn't know any more numbers to sing. We told them we'd do more next time. Shortly after that the Nazarenes were having a church-sponsored event at Disneyland, to which they asked us to come. That was the beginning of the Disciples."[20]

In 1965 Crouch felt himself called to quit his job, sell his car, and begin a choir for drug addicts at the Teen Challenge Center on Hobart Street in Los Angeles. "I'm gonna live on faith," he announced to his skeptical mother. "She looked at me in disbelief," he recalled. "'Yeah, you're gonna call my name faith now, huh? My name is gonna change from Catherine to Faith!'" Eventually, the Addicts Choir began touring and recorded an album featuring a Crouch composition called "The Addict's Plea." "When I sang it at concerts, many people thought I was an ex-junkie," he wrote. "The Lord gave me rapport with the addicts. I'd never been there, but I loved 'em so much."[21]

Working for years at Teen Challenge, Crouch developed his philosophy regarding human difference. "I learned so much at the Center about people," he wrote. "Whites aren't any different from blacks, blacks from Orientals or Orientals from Mexicans. Mankind is born in sin and shaped in iniquity and one race is just as funky as another. But though there's no difference at all, I disagree with making mankind a melting pot. We can have unit in purpose and spirit and still keep our separate ethnic and cultural identities. It's like rice and beans. . . . We need to enjoy the rice *and* the beans."[22]

Meanwhile, Crouch was continuing to direct the choir at his father's church, and the Disciples were beginning to perform locally. He published his first sheet music, "The Blood Will Never Lose Its Power," with Manna Music. In 1968 Crouch met Ralph Carmichael, who had written the slightly dated youth musicals on which many of the Jesus People had cut their spiritual teeth. By then the president of Light Records, Carmichael was impressed by Crouch and the Disciples and agreed to make their first album, *Take the Message Everywhere* — the first of seven albums that Powell asserts "are each as significant to the history of contemporary Christian music as *What's Going On?* (by Marvin Gaye) or *Off the Wall* (by Michael Jackson) are to the history of mainstream rock."[23]

Opportunities started to open up for Crouch and the Disciples. An invitation from an evangelist named John Haggai led to a three-month whirlwind tour through Japan, Hong Kong, Indonesia, the Philippines, Thailand, Singapore, Vietnam, India, Egypt, England, Scotland, and Germany. A week after completing this marathon, the Disciples were off to the South Pacific for more evangelizing. The group added new members in 1971, including Crouch's sister Sandra, most recently a "sanctified tambourine player" with Diana Ross, and a couple of white musicians. Andraé barely survived a mysterious, devastating illness he contracted during an overseas mission tour.

The group's 1971 album, *Keep on Singin'*, was a major hit, and they scored a Grammy nomination with "Christian People." The band appeared on the Johnny Carson and Dick Clark shows. Crouch had opportunities to water down his message for commercial success, but he resisted. "There are people who have made it to the top commercially but in a couple of years haven't stood for what they believed," he noted. "*God needs groups that will stand when they get there.*" Crouch considered himself in the "radical extreme," along with musicians like Larry Norman. "Larry and I have always been good friends," he said. "I really love him. His work is powerful because he knew what he was talking about. He was well versed in the Word. It was great back then to sing with all these groups at the Jesus festivals. When we played in concert, we had one purpose — to see souls saved. That was all we felt when we played. We would get blessed from each other's music."[24]

With the media attention to the Jesus Movement peaking in 1971, Crouch's timing was impeccable. Even more than Norman, the Disciples galvanized audiences of Jesus People, especially those with ears for the integrated, hybrid soul and rock being popularized by Sly and the Family Stone. Brian Vachon caught them live at the University of Southern California. "The auditorium

*On the Road with Andraé Crouch* comic book (Courtesy of Special Collections, Michigan State University Libraries)

was jammed with young people—over a thousand crammed into the bleachers and huddled on the floor," he observed. "The floodlighted platform was draped with a latticework of electrical wires and jammed with amplifiers. It could very well have been a stage to frame the Grateful Dead or Jefferson Airplane, and the crowd could very easily be like the multi-colored groupies that used to swell the insides of Fillmores East and West."

Following a set by Love Song, Crouch and the Disciples took the stage to an "almost deafening" reception, according to Vachon.

> The group was black—one of the few groups of blacks I had seen at any time while looking at the Movement in California. And Crouch himself was a big, authoritative man whose piano was hot soul.

> It's just like walking in the sunshine
> After a long and dreary day.
> I have a satisfied feeling
> *Since Jesus showed me the way.*

> "And how many *have* that satisfied feeling with Jesus in your heart," [Crouch] asked the audience with the melodious singsong of a black revivalist. "Let me see your hands."
> About eighty percent of the people in the room shot their hands up into the air, forefinger pointed skyward.
> "Praise God," [Crouch] said. "Because I trust you're not here just for the foot-stomping and the hand-clapping. We're here singing and talking about Jesus."[25]

Four months after Explo '72, where Crouch's "Satisfied" made such an impact, the Disciples achieved a milestone for Jesus rock, penetrating the cultural citadel of Carnegie Hall. The October 1972 concert was later released as a live album, considered one of the best live albums produced by the Jesus Movement and the first to achieve crossover success outside the Christian music audience. The Disciples were backed by a fine group called Sonlight, which included a rhythm section and a horn player. The show included some scorching music, which matched the infectious, high-energy funk of Sly and the Family Stone with the sort of witnessing you'd expect at a Billy Graham crusade.

Crouch excelled at these messages and invitations. "Hey, this is not a concert tonight—we having church!" he exhorted early on. "Can you imagine how the Lord feels when the world says, 'Hey, everybody's tripping out, and young people today are not really turned onto the Lord'? But here we are, letting the world know that *Je-sus* is the answer!"

He worked the crowd like an evangelist.

> Those of you that have searched through Krishna, through the Bahai faith, just searching through philosophy and religion. . . . Religion is merely man's search for God. But we're speaking about a relationship. And we want to let you know that there are thousands here tonight . . . that have found the answer to life. I want everybody to say who this answer? [Here, Crouch gets the audience into the act, building his own intensity with each question.]
>
> What is his name?
>
> Jesus!
>
> Say it again!
>
> Jesus!
>
> There's power in the name of
>
> Jesus!
>
> There's healing in the name of
>
> Jesus!
>
> There's salvation in the name of
>
> JESUS!
>
> The Bible says that demons tremble at the sound of that name.
>
> JESUS![26]

Crouch ended the concert with an altar call emphasizing the imminence of the end times. "I want you to give respect to these last few moments," he announced. "The Bible says in the last days I'm going to pour out my spirit among all flesh. You see the Devil is mad, so he has a revival going on too. Just because these are the last days all around the world we've traveled several times. And the world is waiting to know who can actually change your life. We want to know the answer to life . . . these last days. Tonight we have a very special announcement, that He has prompted our hearts to tell you. Think about it these last few moments: *It won't be long 'til we'll be leaving here.*"

Despite his musical success, Crouch endured endless condescension and judgmental behavior from audiences. "A lot of 'Christians' hide their prejudices behind scriptures," he wrote. "I call it passing the buck." Some audiences simply walked out when they discovered that a man named Andraé was black and not French. "People have a right not to like black music but as Christians they do not have the right to be rude or to hate a Christian brother or sister," he insisted. Some churches housed the group in substandard ac-

commodations, one time next to a filthy chicken coop. "I've sung for wed-
dings where 'Christians' have asked, 'What are you letting all those "niggers"
in your wedding group for?'"[27]

Crouch often found the attitudes insufferable. "I'm just praying that God
will develop some people so that they'll see that God is black sometimes, so
to speak, and that He is white sometimes," he wrote. "He is really no color at
all, but his vessels are many different colors." Crouch detected among many
Christians an underlying suspicion of rhythm. "Basically, the reason for the
complaint seems to be that the drums come from deep, dark Africa where
all the witch doctors practice," Crouch surmised. "But witch doctors use
candles, and we don't throw those out. We accept the flute in church worship, but the Asian Indians have used flutes for years to charm snakes. So it is
not the object, but *how* it is used."[28]

"We Christians get so wrapped up in 'religious' righteousness trips," Crouch
admitted. "Carrying out preconceived ideas and prejudices into the church
with us keeps us stagnant, makes us proselyte [sic] and condemn others. As I
have traveled, I've found out these hang-ups aren't just in black Pentecostal
churches but for that matter are in loads of churches, black, white, Mexi-
can—churches all over the country." He came to prefer performing in large
auditoriums. "Sometimes I pray, 'Lord, don't let me sing to a bunch of people
in churches,'" he wrote. "'Let me get out there and sing to people who don't
care what kind of clothes I have on, what color my skin is, my religious background or my so-called African rhythm—people who just want to hear my
music which speaks of You. Just let me sing to these people so that right away
they'll hear what I have to say and not waste all that time lookin' me over.'"
Crouch had no patience with "denominational hang-ups," either. "We spend
too much time questioning everybody's credibility," he complained.[29]

Crouch was aware of the church-based opposition to Christian rock, of
which the strident polemics of Bob Larson, David Noebel, and other outspoken ministers were only the public face. "But for some strange reason,
God is using it for these end times," he insisted. "Maybe that's because it's so
raw, not sugar-coated with all the little intricate words that are so pleasing.
It's a cry from our hearts that says, 'I need you, God. I'm desperate.' The world
today is searchin' for reality, not synthetic materials. God knew this would
happen. . . . Maybe He's usin' this type of music because it is a little radical. . . . Maybe we need a loud guitar to stir up the people to listen and think
about what they're hearing. I don't want them to walk away and say, 'Wasn't
that nice? Weren't they charming?'"[30]

Some of the enemies that Crouch faced were worse than human ignorance and prejudice, he believed; they were Satan-sent demons. For a period, he was afflicted by terrifying specters that made heavy-breathing and hissing noises. "I was about to find out what it means to be tormented, for they came back every three or four nights," Crouch recalled. "They would wake me up, be on the side of my bed shaking it, and stomp around my bed. They even swung on my lampshades. I'd be shaving and the door would open, or I'd see my door kicked open." Though the demons would vanish when rebuked in the name of Jesus—"Jesus's perfect love casteth out all fear"—the terror of the experiences lingered. He described it as "like being in a swamp, slowly drowning, with big, slimy snakes slithering all through your legs, weird voices in the trees above, fog all around you, and someone tryin' to take you somewhere but you never know where."[31]

Crouch's mother and sister Sandra were also targeted: "The demons seemed to harbor around my house, and several different people experienced this fear while they stayed there, even when I was away." Members of the Disciples were afflicted during a tour. "At home or on the road, it reached a point where I was being tormented so much that I didn't want to go to bed at night," Crouch recalled. "At concerts I would sing 'I've Got Confidence' and other victory songs. Then, filled with fear, I'd go to my room at night and cry, wondering if demons were going to bother me that night. I kept thinking, I've got to find a way to be rid of this."[32]

The last straw came when Crouch was visited by "a demon of lust" who dangled long hair in his face and blew seductively into his ear. "Instead of a fear trip as in the other experiences, [the devil] was tryin' to attack me with a pleasure trip. He knows I'm not married, that I've been given to the Lord, but he was attacking at a point of need in a weak moment." Crouch studied books on combating the power of Satan and returned home to cast out the demons: "In the name of Jesus, I bind your powers and cast you into the Pacific Ocean!" According to Crouch, the demons never returned.[33]

This sort of overt spiritual warfare was widespread in the Jesus Movement. To be beset with demons was a mark of commitment to the Gospel of Jesus; why else would Satan be taking such interest in the doings of a particular Christian? Jesus People existed in a supernaturally charged world in which both the Holy Spirit and Satan intervened directly and often in daily life. The harrowing challenges offered by the powers of darkness were countered, usually successfully, by a God who responded directly to his human followers who demonstrated the proper faith. This was most pronounced among Jesus People who were influenced by Pentecostalism—believers such as Scott Ross, who recounted several episodes where God seemed to respond in miraculous ways to the perceived needs of his Love Inn community. Eskridge's research shows that nearly all the former Jesus People he surveyed had experienced or observed miraculous phenomena such as baptism of the Holy Spirit, speaking in tongues, prophecy, or divine healing; a majority had participated or seen instances of demonic possession or exorcism. Crouch's dramatic encounters placed him solidly in the ranks of the Jesus Movement.[34]

## Wholy Holy

The very first hymn Aretha Franklin sang at the *Amazing Grace* services in Los Angeles was a gospel number titled "Wholy Holy." The Beatles had pleaded "Come Together" on *Abbey Road* two years earlier, which "Wholy Holy" faintly echoes. The song is a call to power through unity. It slides past in a slow, stately four-four, and Aretha is accompanied by a women's vocal trio intoning "Ho-ly Ho-oh-ly" in angular harmonies. "People we all got to come together, 'cause we need the strength," Aretha sings. The words speak of conquering hate and rocking the world's foundations, but only with Jesus's help.

Aretha's cover of "Wholy Holy" sold well. While the album itself reached number seven, the song was the one single from the album to reach the charts. But it's unlikely anyone in the audience had ever heard it in church; it was a very new song, written by Marvin Gaye for his breakthrough solo album of the previous year. Recording *What's Going On*, Gaye had finally broken the creative stranglehold of Berry Gordy on the Motown machine. It took a long-term battle of wills between Gaye and Gordy to get the album recorded and released. For the first time, a Motown artist had total creative control to record and produce his own album. *What's Going On* was immediately recognized as a sonic and lyrical tour de force.

Most strikingly, it was not a collection of singles but an integrated concept album in which musical themes are introduced and revisited throughout the songs. Far more than any other Motown album up to that time, *What's Going On* has the flavor of jazz. Conga drums and percussion create an underlying Latin vibe. Saxophone and flute solos color nearly every track, often playing in counterpoint to Gaye's multilayered vocals, which weave and merge seductively. He credited a master jazz saxophonist—the same man who influenced Billie Holiday's phrasing—for inspiring a breakthrough in his singing. "One night I was listening to a record by Lester Young, the horn player, and it came to me," Gaye explained. "Relax, just relax. It's all going to be all right."[35] At the same time, strings provide a lush backdrop that heightens the drama of the vocals and instrumental solos, with glockenspiel cutting the lushness of the strings slightly.

Like *Only Visiting This Planet*, Larry Norman's masterpiece, *What's Going On* offers a scorching indictment of American society circa 1971. The album's message might be summed up in one line: "I just don't understand what's happening across this land." Imagining the world through the eyes of his brother Frankie, a recently returned Vietnam vet, Gaye intersperses jeremiads against war, racism, urban blight, pollution, inflation, and drug addiction with pleas for community and agape — Christian love. These social problems might be ameliorated, he suggests, if people would honor the Golden Rule. "Find God. We've got to find the Lord," Gaye exhorts in his liner notes. "Allow him to influence us. I mean, what other weapons have we to fight the forces of hatred and evil? And check out the Ten Commandments, too. You can't go too far wrong if you keep them, dig it. Just a personal contact with God will keep you more together. Love the Lord, be thankful, feel peace. Thanks for life and loved ones. Thank you Jesus."[36]

Like Aretha, Gaye had grown up a preacher's kid but in starkly different circumstances. C. L. Franklin was a major public figure in black Detroit, an irrepressible character who loved ladies and the nightlife and who was once arrested for marijuana possession. Growing up in her father's church, Aretha was surrounded by gospel stars like Mahalia Jackson, Clara Ward, James Cleveland, and Sam Cooke. Gaye's father was an eccentric preacher in a Pentecostal Christian church that followed Orthodox Jewish laws. He physically abused Marvin as a child, burdened him with guilt that would haunt him the rest of his life, and shot him dead as an adult. Gaye would be scarred by his childhood, suffering depression and addiction to drugs and pornography for his adult life. He retained a deeply paradoxical Christian faith throughout his life that some have called gnostic — a clear-cut dualism in which the believer's bodily activities have no significance for his spiritual life.

"I loved my father's religion," Gaye insisted. "At a very early age, I realized I was born into a very rootsy church, and I found it exciting. The idea of tarrying thrilled and fascinated me. That's where you wait for the Holy Ghost, where you repeat over and again, 'Thank you, Jesus, thank you, Jesus, thank you, Jesus, thank you, Jesus,' until the spirit arrives."[37] As usual in Pentecostal worship, music was central and uninhibited, with horns, drums, percussion, and hand clapping all combining to push worshippers into an ecstatic state where the fire of the spirit could break through. As a rising singer in the Motown machine, Gaye had had little opportunity to express his gospel roots until 1971, when he secured total artistic freedom from Gordy.

Gaye went out of his way to acknowledge the divine presence in his album. "God and I co-wrote that album together," he told Smokey Robinson. "It was a very divine project and God guided me all the way," he confided to a journalist. "I don't even remember much about it. I was just an instrument. All the inspiration came from God Himself." Gaye told *Time*: "God and I travel together with righteousness and goodness. If people want to follow along, they can."[38] In "God Is Love," Gaye offers a short sermon on forgiveness. "Oh, don't go and talk about my father," he sings, because "God is my friend (Jesus is my friend)." God is generous and giving. "He loves us whether or not we know it / And he'll forgive all our sins," Gaye sings. "And all he asks of us is we give each other love. . . . And when we call on him for mercy / He'll be merciful, my friends." In "Wholy Holy," the song Franklin covered on *Amazing Grace*, Gaye calls on the community to unite, gather its strength, and spread love and salvation. "Jesus left a long time ago, said he would return," he sings. "He left us a book to believe, in it we got a lot to learn."

"Save the Children" sounds a more world-weary note. "Who really cares to save a world in despair?" Gaye wonders. A sense of the end times creeps in, as he acknowledges a time when "the world won't be singing" and "flowers won't grow." But in the end, he exhorts, "Let's save all the children . . . save the babies, save the babies!" Years later, Gaye would admit: "Revelations is the book in the Bible Father stresses most. It's the book I've studied most carefully. It contains the one script we'll never be able to undo—the final showdown, the day when it all comes down. With that kind of knowledge up in your face, it's hard not to go crazy."[39]

In other words, *What's Going On* was inspired by the same apocalyptic premonitions that ran through the Jesus Movement. "The world was coming down around me," Gaye told journalist David Ritz. "Dr. King's death confirmed my instincts about this country. America couldn't deal with someone that good and just. Suddenly everyone was going nuts. The riots in Detroit hit close to home. We could smell the smoke and hear the gunfire on West Grand." Gaye began identifying with the "white kids" counterculture. "They were smoking weed and dropping acid and I went along with them," he said. "I loved the hippies. They were rebels, like me, and they did this country a world of good. They finally stopped a terribly unjust war. They looked at the status quo and called it bullshit and they were right. They also had the right idea about the power of love. Who else was offering hope? For a while, when

Bobby Kennedy was shot and the cops ran over the kids at the Democratic Convention in Chicago, it looked hopeless."[40]

Unlike Aretha Franklin, though, Gaye expressed some ideas unacceptable to most Jesus People. "I respect the Eastern religions," he said. "Their philosophies are beautiful and wise. They've taught me to root myself in the present. I also believe in reincarnation. We're destined to return to repeat our mistakes if we don't grow toward God in this form. I respect Islam, though I worry that the Koran makes it too easy to kill. I respect all the great religions. But," he continued, "my own beliefs come down to two simple points. One, believe in Jesus, and two, expand love. Both points, you see, are really the same."[41]

Still, Gaye's opinion of organized religion closely echoed the critique commonly voiced by Jesus People. "It's not about this church or that church," he declared. "Almost all churches are corrupt. My church lives within my own heart. Jesus is there when you call him, whether you're strolling through a garden or caught in a storm at sea. He's a lifeline. He's a healer. His name is magic. His example is eternal. His hope is a beacon of light, and with him there is no fear, no death. When we don't follow his example and turn to exploitation and greed, we destroy ourselves." Gaye went even further. "Institutionalized religion is good for the masses but I have a special God who looks over me," he told journalist Steve Turner. "He is the same God that people worship institutionally but I feel I have a special link. Anyone can have a special link if they assert themselves."[42]

Asked if his turbulent personal life had prompted him to seek therapy, Gaye scoffed, saying that "the cure is already inside us. All we have to do is bring it out. All answers are contained within. God is within each of us. If we stop long enough to listen to the rhythm of our heartbeat, that's the rhythm of God's voice. After leaving Washington, I've never regularly attended church, but neither did I ever leave the church. The church never left my heart. I had religion, so why did I need head doctors?"[43]

These spiritual reflections aligned Gaye with two other artists who would dominate the pop and R & B charts for the remainder of the decade: Stevie Wonder and Maurice White of Earth, Wind & Fire. Wonder was eleven years younger than Gaye but had begun cutting records at Motown just a year after Gaye had (Gaye played drums on Wonder's first recording). He was not preacher's kid like Franklin and Gaye. He would claim to have been a junior deacon and occasional soloist at the family church, Whitestone Baptist, although an old friend brushed that off as a Motown invention. Singing outside in a neighborhood duo with a friend, Wonder recalled a sanctified church lady coming along to express her displeasure: "Oh Steve, I'm ashamed of you for playing this worldly music out here."[44]

But Wonder was clearly not troubled by the competing claims of Jesus and worldly pleasure. "Music is like a religion to me, and the more sharing that takes place between the musicians and the audience, the more spiritual the music becomes," he said. "We've still managed to make a lot of people have soulful experiences." Compared to soul artists like Franklin, who remained more rooted in black music, Wonder, with his early attraction to Dylan and the Beatles, "lit out for territories usually controlled by the 'white' counter-culture," according to Craig Werner. "Without losing black listeners raised in the church, he renewed his attempt to reach young whites whose sense of spirituality might come from transcendental meditation or the Grateful Dead."[45]

To a surprising degree, though, Wonder took up a rather traditional Christian position in the recordings he pushed through Motown during his astonishing burst of creativity in the early seventies. Wonder had been the first Motown artist to benefit from Gaye's successful securing of creative independence the previous year in *What's Going On*. Turning twenty-one in May 1971, Wonder demanded millions in earnings that he was owed by Motown, as well as creative control over future recordings. For the next five years, he dominated the charts and Grammys with a series of self-produced and -performed masterworks: *Music of My Mind* and *Talking Book* (1972), *Innervisions* (1973), *Fulfillingness' First Finale* (1974), and *Songs in the Key of Life* (1976).

At the end of his first solo album, *Music of My Mind*, Wonder takes on the problem of sin. "Evil, why have you taken over God's children's eyes," he sings. "Evil, before they could really grow to see / That your way is not the way to make life what it should be." "Superstition," his big hit of 1972, catalogs the popular images of deception: ladders, broken mirrors, mysterious writings on the wall. "When you believe in things that you don't understand," Wonder concludes, "then you suffer; superstition ain't the way." *Talking Book* also contains the song "I Believe (When I Fall in Love It Will Be Forever)," which addresses a young woman in a prayerful way common to soul music since Sister Rosetta Tharpe and Ray Charles: "You know God surely answered my prayer, God always will answer your prayers / Believe in one who will answer my prayer, Thank you God."[46]

One song from *Innervisions* directly references the high-profile young Christians of the early seventies. In "Jesus Children of America," Wonder asks his listeners if they hear what Jesus is saying and feel what they are praying. He addresses a "holy roller," wondering if he is true to his words, and a "junkie," asking if a needle in a vein brings happiness. The song turns more theological. "Jesus died on cross for you, Mary is just looking at you," Wonder sings. "Mother Mary feels so much pain, looking at him." Elsewhere on the album, Wonder sings: "God is gonna show you higher ground / He's the only friend you have around." Synthesizing Christian and Eastern belief, he expresses relief that he's being allowed to live his life again, "'cause my last time on earth I lived a whole world of sin." This time around, he knows "more than I knew then."[47]

Like Gaye, his mentor, Wonder gives voice to the sort of unorthodox religious views that the Jesus Movement found most repugnant. "Jesus Children of America" includes the line: "Transcendental meditation gives you peace of mind." His first wife, Syreeta Wright, a singer and a secretary at Motown, taught TM and encouraged Wonder's interest Asian religion. "I would like to believe in reincarnation," he said. "I would like to believe that there is another life." But reincarnation could be another way of describing born again. On his way to a benefit concert in North Carolina in the summer of 1973, he was nearly killed in an automobile accident. "This is like my second chance for life, to do something or to do more, and to face the fact that I am alive. God was telling me to slow down, to take it easy."[48]

Though Earth, Wind & Fire (EWF) never recorded for Motown, its members engaged many of the same spiritual issues that Gaye and Wonder did in their music. Founded in Chicago by Maurice White, who sang and played drums, the group moved to Los Angeles and began recording for Warner Brothers in 1970. An early break came when Melvin Van Peebles recruited them to play the soundtrack for the surprise smash film *Sweet Sweetback's Baadasssss Song*. In 1972, the same year that Stevie Wonder went solo, they began releasing an extraordinary string of spiritually themed, singles-chart-busting and mostly platinum-selling albums for Columbia. The music of EWF was infused with an eclectic grab bag of blended spirituality, drawing on Christianity, Eastern mysticism, and African religion. The aura was further heightened by the group's spectacular stage shows, which featured extravagant special effects, some provided by magician Doug Henning.

Raised in Memphis, White grew up in a Baptist Holiness church, where he accepted the existence of a distinct boundary between godly and ungodly music. He began singing at age six, took up drums at twelve, and became a seasoned session drummer. In Chicago, he worked at Chess and backed everyone from the Impressions and Chuck Berry to Muddy Waters, Bobby Blue Bland, Howlin' Wolf, and jazz saxophonist Sonny Stitt. At Motown,

White played on session for the Supremes, the Four Tops, and Martha and the Vandellas (including on their hit single "Heat Wave"). During the sixties, White also worked with jazz artists, including John Coltrane, Sonny Stitt, and Ramsey Lewis, all of whom expanded his spiritual outlook.

Unlike many of the funky, Sly and the Family Stone–influenced bands with whom they were compared—from Parliament/Funkadelic to the Ohio Players, Kool and the Gang, and War—EWF kept their message conspicuously wholesome. Recorded in 1972, their first album for Columbia had the vaguely end-times-sounding title *Last Days and Time* and included such above-board songs as a cover version of Pete Seeger's "Where Have All the Flowers Gone?," "Remember the Children" (which echoes sentiments from Gaye's *What's Going On*), and a tribute to motherhood titled simply "Mom."[49]

White explained in an interview "that Sly's being from the church and my group being from the sanctified church is why we might have similarities in our vocal sound." But EWF's spiritual agenda went well beyond sonic affinities. "We want to almost have old-time revival church meetings," White confessed. "One day I hope that we can come to the point where people won't have to just come to a show. We want them to come to have meetings of the soul. It should be able to carry them through the next week, or the next month, just like church used to, and this is just the beginning of it. I know we have a high energy level, but that's to keep your eyes up there and that's what we feel, too, but at the same time we want everybody to be able to come and partake in old-time communion."[50]

Despite such aspirations, artists like White, Wonder, Gaye, and even Franklin assimilate uneasily into the musical world of the Jesus Movement. The eclectic nature of their spirituality, among other things, set them apart from the majority of boomer evangelicals, and there's no evidence that they were embraced as fellow travelers in the movement. "The basic symbol of evil for the Jesus movement seems to be multiplicity," observed Robert Ellwood in 1973, referring to the "countless options, symbols, and alluring paths" open to those living the "unconverted life."[51] But the boundaries separating worldly and "anointed" music were never crystal clear, especially in the case of African American artists. If Marvin Gaye was positioned outside the world of Christian pop music, Andraé Crouch was clearly a central figure, with his old fellow COGICs member Billy Preston occupying some ambiguous middle ground. During the seventies, the real gatekeepers of the Christian music scene were formidable antirock crusaders like Bob Larson and David Noebel, who viewed a Christian rocker like Larry Norman with nearly as much suspicion as Mick Jagger. More subtle policing of the boundary of Christian pop music would come later in the seventies with the development of a more independent Christian music industry.

Moreover, when taking a long view of the sixties and their aftermath, it's clear that this music—whether or not it was endorsed by Campus Crusade or Calvary Chapel—shared a similar structure of feeling, both musically and lyrically, with the most powerful (if not always the most popular) of the early Christian rockers: a grounding in African American vernacular music, a comfort level invoking the name of Jesus, regard for Golden Rule morality, a prophetic stance toward U.S. society, and the sense of an impending apocalypse. These are the affinities that position the Jesus Movement and its music as eddies in the much larger, longer cultural front of the sixties.

## Chapter 5

# HOLLYWOOD'S GOSPEL ROAD

"Last night I had a dream," June Carter told Johnny Cash in 1966. Not yet married, they were staying at the King David Hotel in Jerusalem. "I saw you on a mountaintop in Israel, and you had a book in your hand—maybe it was a Bible—and you were talking to millions of people about Jesus." The idea unnerved Cash, because he knew at that point he "wasn't physically and spiritually able for such a role"—he was just beginning to think about fighting a crippling addiction to pills. But they continued to think about the dream. "A few days later, when we got to Galilee," Cash recalled, "the land where Jesus had lived, June tugged my sleeve and said, 'There's the mountain I dreamed about where you were standing.'" In 1968 the couple recorded an album called *In the Holy Land*, but it still seemed incomplete. "That wasn't my dream," June said, glancing at the album cover.[1]

Five years later, in 1973, the vision was realized with the release of the movie *Gospel Road*. Starring June Carter Cash as an emotionally incandescent Mary Magdalene and Cash himself as the host and narrator, the movie alternates Cash's folksy retelling of the life of Jesus—delivered in his deep, craggy voice—with a series of country-gospel songs keyed to key moments in the Gospel narrative: John the Baptist baptizing Jesus; the wedding at Cana, where water was turned to wine; Jesus's nervy rescue of a woman caught in adultery; Jesus cleansing the Temple of money changers; and the Last Supper and Crucifixion. Cash quotes liberally from the King James Bible as well.

Filmed on location in Israel, the film intersperses dramatic and fairly authentic-looking reenactments of the scripture stories with shots of a black-clad (including Converse high-tops) Cash delivering his story, rolling a Bible in his hands, perched high on a mountain with wind tousling his longish hair or traipsing/striding along the Sea of Galilee. Early in the film, before the title appears, the camera pans up the Jordan River, explaining the desire of many believers to be baptized in that river: "They walk the way of the cross, they shout, 'Praise the Lord!'—and they mean it. Now come along with me in the footsteps of Jesus, and I'll show you why they do."[2]

"Never a man spoke like this man," Cash intones near the beginning of the film. "Never a man did the things on this earth that this man did. And his words were as beautiful as his miracles." Cash had spoken these exact words to the huge final-day crowd at Explo '72. In many ways, the Jesus of *Gospel Road* was pitch-perfectly attuned to the Jesus Movement. Played by Robert Elfstrom, who also directed the film (he had earlier made a documentary film about Cash), the long-haired, blond Jesus is clearly a man of the people determined to save the wretched of the earth. To do so, he has to take on the entrenched powers of the Establishment.

"Jesus loved all men," Cash explains in a voice-over, "but I guess if there was one thing he really couldn't stand, that was a hypocrite. And he saw in the scribes and the Pharisees and the elders of the people in the Temple, total hypocrisy. Blasphemer, they all call him, for saying that he's divine, the son of God in the flesh. But the mass of the people, especially the poor and the underprivileged, followed him in such numbers that they walked on top of each other just to touch the hem of his garment."

But because his teachings called for "repentance and reform," Jesus was "followed and spied on throughout his ministry." As Jesus's life unfolded, Cash narrates, "he would be branded by skeptics as a false prophet, by the wicked as a fool, and by the scribes and Pharisees, the keepers of the law, as a radical, as a revolutionist, as a man to be feared. For his words represented change. He knew his purpose in this world. And he knew that scripture; he knew the Word." Many attempts were made on his life; he lived in mortal danger. "The crowd cries for his death," Cash says as the story reaches its denouement. "And in the face of authority, he never backs down."

Though grounded in the specific conditions of his time and place, Jesus was also a radical democrat. Cash explains that while Christ was born a Jew, "he made it clear that he was sent to all men for all time. . . . Jesus addressed men as men and not as members of any particular class or any particular culture. The differences that divide, such as wealth, position, education, so forth, he knew were strictly on the surface."

Besides fitting the favored subaltern Christ of the Jesus Movement, *Gospel Road*'s Jesus was to a degree formed in Cash's own image — an image that itself reveals much about the larger sixties cultural front from which it emerged. For his own songs and persona, especially after the release of the albums recorded at Folsom and San Quentin prisons, were that of an outlaw speaking truth to power, the Man in Black taking the side of the underdog against the entrenched power of the law. When Cash repeatedly blasted the scribes and Pharisees for their hypocrisy, he was sounding a theme that had roots in his own experience and the populist milieu from which he sprung. He himself had been criticized for playing Las Vegas, for consorting with dangerous men, whores, and gamblers. "My response was that the Pharisees said the same thing about Jesus," Cash wrote. "'He dines with publicans and sinners.'"[3] Cash emphasized that Jesus was a carpenter, a real man who knew how to work with his hands.

Like the Jesus of *Jesus Christ Superstar*, Cash's Christ is not immune to the appeal of an attractive, godly female. "Mary was the kind of woman that Jesus had a lot of love and compassion for," he explains at one point. "*A lot* of love and compassion." And simply by virtue of the fact that his own unmistakable voice is narrating the life of Christ and reading the scripture, Cash imbues him with some of his own charisma and star power, then near their peak.

In 1971 Cash had written his signature song, "Man in Black," to answer questions people had about his views on "social issues, problems, and prejudices." He wears black, the song explains, as a symbol of solidarity with the downtrodden: "the poor and the beaten down"; "the prisoner who has long paid for his crime"; those who have never heard "the words that Jesus said"; "the sick and lonely old"; "reckless ones" scarred by bad trips; lives lost in combat "believin' that the Lord was on their side"; victims of combat and war. Cash offers himself to take the burden of this human suffering, refusing to wear white or bright colors as if "everything's OK": "I'll try to carry off a little darkness on my back / Till things are brighter, I'm the Man in Black."[4]

The Cashes' approach to making the movie had a kind of improvised, seat-of-the-pants style that was in step with the prevailing style of the Jesus Movement and youth culture more generally. "We were stepping out on blind faith, using our own money and resources, with no outside sponsorship or any arrangements for distribution of the film," Cash wrote. "We took almost forty people with us, just about everybody who worked for me in the music business, and while many of them volunteered their time, I paid everyone's travel and room and board."[5]

The cast was assembled in Nashville from among family and friends. In addition to June as Mary Magdalene, Cash brought on his sister Reba, his pastor to play Pontius Pilate, and his manager to play Caiphus. The disciples were hired on location after Cash ran an ad in the *Jerusalem Post*; he chose the twelve from an international pool of backpackers, dropouts, and draft resisters who had somehow landed in Israel. Cash hired two guides, an Arab and a Jew, who between them could get the cast almost anywhere in the war-scarred region. He also witnessed to a particularly worldly and unruly film crew, apparently winning them over. "We shot in Israel for thirty days with two cameras running almost all the time — a nightmare at editing time — and for me those days were intense and exciting," he recalled. "Much of what happened was self-evidently true, but it seemed strange; mysterious, often almost magical."[6]

Returning to New York right after the shooting, Cash and Elfstrom spent much of the next year editing the film and dubbing in the songs, most of which Cash sang but were written by others, including Larry Gatlin, John Denver, and Kris Kristofferson. This was the year Cash and Kristofferson had bonded as new (or newly energized) Christians; both had appeared the previous summer at Explo '72, where Kristofferson sang his gospel hit and gave testimony. Kristofferson visited the Cashes when they were working on the "rough cut" of the film and offered to sing a couple of new songs. It came out that he had also attended the Cashes' home church near Nashville, where he was affected by the preaching and became inspired to write the two songs.

"Well, one of the songs I wrote is called 'Why Me, Lord?'" Kristofferson told Cash. "Gatlin sang 'Help Me' at church when I was there, and it about killed me. Then Snow started talking about Jesus and how He loved me no matter if I am a rotten so-and-so, and I just had to write one called 'Why Me, Lord?'" Then Kristofferson sang it, to praise from June; it became a hit and a classic. The next song, "Burden of Freedom," gave Cash an image of "Jesus carrying his cross, falling, struggling, making the long, torturous journey to Calvary," and it was used for that scene in *Gospel Road*. Kristofferson also sang an affecting version of Gatlin's "Help Me" for the film.[7] Most of the songs carried the spare "boom chicka boom" beat that had been Cash's signature sound since his first Sun recordings with Marshall Grant and Luther Perkins in 1955.

Finally, the film was finished, and it premiered early in 1973 in Charlotte, North Carolina. Getting the film distributed and screened would prove another mountain for Cash. Though Twentieth Century Fox provided some feeble distribution, it would fall to Billy Graham to distribute the film after he acquired the rights from Fox for his World Wide Pictures. Meanwhile, Cash himself would spend the next year energetically promoting *Gospel Road* around the country amid his already packed concert schedule, introducing it at theaters and giving interviews in support. A pastor that Cash knew from California brought it coast to coast to any prison that would let him in; Cash proudly estimated the film had been seen by 150,000 inmates. Despite Cash's best efforts, the film and the soundtrack had disappointing sales. "It wasn't long before *The Gospel Road* settled into the church basements of America," writes biographer Michael Streissguth, "where it flickered for many years on white painted walls and portable screens."[8]

## The Gospel of Cash

There is a striking moment near the end of *Gospel Road*. As Christ hangs near death on the cross, raising and dropping his head, grimacing in pain, the camera pans back to reveal several landscapes in modern America: a warehouse district in a city, a commercial strip, and, finally, a large smoggy city stretching below. It is the only anachronistic scene in Cash's entire film. Jesus, the film seems to be saying, is still completely of our time and continues to be sacrificed in our time.

Films are by nature hugely collaborative projects that require input from large teams of people, but *Gospel Road* was about as close to a solo (or perhaps duet) as a movie could be. From conception and script to distribution and publicity, it was an enormous undertaking. Reflecting back on his life, Cash called it "the most ambitious project I've ever attempted." Streissguth considers it a "tragedy" that Cash's achievement in multimedia expression hasn't been more recognized by critics or the public: "Cash poured years of his life into *The Gospel Road*, first lending his name to advertisers such as Amoco and Lionel Trains in order to raise money for the project, and then doggedly pursuing the concept in recording studios, atop rock peaks outside Jerusalem, and in editing suites with Elfstrom." Streissguth blames "America's arbiters of chic" for rejecting it: "The image proffered by the film clashed with the dark countenance that fascinated them."[9]

At least Cash's timing was right; he picked a window in time when Jesus was all over mass culture and less stigmatized among the chic than he was before or would be after. It would be a stretch to classify Cash with the Jesus People, of course; he was half a generation too old, and his Arkansas/Tennessee roots were remote from the Calvary or Bay Area Jesus scenes. He retained musical friendships with younger artists like Bob Dylan and Kristofferson, to be sure, and he was a close enough fit to be chosen as the headliner at Explo '72, the man who introduced Billy Graham to the youthful multitudes. Like nearly all the musicians who became popular among the Jesus People, though, Cash had grown up religious and continued to think about his faith. By the time the Jesus Movement burst into the national media in 1971 (and *Gospel Road* came out two years later), Cash had been reflecting on his relationship with Jesus for more than thirty years. And like many of the popular musicians who turned to the Bible around this time, Cash had just come through a time of enormous turbulence in his personal life.

Growing up in Dyess, Arkansas, a New Deal agricultural colony built from scratch in northeast Arkansas for destitute farmers as part of Franklin Roosevelt's Federal Emergency Relief Program, Cash attended several churches. His earliest memories center on a small Pentecostal church whose ecstatic worship style terrified and captivated Cash — especially the young preacher who shouted and cried and gasped for breath like he was choking to death. The music, on the other hand, was wholly compelling. "The Church of God allowed all kinds of musical instruments, and they'd have guitar, mandolin, and banjo to accompany the singing," he recalled. "But as far as I was concerned, the service might as well have ended when the songs were over. Because it was the songs I was beginning to feel."[10]

Neither of Cash's parents were Pentecostals, though; his mother was Methodist and his father was Baptist. And he could pinpoint quite specifically when he first accepted Christ in a meaningful way. Cash claimed that at age twelve, he attended every night of a two-week revival at the First Baptist Church in Dyess. The church seated perhaps 500 people. "I remember the hard oak benches and the small amounts of oily sawdust on the floor to keep the dust down when they swept," he wrote. "There were the little brass chandeliers with four naked light bulbs and the windows wide-open to let in fresh air." (The church actually carried out its baptisms at the local swimming hole in the Tyronza River.)

Cash's moment of truth arrived as the congregation was singing "Just As I Am." He felt "miserable and twitchy and nervous," and he wanted to bolt. "As the song kept on flowing, I started thinking of all of those songs I'd been hearing at home on the radio and how they were pointing out the direction for me to turn right then. It was time to make a move." Either leave — or walk forward for the altar call. Cash vacillated, then caught sight of his beloved brother Jack up front clutching his Bible and singing. Johnny went forward and took the preacher's hand. "There was not any big burst of shouting or fireworks," he recalled, "but a beautiful peace came over me that night. . . . It wasn't like a drunkard's conversion or that of a long-time-gone sinner. It was the surrender of a young boy who had reached the age of moral and spiritual accountability."[11] Cash's next walk to the altar, twenty-seven years later, was more that of a fallen sinner.

After three years in the army stationed in Germany, Cash ascended quickly in the Memphis music scene. "Cry, Cry, Cry," the first single released by Johnny Cash and the Tennessee Two, reached number fourteen on the *Billboard* chart in 1955. The following year, "Folsom Prison Blues" reached number five, and "I Walk the Line" peaked at number two, spending forty-three weeks on the charts. Cash's addiction to pills, mainly amphetamines, began at about that time. The addiction recurred throughout his life, but it nearly killed him in the sixties. "Inside that bottle of white pills, which only cost eight or ten dollars for a hundred, came at no extra cost a demon called Deception," he would later write. Drinking and "carnal" pursuits also dominated Cash and destroyed his first marriage to the devoutly Catholic Vivian Liberto, whom Cash had courted assiduously during his stint in the military.

But, according to Cash, he never abandoned his childhood faith. "Though I kept company with those demons and allowed them to court me, badger me, hassle me, and taunt me, they could never claim me," he stated. "Friends, loved ones, casual acquaintances, and even fans who didn't know me personally but knew my problems and cared for me were praying for me all across the country. . . . A still, small voice would breath forth inside my being: 'I am your God. I am still here.'"[12] He struggled to reconcile his success singing secular songs with his desire to record sacred songs, something that producer Sam Phillips discouraged. He resolved to "tithe" his recordings, meaning some of them would be gospel even if they didn't sell; he jumped from Sun to Columbia in 1958 partly for this creative freedom.

That same year, Cash gave his first prison concert at San Quentin. "He brought Jesus Christ into the picture, and he introduced him in a way that the tough, hardened, hard-core convict wasn't embarrassed to listen to," explained Merle Haggard, then an inmate at San Quentin who saw the New Year's Day concert. "He didn't point no fingers; he just knew how to do it." Paroled after three years (and later pardoned by Governor Ronald Reagan), Haggard would begin his own career as a country legend. But singing the gospel songs wasn't enough for Cash. "My policy of aloneness and severed fellowship from other committed Christians would weaken me spiritually," he realized later. "Not that missing church necessarily meant missing God.

It was just that Jesus never meant for us to try and make it on our own." And it left him "vulnerable and easy prey for all the temptations and destructive vices that the backstage of the entertainment world has to offer."[13]

Cash spiraled ever deeper into substance abuse, worsening after the family moved to California in 1959. His October 1965 arrest in El Paso on federal drug charges made national news, though he got off with a fine. But in true country music fashion, the love of a good woman would soon redeem things. Cash had seen June Carter, the daughter of one of the three members of the seminal Carter Family, sing at the Grand Ole Opry when he was a high school senior on a class trip, and he flirted with her when he debuted at the Ryman Auditorium in 1956. Five years later, while still married to her second husband, Carter was invited to join Cash's road show, and the romance Cash had long wanted began to kindle. Musically, it bore fruit in the 1963 hit "Ring of Fire," written by Carter. She bravely attacked his pill habit and, over time, shored up his evangelical faith. In March 1968, after six turbulent years on the road, Cash married the woman who would turn out to be his "lifetime duet partner, show opener, lover, booster, seamstress, caretaker, and nemesis."[14] Shortly afterward, the couple made their second trip to Israel. The experience became the basis for Cash's *The Holy Land*, an album that combined songs with narratives recorded on a cassette player.

Meanwhile, Cash was slowly cleaning up his life. "You stayed off pills but you're still awfully carnal," he wrote to himself on New Year's Day 1969. "You need to pray more. You hardly ever pray." But people close to him noticed a difference. "Starting in late '68, '69 and '70, John got ninety percent straight, not a hundred percent but he got 90 percent straight," longtime sideman Marshall Grant told an interviewer. "And he come around, and he looked like a million dollars, but there was always just a little there, not a lot, but just a little. And then the day that John Carter was born he quit cold turkey, period. From 1970 until 1976 he was as straight as any man that has ever lived, and there was a great, great, great, great human being for all those years." He even quit smoking.[15]

In 1971 the Cashes joined Evangel Temple, a small Pentecostal church in Nashville pastored by an old friend named Jimmy Snow, the son of country legend Hank Snow. The pastor had invited Cash to bring his guitar and sing in the church. Cash was impressed by their "off-the-fence kind of worshiping," the kind that scared him as a little boy in Dyess. He identified with "the bunch of would-be down-and outers" who worshipped at Evangel: people from the music business who Cash knew struggled with drugs or liquor, and a piano player who "must have taken a trainload of dope in his day." "There's just enough underdogs and second-lifers over there to make me comfortable — my sister Joanne for one," Cash said. "I've got a lot in common with them."[16] This was the Nashville version of the sort of Bible study and informal worship scene that had developed among musicians in Los Angeles.

When Cash wasn't on the road, he tried to attend Evangel regularly. A guest appearance by Larry Gatlin, who sang "Help Me," clinched it. (The first time Cash heard the song, he decided to feature it in *Gospel Road*.) "I thought of the time when I was twelve when I had gone to the altar, when I had made my original decision," Cash wrote. "Twenty-seven years had gone by. I had learned the long-suffering and complete forgiveness of God. What a joy to know that He'd clean the slate for all those years."[17]

At about this time, Cash struck up a friendship with Billy Graham that would further shape his career. Graham was just then in the thick of trying to figure out the Jesus People, to reach out to a generation of baby boomers he felt were promising but profoundly misguided. Graham was looking for allies, and his own troubled son Franklin was a big Cash fan, so he sought out the star, finally meeting him just after John Carter's birth. The two would remain slightly in awe of each other. Graham echoed what Sonny James had told Cash many years earlier about his vocation as a Christian musician: do what you do best and leave the preaching to others. "He advised me to keep singing 'Folsom Prison Blues' and 'A Boy Named Sue' and all those other outlaw songs if that's what people wanted to hear and then, when it came time to do a gospel song, give it everything I had," Cash recalled.[18]

Immediately after meeting Graham, Cash wrote "What Is Truth?," a song that captured what both men were thinking about the boomers and Jesus People. Youth were simply asking about truth in an era that made little sense to them. An old man complains about "funny music." A seventeen-year-old boy is taught the Golden Rule in Sunday school and sent off to die in a war that seems meaningless. A young man's long hair and mod clothes mean he isn't believed on the witness stand. A young woman dances to the latest beat, and a young man publicly speaks out for what he believes. "Yeah, the ones that you're calling wild / Are going to be the leaders in a little while," goes the final stanza. "This old world's wakin' to a new born day / And I solemnly swear it'll be their way."[19]

Graham may have counseled Cash to leave explicit evangelism to others, but by then Cash had a prominent pulpit. ABC's *The Johnny Cash Show* debuted in June 1969 from the Opry's Ryman Auditorium, and from the beginning, Cash made it clear he was crossing boundaries — racial, generational, and spiritual. The first broadcast featured both Joni Mitchell and Bob Dylan;

Cash had begun hanging out and trading songs with Dylan after the 1963 release of *The Freewheelin' Bob Dylan*, an album that impressed the older singer immensely. By 1969 Dylan's own music had taken an unexpected turn toward country with *Nashville Skyline*. In addition to older stars like Bob Hope, Peggy Lee, Al Hirt, Patti Page, Roy Orbison, and Ray Charles, Cash invited plenty of young stars: Arlo Guthrie, Linda Ronstadt, James Taylor, Ramblin' Jack Elliott, and Derek and the Dominoes (with Eric Clapton). (Cash also won a power struggle with the network to get the controversial Pete Seeger on the show.) Cash continued to "tithe" his repertoire, offering a steady diet of gospel songs. "The songs and hymns I'd been singing since I was a kid were brought into the format of the weekly TV show," he wrote. "I sang all the ones I loved. The Carter Family, the Statler Brothers, and Carl Perkins joined in on them, as did June."[20]

A manifestation of the sixties cultural front that stretched across disparate sectors of American society, *The Johnny Cash Show* represented a precarious alignment at a time of unusual social tension in the United States. Before long, its host was in peril. Cash's gospel songs and public professions of faith were raising hackles at ABC and, presumably, among those of his fans who preferred their Man in Black to be an outlaw who consorted with mavericks like Dylan. "Any combination of religion and TV or religion and secular celebrity, makes for dangerous ground, full of traps and pitfalls, marked out with lines that can be too fine to see, and that's especially true for the man standing in the glare of the spotlights," Cash reflected later. "I should know; I've crossed a few lines myself and found trouble on the other side."[21] The episode was vivid enough to compel Cash to recount it fully in both of his memoirs. (He brings it up twice in the second book.)

Many viewers apparently wanted to know if Cash was a genuine Christian or just another performer who had learned to sing in church and knew the songs. He decided to oblige them while introducing the show's closing hymn: "'Well, folks,'" I began, "'I've introduced lots of hymns and gospel songs on this show. I just want to make it clear that I'm feeling what I'm singing about in this next one. I am a Christian.'" The world is ruled by two powerful forces, Cash continued, good and evil—God and the devil. "The number one power in this world is God," he declared. "The number two power is Satan, and though he manages to fight for second in my life, I want to dedicate this song to the proposition that God is the victor in my life. I'd be nothing without Him. I want to get in a good lick right now for Number One." Then he launched into "I Saw a Man" ("He turned and then I saw / The nail-scarred hands that bled for me").[22]

*The Johnny Cash Show* never recovered. Producer Stan Jacobson recalled that "after that statement, the show took a nosedive. Let me tell you: bang, into the toilet. And Screen Gems–Columbia Pictures got nervous. ABC got nervous." The network cancelled it in March 1971, along with *The Lawrence Welk Show* and *Let's Make a Deal*.[23] Hearing the news on tour in Australia, Cash claimed he was "relieved" to be free of the all-consuming obligation. But there were other costs. "The worldly consequences of my declaration were severe," Cash admitted in 1997, "not just in lost record sales but also in some of the reactions from religious people, which ranged from attempts to use me for their own purposes to condemnations and exclusions from their particular folds."

Cash was unrepentant. The last broadcast of *The Johnny Cash Show* in the spring of 1971 featured Mahalia Jackson, the Edwin Hawkins Singers, the Blackwood Brothers, and the Oak Ridge Boys—capped by the preaching of Billy Graham himself. "The whole show was a closing hymn," Cash wrote later.[24] Rumors circulated in 1972 that he had issued an altar call from the stage of the Hilton International Hotel in Las Vegas, and he talked about mounting a Johnny Cash Crusade. He was also featured at Explo '72.

At the very peak of his fame and success, Cash struggled to retain his hold on two divergent audiences: a largely secular crowd that admired his friendship with Dylan and his support for prison inmates, American Indians, and the voices of protest; and a Silent Majority faction that responded to his patriotism, Christian values, and friendship with Billy Graham. At a December 1969 concert at Madison Square Garden, Cash appeared to offer support for Nixon's Vietnam policy. A few months later, he was invited to perform at the White House and asked to sing, in addition to his hit "A Boy Named Sue," two politically charged songs he'd never performed: Merle Haggard's "Okie from Muskogee" and Guy Drake's "Welfare Cadillac." Cash's demurral made headlines. The request had come from Bob Haldeman, it turned out, so Cash wasn't actually refusing the president. He later insisted that "the issue wasn't the songs' messages, which at the time were lightning rods for antihippie and antiblack sentiment, but the fact that I didn't know them and couldn't learn them or rehearse them with the band before we had to leave for Washington." He admitted feeling "fortunate" that this spared him from having to deal with the messages.[25]

As the sixties cultural front pushed on into the early seventies, there was little neutral ground for an artist who crossed as many audience boundaries as Cash did. Despite a strong youth vote for McGovern, Nixon had been re-elected amid signs of peace; but the month after the election, the United

States unleashed the "Christmas bombings" of North Vietnam amid international protest. The last American troops left Vietnam in March 1973, but the war continued, tilting decisively against South Vietnam—where the United States had invested so much blood and ambition. The defeat of George McGovern seemed a decisive rejection by American voters of the social and cultural politics of the sixties. Still, the armed occupation of Wounded Knee by American Indian radicals in 1973 reminded Americans that sixties-style causes and tactics were not completely a thing of the past.

Meanwhile, the United States faced increasingly daunting challenges in the Middle East. In 1972 the world had been horrified by the murder of Israeli athletes by Palestinian terrorists at the Olympic Games in Munich. In 1973, in terrain where Johnny Cash and Norman Jewison had recently shot their respective movies, war broke out between Arabs and Israelis. The conflict threatened to draw in the United States and the Soviet Union, heightening fears of nuclear Armageddon (and providing yet more evidence to Christians convinced that the end times were imminent). To punish the United States for its support of Israel, the Arab oil-producing nations announced an oil embargo against America, Europe, and Japan and raised prices 400 percent.

This dramatically worsened an already faltering U.S. economy—one area that had not been a concern in the sixties. Inflation began creeping up in 1967, reaching 9 percent by 1973 and remaining in double-digits for most of the seventies. Unemployment also increased notably, raising the specter of a new economic curse known as "stagflation," a theoretically impossible conjunction of economic recession and inflation. No one in the United States could miss the fact that the stuff of everyday life, from food and gasoline to appliances and toys, seemed to cost noticeably more. Predictably, the stock market plummeted.

A constitutional crisis added a final twist to the sense of national breakdown. In the summer of 1972—coincidentally, the same day Explo '72 reached its climax in Dallas—burglars were arrested in the act of breaking into the Democratic National Committee headquarters at the Watergate complex on the Potomac River in Washington, D.C. Through a grand jury investigation and Senate hearings, a cover-up scandal emerged. In 1973 key White House aides John Ehrlichman and H. R. Haldeman, along with the attorney general and the acting director of the FBI, resigned in the face of the scandal. Increasing evidence pointed to President Nixon's intimate involvement in the cover-up, despite his profession to a television audience that "I'm not a crook." Special prosecutor Archibald Cox took Nixon to court in order to obtain secret White House tapes whose existence had come to light in Senate hearings; when Nixon fired Cox, the replacement prosecutor, Leon Jaworski, continued the campaign to obtain the tapes, the contents of which ultimately led to Nixon's resignation the following year. Meanwhile, in 1973 vice president Spiro Agnew himself resigned for accepting bribes both before and during his term in office.

"I couldn't leave 'till the Watergate hearings were over," admitted Marvin Gaye, who was mustering his courage for a national tour while his 1973 album *Let's Get It On* was on the charts. "It'd be like watching a cowboy movie without seeing the bad guy punched out. I had to see Tricky Dick go down, down, all the way down." Meanwhile, Cash and Graham would periodically sit on Cash's porch in Jamaica, listening to reggae music. When Nixon finally resigned, Graham talked Cash into giving him a Christmas call to boost his spirits. "Cash didn't want to do it because he thought Nixon was a skunk," the story went, "but Graham is such a good man that he reminded him that every sinner can be redeemed."[26]

All of which underscored the sense of end times, whether based on Bible prophecy or on its secular counterparts. In a way, it was even more debilitating than the traumas of 1968. "Despite all the terrible things that happened in the sixties, there was a sense of idealism and cause," recalled Bernie Sheahan. "The seventies didn't have all that." Graduating from high school in 1974, she considers herself "a real child of the sixties" and remembers the way the national mood changed, especially after the loss of Vietnam: "Disillusionment and really sort of a blah feeling: things aren't going so great. But people weren't rallying. There was nothing to rally around like there was in the sixties," no galvanizing political movements like civil rights, antiwar protests, or women's rights. "There was no passion that I recall. There was just a sense of malaise."[27]

## Jesus on Location

*Gospel Road* wasn't the only Jesus Movement–tinged film to reach movie theaters in 1973; it wasn't even the most widely viewed. Released a few months after Cash's film was *Godspell* the movie, also filmed on location—not in the Holy Land but in Manhattan. Malaise is conspicuously absent from *Godspell*. The mood is Tompkins Square hippie slapstick, the ten cast members hamming it up like flower children in clown costumes and face paint. A lanky Victor Garber plays Jesus, looking something like Abbie Hoffman with an expansive Afro and Superman shirt with a large *S*. There are only nine "disciples" in the film, five women and four men. Except for David Haskell, who plays both John the Baptist and Judas in a Sgt. Pepper–like jacket with epaulets, the disciples are known by the first names of the actors who play them: Katie Hanley plays Katie, Lynne Thigpen plays Lynne, and so on. Each is called out of his or her day job—fashion model, taxi driver, dancer, business executive, waitress—by a blast on the shofar, a Jewish ram's horn sounded by John the Baptist.[28]

Suddenly midtown Manhattan is emptied of people, and the cast has the city for its playground. The disciples are baptized in a fountain in Central Park. They cavort and prance through the various parables and episodes from Matthew: the Good Samaritan, Lazarus and the rich man, the sower and the seeds, a woman caught in adultery. The mood throughout is light and whimsical—even the scene where a servant is subject to torture for capriciously forcing a fellow servant to pay a debt when the master has forgiven his own debt. A typical exchange:

> Jesus: Did I ever tell you I used to read feet?
> Jeffrey: You used to what?
> Jesus: Some people read palms or tea leaves. I read feet. Look what it says. (He examines Jeffrey's foot.) Ah, it says, Rejoice!
> Jeffrey (also checking): It says, Keds!

Christ serves matzoh at the Last Supper and gives a blessing in Hebrew while we hear a version of Psalm 137, with its famous line: "How shall we sing the Lord's song in a strange land?" Even Judas's betrayal seems innocent, almost compassionate. Jesus refers to the disciple as a friend and kisses him on both cheeks. It's clear that Judas is reluctant to carry out the deed. Squad cars arrive with lights flashing but no officers actually emerge. Jesus is gently crucified on a chain-link fence while the disciples hurl themselves against the wire.

Although most orthodox Christians preferred it over *Jesus Christ Superstar*, *Godspell* does not depict anything like an overt resurrection. The morning after the crucifixion, the gathered disciples gently take Jesus down from the fence and carry him through the streets until they round the corner of Park Avenue. Instantly, the streets and sidewalks again fill with the busy crowds of an ordinary workday—the tableau with which the film began. Normal life has resumed.

Falling somewhere between the biscuits-and-gravy sincerity of *Gospel Road* and the gentle irreverence of *Godspell* was the film version of *Jesus Christ Superstar*, which hit movie theaters in August 1973, just a month before *Godspell* and several months after Cash's film. Directed by Norman Jewison, whose credits included *In the Heat of the Night* and *Fiddler on the Roof*, *Superstar* the movie was also filmed in Israel less than a year after Cash's crew wrapped their work. Though Israeli government policy provided incentives and encouragement to foreign filmmakers, there was some controversy about shooting this particular story, especially among Orthodox members of Parliament.

"Jesus Christ still does not command much admiration," said an assistant to the mayor of Jerusalem. "And there are rumors that the Arab guerillas are threatening sabotage on the production, since the American film industry is largely controlled by Jews." A policeman in Tel Aviv put it more bluntly. "We already had one Jesus here and he gave us more than enough trouble," he said. "He may be God to some or a superstar, but none of that matters to us."[29]

Tim Rice and Andrew Lloyd Webber wanted the film version (which was anticipated even before the show was staged) to reflect more faithfully their original vision for *Superstar*. Coming on the heels of Tom O'Horgan's over-the-top onstage surrealism, which drew mixed reviews, Jewison's vision of the film was closer to what Rice and Webber had in mind. His model was Pasolini's somber *The Gospel According to Saint Matthew*, not the spectacle-heavy *King of Kings*. The locations—which ranged from fortresses near Bethlehem and the Negev Desert to the Dead Sea and an ancient Roman amphitheater near Nazareth—were clearly authentic, but costumes provided contemporary flavor. The soldiers wore Roman centurion helmets along with Israeli army fatigues and boots, and they carried machine guns. At a dramatic point before Judas's suicide, Israeli tanks and jet fighters appear to give chase. Costumes range from earth-tone hippie garb to high camp and drag.[30] Jewison further demystified the story by staging it as a play within a play. As the film begins, we see the actors arrive in the desert in an old hippie-style bus, getting off in high spirits to set up for the show. After the crucifixion, all but Ted Neeley, who plays Jesus, solemnly board the bus, looking spent. They slowly drive off as the film ends.

The big-screen *Superstar* retained some of the Broadway cast—Yvonne Elliman as Mary and Barry Dennen as Pilate—but brought in some new actors. Zero Mostel's chubby, frizzy-haired son Joshua was hired to play Herod. Carl Anderson, who replaced Ben Vereen, plays Judas somewhat like a cross between H. Rap Brown and Al Green. Embodied by Anderson—a twenty-six-year-old from Washington, D.C., who played the role onstage in Los Angeles—Judas seems to be the most contemporary and three-dimensional character in the film. He worries a lot about Christ's character and fitness to lead, about where the disciples are headed, about provoking a crackdown by the authorities, about his own mental stability. Far more perceptive than the other disciples, he wants to do the right thing, but he fails miserably. Competing egos have much to do with it.

A power struggle smolders between Jesus and Judas but also between Judas and Mary Magdalene, who, in very different ways, vie for Christ's favor. As she famously sings, "I don't know how to love him . . . he's a man, just a man." When Jesus appears to side with Mary, Judas turns bitter. "To think I admired you, for now I despise you." But shortly before his suicide, Judas reprises both Mary's song and sentiments. Judas admits he doesn't know how to love Christ, either, and doesn't understand the hold he exerts: "He is not a king, he is just the same as anyone I know / He scares me so."[31]

Ironically, Ted Neeley essentially shared Judas's view on the divinity of Jesus. Neeley was raised a Southern Baptist in Ranger, Texas, and had won praise for his role in the L.A. production of *Superstar*. He was also a friend of Larry Norman, who had hired Neeley for his musicals. But Neeley was a fellow traveler, not a bona fide Jesus person. "The Jesus I portray is a man, not God," he said. "The stress is on the humanity of Jesus, not his sanctity. . . . Jesus was a great, charismatic leader. He was a theologian and thinker, but not God. He was a man who got beyond himself and went too far."[32] Jesus is world-weary, exhausted by the demands on his energy that come from all sides, and ambivalent about the agonizing gauntlet he knows he must run.

By the summer of 1973, with the New Left long since debilitated by similar power struggles, cults of personality, and government-sponsored infiltration, older boomers could view *Jesus Christ Superstar* as an allegory for what became of their own youthful idealism. Historian Richard Fox aptly observes that "*Superstar* delivered a crushing judgment on the political sixties: cease and desist, seek your salvation in another world, resign yourself to the fate God has in store for you. In *Superstar* the counter-culture in effect turned its back on SDS, the anti-war movement, and the black-power movement (which had already subsumed the civil-rights movement), not to mention abandoning the entire Social Gospel tradition that stretched from Washington Gladden in the 1880s to Martin Luther King in the 1960s." *Superstar*'s Jesus refuses to preach revolution or even reform, as some around him urge. "He does scarcely any teaching at all," Fox notes. "The 'end' he preaches is his own end, his own death, not the end of the world or the end of the reign of death."[33]

Rather than a political parable, Fox argues, *Superstar* is a meditation on the seduction and destruction of celebrity in modern American life. Historically, people have turned to the figure of Jesus in order to borrow his authority to support their particular interests, but in doing so they create a new image of

Christ that reflects the context of their times. By 1970 the time was ripe for a depiction of Jesus Christ as a historical figure ultimately destroyed by the passions unleashed by his own celebrity.

As the story progresses, we see Jesus lionized by the people for his charismatic gifts then rejected by them as his stock unaccountably plummets and his enemies mobilize. Even his inner circle deserts him. "*Superstar* shrewdly combined what everyone knew about modern celebrity with what everyone knew about Jesus," Fox writes. "Celebrity means sacrifice and defeat as much as it means fame and success." As Jesus proves, it is not always ephemeral. "At its core, celebrity is not so much transitory as corrosive," Fox concludes. "Immortality—as Jesus, Marilyn, and (a few years later) Elvis demonstrated—is possible, but its price is unbearable physical and psychic suffering."[34]

This was not true so much for Marjoe—at least the unbearable suffering part. Named by his evangelist parents after Mary and Joseph, Marjoe Gortner was the subject of yet another extraordinary Jesus film of the early seventies. As much as *Superstar*, the film, released in 1972 with the simple title *Marjoe*, is about the symbiosis between religion and celebrity, although both terms are valued very differently. Representing the fourth generation in a dynasty of evangelists, Gortner began preaching at three, was ordained and conducted his first wedding at four—for a Paramount newsreel—and was baptized in the Holy Spirit at five. His prodigious childhood is well documented in his scrapbook of newspaper clippings and film clips. Not surprisingly, Gortner eventually bridles at the role his parents have cast him in, leaves home at fifteen, moves in with an older woman, and starts a rock band.[35]

Gortner is back on the revival circuit part-time during the filming of *Marjoe*, both for the money he can raise as a traveling evangelist and, we gather, for the publicity he can glean for exposing the inner workings of itinerant Pentecostalism. We watch him instructing the worldly film crew on how to blend in so as not to raise suspicion among the holy rollers who make up Gortner's audience. He parties with sophisticates who laugh at his well-honed shticks. "Religion is like a drug," he tells them. "It's addictive." One scene finds him divvying up money with his partner, another reveling in the bills as he sprawls in bed. It feels almost like going backstage with a cynical, sixties-version Huck Finn who gleefully exposes his mountebank sidekicks, the Duke and the Dolphin.

The Marjoe we meet in the film is in his twenties. He is tall and gangly; his long curls give him the look of a blonde Victor Garber (*Godspell*'s Jesus), and he dresses in the loud, clashing clothing of the *Godspell* cast. Gortner gives one riveting performance after another at Pentecostal revival meetings (including one mostly black congregation), strutting and gyrating like a rock star. His sermons often address the delivering of young people from drugs. Afterward, he blesses processions of worshippers, apparently healing a lame man. Many of the women he lays hands on fall over in spiritual transport.

Unlike the world-weary Jesus of *Superstar* who is overwhelmed by the numbers of lame and sick clambering for his healing touch, Gortner seems genuinely enthusiastic about his role. He confides at one point that if he had to choose a form of Christianity to actually believe, it would be Pentecostalism because of the great music and interesting people. It's worth remembering that the same year that Marjoe was being filmed, Lonnie Frisbee was securing his reputation by demonstrating the same spiritual gifts at Calvary Chapel. The music of Marjoe is not Jesus music, though; it is pure southern Gospel, twangy with the sound of country.

Marjoe admits he loves performing but would rather be a rock star or an actor than a preacher. *Marjoe* helped him get the chance. Made by filmmaker Sarah Kernochan and *Village Voice* columnist and radio host Howard Smith, the film made a splash at Cannes and won a Best Documentary Oscar for 1972, generating scads of national media attention for Gortner. Reviewing the film in the *New York Times*, Vincent Canby described it as "less a documentary about Marjoe's final weeks on the pentecostal church-and-tent circuit than a feature-length screen test for Marjoe, who apparently hopes for a career in showbiz, either as an actor or as a rock star like Mick Jagger, whose dress and mannerisms he so carefully imitates." Gortner had hired an agent and a manager and moved to Manhattan, according to Canby, where he hung out with hipsters at Elaine's and Max's Kansas City.[36] Before long, he was getting parts in B movies like *Food of the Gods*, *Viva Knievel!*, and *Hellhole*.

But southern audiences never saw *Marjoe*. "The distributor was too afraid of the furor it would cause," according to Kernochan, "so he refused to open it in any city south of Des Moines."[37] If Bible Belt audiences saw any of the Jesus films of 1972–73, it was most likely Johnny Cash's *Gospel Road*. Which was probably just as well with Gortner, since the audiences he intended to reach were on the coasts. *Marjoe* represents the revenge of the celebrity-healer against the parents that pushed him into evangelism as a small child and the community that supports old-style evangelism with their donations. Instead of being overwhelmed and ultimately destroyed by the pressures of celebrity, as was *Superstar*'s Jesus, Gortner exploits the new media of the era to win wealth and launch a new career as a rock star–actor–celebrity. He is the anointed one who eagerly seizes hold of all the celebrity he can conjure up.

With Jesus enjoying a brief moment in the Hollywood spotlight, the sixties cultural front was stretched nearly to the breaking point. It had been only five years since *Hair*, but they had been long, demoralizing years. The giddy exuberance of *Godspell* was glaringly out of synch with the mood of 1973. The cynicism of *Marjoe* rang true, but the final scene of *Superstar* got it best. The movie's Jesus Freaks had just enacted the roller coaster of the Passion, watching in disbelief as their man was condemned and crucified. Now they were dressed in street clothes, wearily climbing back on the school bus that had dropped them off in the desert at the beginning, stealing a glimpse of the empty cross, the desert sun setting behind it. Show over, destination unknown.

Chapter 6

# LET'S GET MARRIED

In October 1974, two months after Nixon stepped down, Al Green had his hands full. The twenty-eight-year-old soul sensation was spending long hours at a ramshackle recording studio in a Memphis ghetto with his producer, Willie Mitchell, trying desperately to keep alive a series of Top 10 hits that began in 1970. And he was juggling women. He had a longtime girlfriend named Laura Lee, but he had recently met a "radiant and ravishing" femme fatale. "I loved Laura and there were times . . . when she was closer to me than any other human being had ever been," Green recalled in his autobiography. "But there also comes a time when friendship isn't what a man is looking for, and a woman who's as loyal to him as a sister can't take the place of a woman who treats him like a man. And this was one of those times."[1]

Green had met Mary Woodson at a prison concert in New York (she was not an inmate), and they had begun to flirt. At twenty-nine, Woodson had had a tumultuous life since getting married at sixteen. She had a husband and young children in New Jersey, but she followed Green to Memphis. She got arrested for smoking pot at the historic Peabody Hotel. Green got her released and took her back to the legendary Royal Recording Studios with him, promising to write her a song. "But I was nervous and upset by the events of the evening, so I ended up just riffing on 'Sha-La-La,' hoping the refrain would calm her down and soothe her anxious spirit."[2]

Then another woman friend showed up, an airline stewardess in town on a layover. Hoping to defuse a tense situation, Green invited both women back to his mansion. "I made sure they understood I had lots of spare bedrooms where they could spend the night—the last thing on my mind right then was some kind of kinky encounter." Driving them home in his Rolls, Green was unnerved by glimpses he caught of Mary in the rearview mirror: "Once she caught me looking at her and fixed me with a cold, appraising stare that set my nerves on edge."

The stewardess went to bed, and Green joined Woodson in the kitchen, where she was boiling a pot of water. "She turned when she heard my footsteps and smiled, a wistful, sad smile. 'Al, honey, have you ever thought of getting married?' she asked. It took me a minute to register what she was actually asking." Green, the singer who had had a hit single with "Let's Get Married," suggested they talk about it the next morning. He went upstairs to shower and brush his teeth. He heard a sound from the bedroom, but he saw nothing. A few moments later, he heard the bathroom door opening. "I looked up just in time to see Mary's reflection in the mirror," he remembered. "She had the steaming pot in both hands."[3]

Like the great majority of soul singers, Green's roots were in the church. Born in rural Arkansas, Green moved with his family—five older siblings and four younger ones—to Grand Rapids, Michigan, when he was nine. They attended a storefront revival church called Mother Bates's House of Prayer. Green's father pushed four of the boys, including Al, to sing in a gospel quartet, which toured the state and eventually went as far as Canada and New York City in pursuit of a breakthrough hit. Though Green senior had enjoyed the secular music of juke joints, he forbade it in the family. At age eighteen, Al was thrown out of the house for listening to Jackie Wilson 45s once too often; "A Woman, A Lover, A Friend" was the straw that broke the camel's back. Then began a decade of hustling, drifting, and pursuing the dream of being the next great Soul Man. Green had a minor hit with "Back Up Train" and got as far as the Apollo Theater, where he stole the show, but anything that felt like genuine success was elusive.

A chance meeting in late 1968 with semilegendary trumpet player, bandleader, talent scout, and producer Willie Mitchell began to turn that around. After a rendezvous-with-destiny encounter in a Midland, Texas, roadhouse, Green followed Mitchell to his Memphis stomping grounds. (Green had to leave Juanita, a Grand Rapids hooker he had been living with since leaving home.) Together, Mitchell and Green worked out a signature ensemble sound: "Silky on top. Rough on the bottom," Green described it. "Jazz vocal style with those mellow chords and progressions laid lightly over a sandpaper-and-grits R & B rhythm section."

But the key alchemy was with Green's voice itself.

What Willie was trying to bring out in me was something more private and personal, something I was almost afraid to let another person hear. It was a soft, tender, vulnerable side of myself that could only express itself through singing, like a little boy crying out for his mama or a grown man weak for the love of a woman. To sing like that, you've got to let something inside of you loose, give up your pride and power, and let that surrendering feeling well up inside until it overwhelms you and uses your voice to cry out with a need that can't be filled.[4]

It took some time, but by 1971 Green's singles were climbing high on the charts. And he was starting to enjoy the perks. "I have had carnal relations with more women than I can remember or confess," Green admitted. "Their names and faces, their bodies and voices have blended together long ago, one lonely form all blurred and transparent, like a restless ghost that wanders through my memory." But in contrast to Green's sexy persona, his greatest hits weren't about casual flings. They enacted do-or-die romances between couples that literally couldn't live without each other. Often they were from the perspective of a man yearning for romantic stability: "Let's Stay Together," "So Tired of Being Alone," "Let's Get Married." "I know that without the love of a woman, the world is a hard, dry, and unforgiving place," Green wrote. "I know that our Creator fashioned the love between [a] man and a woman as a holy sacrament and, speaking personally, I could not live without it. I've never believed in the war between the sexes."[5]

"During those strange and unreal times," Green continued, "God gave me a true friend and boon companion, someone I could trust and who called on me to be trustworthy, maybe the most selfless and loyal person who ever crossed the path of my life." Raised in Chicago, Laura Lee had begun as a gospel singer like Green before signing with Chess Records in the midsixties. For Chess, she cut down-and-dirty songs and "long spoken sermonettes, mostly on the subject of female liberation." She recorded at Muscle Shoals, where Aretha Franklin cut her monster soul records for Atlantic. Lee met Green in Atlanta, where they shared a bill in 1972, and they began dating. "We were soul mates," Green explained, "birds of a feather, two halves of one whole."[6]

Green was with Lee when he was spectacularly born again—fittingly enough—in Orange County, California, in a hotel room at Disneyland. He described his experience to filmmaker Robert Mugge.

> I was born again in '73. And I was converted, or changed about, or turned around, which is what converted means. . . . And I felt so good, so perfect, so uplifted, so forgiven, so clean. (How did that happen?) I went to San Francisco to do a concert, and I flew my girlfriend [Laura] from Detroit to Los Angeles. At that time, I had nothing any better to do. . . . We had a midnight concert at Disneyland. This is great, boom. I did San Francisco that night with Smokey Robinson and I did Disneyland at 12 o'clock. I flew us up on a private plane. But when she got there, I says, I am *pooped*, I am *tired*. So goodnight, *right*, on the other side of the suite, *right*, 'cause I am going to hit it, *right*. Man, I got in bed and I went to sleep. Simple, like the rest of the twenty years I went through.
>
> Around 4:30 that morning, I woke up praising and rejoicing, and I had never felt like that before and I never felt like that again. I felt, man, so many things were changing so fast. And I had this input, you know, it's like a charge of electricity to create a new person. And I said, oh . . . to actually come in, just change your whole personality. And I said, man, I don't understand. So I ran into the bathroom. My girlfriend is knocking on the door, "What's happening, what's happening?" I'm saying, thank you Jesus, hallelujah, praise God—I never said that before. . . . I try to cover my mouth to keep from saying this stuff, you know, try to keep from saying all these things 'cause she's gonna hear me. And I heard this voice saying, "Are you ashamed of me?" And I came out of there, I think . . . no, I'm not ashamed. I am not ashamed. I never will be ashamed. I was feeling so good I tried to keep that feeling for as long as I could.[7]

That same year, for reasons he couldn't quite explain, Green had written a gospel song for his Grammy-nominated album *Call Me*. He called it "Jesus Is Waiting." "I could recite the words of repentance, the formula for forgiveness, and the attitude of saving grace," he explained. "But behind that knowledge was spiritual ignorance. I had forsaken the faith and, in the process, sold my birthright." This alarmed Mitchell, who had no interest in doing gospel and saw no reason to tamper with a formula that had made Green a superstar. During his road tours, Green resolved to attend church every Sunday, wherever he was. "I was hungry to hear the Gospel preached and, on occasion," he claimed, "I'd even end up with some Korean or Spanish congregation where, even if I didn't understand the words, at least the Holy Spirit was there to welcome me." At concerts he would spontaneously break into testimony or scripture. "I didn't know what to think when those spells came over me, didn't even know where I had heard or remembered the Bible quotations I was spouting, and sometimes thought I was going crazy for sure."[8]

He expanded on his predicament in Mugge's film interview:

> I got to figure out what to do. I mean, I got a million-dollar career going here. And I'm telling folks they need to be born again? I mean, man, this is tripping me out, I'm telling you. I have never experienced anything like that, Bob, before in my life. And onstage I'd be doing great. I'd sing "Love and Happiness," "I'm Still in Love," all that stuff. Now when I get down to the point of, like, "You ought to be with me," I get down to the point of "For the Good Times"—man, I don't know. Something started happening, man, I get these impulses—boom. . . . And I thought: scriptures. Well, I asked the people in San Francisco. I was very serious and I haven't forgot that night yet. I sang "I Want to Take You Higher." And all of the 17,000 people say, "Yeah, yeah." Okay? And when you talk about man and woman, boy and girl relationships. . . . That's wonderful—you're supposed to have companions. Not good for man to be alone . . . be fruitful, multiply, have children, all that, great. But see, when you talking to people in a club, after they've had about three or four joints, you know, after a few martinis, a little scotch on the rocks. . . . Man, give me the chick, this is my neighbor's old lady, right? We're just out for the party, see. Now you're going to tell me about the Lord? Da da da. We'll get to that on Sunday. And that's the way it was. So the concerts started going crazy. Records started going crazy. Al was most certainly going crazy. Willie was going crazy. Everybody was going crazy.[9]

Pulled in opposite directions—whether to continue his career as a sexed-up soul man or dedicate his life to the Lord—Green "did what most of us poor frail humans do. I tried to have it both ways." Not long after deferring his decision, Green met Mary Woodson. On one of their first dates—a spring picnic in a park—she had surprised him by prophesying that he would be a great minister one day, saving many souls through his sermons. "When you preach in your church," she asked him, "will you save a seat up front for me?"[10]

On that October night in Green's Memphis mansion, Mary faced Green with a steaming kettle full of boiling grits. "In the next second, my world ex-

Al Green in 1974
(Image © Michael
Ochs Archives/
CORBIS)

ploded into a thousand splatters of pure agony," he recalled. "With all her strength, she hurled it at me, splashing the bathroom walls and scorching my naked back. The pain was so intense that I wasn't sure what was happening for a moment before I heard screaming." They were his own screams. Williams burst into the bathroom, nearly fainted, and pushed Green under a torrent of ice-cold water in the shower. Then they heard two loud reports from down the hall, followed by "the sickening, unmistakable sound of something heavy hitting the floor." They moved down the hall, checking bedrooms, until they got to the last one. There, they found Woodson's lifeless body, a gun in her hand. She had killed herself.

As Green began an eight-month recovery process in the hospital the next day, he faced interminable interrogations by teams of police, who suspected foul play. He was eventually invited to take a polygraph, which he passed.

But the rumors circulated: Green had murdered Woodson, or his bodyguards had, or his physical abuse had driven her to take her life. "It was also spread around that my religious 'conversion' had come from almost getting scalded to death that night," he said, "and being caught up in so disgraceful a mess that I had to do something to redeem my image." Indeed, that impression persists to this day. "Whatever happened there traumatized him to leave pop music," insisted music writer James L. Dickerson. "I think it affected Al, and I'm sure it still does," agreed Isaac Hayes, another Memphis man. "I think it drove him a little closer to God. Life-and-death situations do that."[11]

The chronology is more complicated, though. Green had been moving closer to God, musically and personally, for some time before that horrific October night in Memphis. As Green described it, the relentless demands of staying at the top began to take their toll not long after his first breakthrough hits, "Can't Get Next to You," "Tired of Being Alone," and "Let's Stay Together." The pressure was always on to produce new, bigger hits, and the tours required to promote those hits and albums stretched out endlessly. "After a trip to the top that pretty much took my breath away and more than I could imagine of the kind of success that was supposed to matter," Green wrote, "I was already beginning to ask a question that has come to haunt more than one rich, famous and fabulously happy celebrity: *Is this all there is?*"[12]

### Sex and the Single Jesus Freak

The struggle between the flesh and the spirit is a familiar one in the world of music, never more than in the golden ages of R & B and rock 'n' roll. Davin Seay, who collaborated with Al Green on his autobiography, wrote of the "bondage to an overpowering, unending conflict" that marked the lives of singers like Sam Cooke and Little Richard, and one could easily add Green to the list. "It was for the Church to rub salt in those wounds," Seay added. "Doctrines that rammed home the implacable enmity of spirit and flesh would find their outworkings in the creative process. Music, not allowed to exist for its own sake, was sacrificed on the altars of piety or profanity."[13]

Churches had to work extra hard to rub salt during the seventies, the most hedonistic decade in American history, a period when social control over sexuality appeared to have broken down irreversibly. The sexual perks of power and stardom had filtered down from the upper echelons of wealth, power, and celebrity. "The early '70s was a period of time when you could meet somebody, and you could go out and have lunch with them, and if you could make each other laugh enough by the end of lunch, you'd say, 'You want to take another hour and check into a motel?'" explained an L.A. record producer named Michael James Jackson.[14] Not that many rank-and-file Jesus People had inhabited this world, but there was considerable overlap, especially in the case of musicians and religious leaders (who were often one and the same). Charismatic leaders have always faced an inordinate abundance of fleshly temptation, not least the charismatic leaders of religious communities, their obligations to represent and embody sexual restraint and morality often inspiring them to be even more creative in rationalizing their conduct than mere political leaders.

"You can still be a star and sin not," Green wrote in his memoir. "But I speak from experience when I say that the temptations that beset a man of wealth and fame are all but overwhelming, except to the strongest and most resolute among us. Ask yourself: If you were able to get whatever you wanted— the finest meals, the fastest cars, the most beautiful women—whenever and wherever you wanted, what would hold you back, what would restrain you from losing yourself in the desires of the flesh in all their endless variations?" Green continued: "There's no way in the world a man can stay humble and contrite beneath the blinding light of fame. And there's no way he can stay pure—if not in deed, then surely in his heart—when he sees firsthand how fame and fortune can turn a woman into a harlot, hungry for his power."[15]

These temptations intruded even into the world of Jesus music. Matthew Ward, who sang with his two sisters in 2nd Chapter of Acts, one of the key Christian groups of the seventies, began touring when he was a young teen and by age sixteen had traveled to every state except Alaska. Usually, the group stayed in homes rather than hotels, sometimes with daughters who could be quite demonstrative. "More times than not," Ward recalled, "the PKs [preacher's kids] proved to be the most rebellious, most out-of-control kids. As a young teenager, I had a hard time because many of these girls were pretty and more than willing to do things with me that I knew I just couldn't do. Fortunately, for the most part I was able to resist the devil, so to speak, but I certainly made out with some of them." One mother regularly brought her daughter to concerts, hoping to fix her up with Ward; one time, the girl pulled out a Polaroid snapshot of "her climbing into her bunk bed wearing nothing but a skimpy piece of lingerie." Ward tore it up. Another girl came up after a concert and asked to talk in private. Expecting that she wanted to pray with him, Ward was nonplussed when she uncovered her breasts and asked him to sign them. "I don't sign flesh," Ward informed her.[16]

As mentioned in chapter 4, Andraé Crouch faced temptations of a less corporeal variety. During the period when he found himself targeted by demons, the climactic encounter involved "a demon of lust." Sleeping in after a Disciples concert, Crouch awoke to something crawling on his body. "I felt long hair in my face," he recalled. "Then it began to blow softly in my ear, like an intimate moment between lovers. I thought, *This is a woman on me!* My mind just froze with fear." According to Crouch, the guise nearly worked. "The force was so powerful it pulled on my mind as if it was temptin' me, 'Why don't you see if you can go on with her? See if it would really work, if there could be some type of episode. Why don't you?'" Remembering his earlier run-ins with demons, Crouch "yelled 'JE-SUS'" as loud as he could, and the demon vanished instantly. But it was a close enough call to send Crouch to a Bible bookstore to read up on Satanism and the occult and conduct an exorcism of the house that, by his account, removed the demons once and for all.[17]

Scott Ross, founder of the Love Inn Christian community in upstate New York, faced sexual challenges as both a celebrity and a leader in the Jesus Movement. A cutting-edge disk jockey in New York City, Ross had played a sybarite's life to the hilt. He hung out with the Beatles and partied with the Rolling Stones. He smoked his first joint and dropped his first pills with Brian Jones. He often crashed with a rich playboy named Martin in an opulent penthouse on Central Park South—appointed "like a Hollywood movie set" with real Picassos on the wall—enjoying "the wildest living I had ever imagined." Martin bought marijuana by the shopping bag, but what stuck with Ross were the girls: "Warm young bodies who drifted in and out of our lives for an evening or a weekend, then disappeared into whatever fantasy had brought them."[18] One of these young women "freaked out" and ran "half naked" out of the apartment into Central Park. Not long afterward, Ross was busted at the apartment, consequently losing his radio show at age twenty-six. Then he began dropping acid frequently and in large doses.

About this time, a young lady began leading Ross back to the Lord, but she was not one of the usual suspects. It was his girlfriend Nedra—one of the Ronettes, a first cousin of Ronnie and Estelle, and to Ross's eye the prettiest of the three. "Nedra with her mixture of black, Spanish and Indian blood was petite, amber skinned, high cheek-boned," Ross wrote. "She was something else too. Naïve? Unassuming—I don't know the word for it." Nedra's dating of Ringo Starr gave Ross pangs of jealousy, but Ross ultimately won her. Their spiritual odyssey eventually led them into the Jesus Movement, with its intense visions, prophecies, demons, faith healing, and a young Pat Robertson. They had one child, then another. Their call took them to upstate New York, where Ross pursued his ambition of Christian radio along with founding the intentional community Love Inn. Their leadership attracted a large, dynamic group of Jesus People.

But Ross's past continued to act as a thorn in his Christian flesh and undermine his leadership. "How could I share with anyone else the struggles I was having with my thought life?" he wrote. "In the days before I became a Christian my sex life was pretty free-wheeling. When Nedra and I walked to the front of the church in Hagerstown, I knew that, among other things, the actual sex adventuring had to stop, and it did. Only, there was an interior sex life—a fantasy life—that kept right on. It was, I said to myself, an innocent enough way to handle drives that the Lord had given me and I made no special attempt to stop it."[19]

Ross thought marriage would end his unwelcome fantasies, but it didn't, and he felt they threatened his leadership of Love Inn. "The most frequent problem area for the young people who came to the barn was sex," he explained. "From masturbation and sex before marriage, to homosexuality and a lot weirder perversions, they were generally hung up on sex in one way or another. When people talked with me about their problems they didn't want theories, they wanted help that worked. If I hadn't won the battle myself, what could I tell them? Whenever I talked to some guy about the beauty of sex the way God created it to be, I could see in his eyes that I wasn't getting through."[20] It was part of a several-year battle Ross waged against his own pride and willfulness, his hot temper, and his unwillingness to submit to authority, especially God's.

Ross's spiritual crisis came to a climax in April 1974, when he stormed out of a weekly basketball game at the local high school, "sick of the whole stupid scene at Love Inn." He invited a friend to get drunk with him at an Ithaca bar. But after a girl with a "tremendous figure" came in, Ross dismissed his friend and began to flirt. "An hour passed on the Four Roses clock on the wall," he remembered. "The girl put her hand on my arm and asked for another drink. When it came she didn't take her hand away. And suddenly I knew for sure that in addition to the sin of murder, I was also capable of adultery." But when the two prepared to leave together, Ross unexpectedly began to witness to the woman, blurting out: "At-Love-Inn-we-help-people-find-the-Lord." Once the tension passed, both burst into laughter, and she gave him a lift to Love Inn. In Ross's telling, the bar incident marked a watershed of "effective, permanent healing" that would stick.[21]

Sexual morality was a widespread concern in the Jesus Movement. "It was an age when all those things were clashing," recalled Jerry Bryant. "There were a lot of criticisms because early Jesus Freaks—no one was there to mentor us and pastor us and father us—thought, I can smoke dope and have sex with my girlfriend and still be madly in love with Jesus. So the Holy Spirit had to show us that that was a nonnegotiable." Melody Green, wife of musician Keith Green, agreed that "the attitude of many Christians was pretty lax. It seemed like you could be a Christian and do almost anything you wanted— sleep around, smoke dope, and swim nude in mixed company."[22]

Some young evangelicals had considerable sexual experience lodged in their memory, even if a major draw of the Jesus Movement was to escape the emotional scarring that free love sometimes imposed, especially on young women. And it's unlikely that these memories were all bad; chastity could be a tough sell. A so-called Sweet Jesus Rock Concert at Stanford University, featuring the Spokane-based rock band Wilson McKinley, drew 8,000 people. "The Jesus People almost lost the crowd," *Time* reported in its cover story, "when one evangelist told the collegians they should 'abstain from sexual immorality, and that means abstain except in marriage. We're finding this is the last area people want to give up.' There were no cheers but, astonishingly in the Age of Aquarius, no hoots either."[23]

"Sexuality is one of the greatest gifts God gave to man," opined a Jesus Freak from Palo Alto who had tripped with Timothy Leary and sold drugs. "It's his most powerful force. To misuse it and to make a mockery of it is just of the devil. The proper use of sex is in marriage. To keep people together and have kids. I don't believe everyone should have kids now with the population explosion, but it is very deep. It is the root of you, and it should not be taken lightly. It should be shared among life-long partners." He turned to the subject of homosexuality, which he described as "becoming a tremendous problem. Maybe it's good that it's coming out into the open, all the latency is becoming overt today. Psychiatrists don't seem to have any answer to it. I believe it is a spiritual problem. Jesus can fill all those empty holes in our lives, if we just let him."[24]

Billy Graham recognized that sex was a particular danger zone for the young baby boomers he was so concerned to win for Jesus. (A hot-blooded youth, he knew something about the war between spirit and flesh, resolving early in his ministry never to be alone in a room with a woman not his wife.) In *The Jesus Generation*, Graham devoted an entire chapter to what he titled "The Sex Hang-up." "Most young people today have some sort of sex hang-up," he began. "This has been true in every generation. But today it is probably more acute than at any other time in history. But I doubt if you know the extent to which you are coerced, maneuvered, tempted, exploited, and bedeviled by commercial interests who support sex for their economic advantage. Wherever you turn, sex rears its head."[25]

Graham listed some of the culprits: "a sex-saturated culture" celebrated by the media, "cultural anthropologists" with their findings about permissive sexual practices in other societies, and peer pressure. Quoting liberally from Norman Vincent Peale, he patiently explained a variety of practical reasons why sleeping around comes back to haunt. "It takes no poll for those of us who have communicated with young people to know the devastation that permissive sexual activity generally causes," Graham insisted. "It becomes a cancer in the bodies and minds and characters of those who indulge, almost without exception. And there are other victims, such innocent bystanders as parents, grandparents, old family friends, teachers, and advisors, all much more concerned than you can understand. They want only the best for you. Anything less than a happy marital voyage gives them pain." But most important for Graham, fornication and adultery are condemned throughout the Bible. "Recognize that premarital or extramarital sex brings misery and tragedy into your life and the lives of others," he concluded. "But most of all face the fact that sex outside of marriage is a sin against God."[26]

The famous evangelist occasionally donned a disguise in order to blend in and spend some time with Jesus People, but those who took the time to get closer to the Jesus Movement found a range of attitudes and behaviors not atypical of any young American of the era. "I would say the sexual life of the Jesus youth is fairly normal, at least by middle-class standards," reported Hiley H. Ward. This appraisal was shared by Graham, who reassured his young readers that they weren't really missing out on much, despite what the media was reporting: "The middle-class church code expects chastity, celibacy of the nonmarried, and fidelity in marriage. The Jesus People try to put down sex, pretending it is not very important, when Jesus is all." But as he traveled around the country, Ward found plenty of evidence of physical attraction and occasional carnal activity. "When five young men trying to live in the Spirit of the Lord in Phoenix, began to confess their sins," he wrote, "they found they all had the same 'lust for Tina,' a member of their Bible study group." He witnessed quite a bit of late-night kissing at the Children of God's commune in Los Angeles, mostly among girls, "as part of the after-midnight exuberance of dancing, singing and praising God." A few young men offered each other "a holy kiss" as well. "Sexual problems have not yet all been overcome," concluded researchers who visited Harvest House in San Francisco, where they met a young man rocking a baby whose unwed mother was also a resident. "The father reluctantly admitted that his sexual activity was wrong, but added that he was not the only one who had trouble in this area. The situation, he said, was now fully under control."[27]

Ward decided that "normal boy-girl dating relations or even normal familial sister-brother relations are not always easy to establish in the young communes of Jesus People." Another observer, Lowell Streiker, was surprised by "the disembodied, physical up-tightness" of the young Christians: "After my exposure to the sensitivity training or encounter group scene with its 'touch me, feel, heal me' emphasis on physical contact as a means of expressing oneself, I was aghast at the 'keep your hands to yourself' spirit of the Jesus people's praise and worship services and their communal life. My temperament is so different," he admitted. "I hugged kids who were ecstatic with joy, placed an arm around a shoulder of a brother in anguish, stood toe-to-toe with my hands on the forearms of those I disagreed with, embraced new-found friends when I left them. But for the most part the Jesus people seem disgusted by physical contact." Ward was struck by the wide range of moral codes in the communities he visited. "The Jesus People communes—most of them run by peers no older than the other members—cover a variety of disciplines, all of them aimed at the Christian ideal," he wrote. "Many are outright puritanical, allowing no mixture of the sexes, except at mealtime or on street corners when evangelizing. Others allow dating, recognizing their members as mature adults. Others allow no dating or marriage plans without consent of the leaders."[28] Often people outside the community were considered off-limits. Of course, some communes were single-sex, which simplified matters.

The Children of God had begun as a particularly puritanical group within the Jesus Movement. Dating and "smooching" were forbidden, and marriages were arranged by elders and could only involve fellow members. As was true for other Jesus communities, the Children's Texas Soul Clinic was markedly paternalistic. "There is no women's liberation movement at the Soul Clinic," reported NBC's Robert Rogers. "The girls handle the cooking and serving of meals. They also wash the men's clothes. . . . Many of them had refused even to wash dishes at home. Here they labor without complaint and most seem grateful for the opportunity." Members also accepted arranged marriages. One young woman, married for nine months in the Children of God, admitted, "I had gone with a number of men before I joined the team, and I was sick of guys. I decided when I was twenty that I would never get married, and especially never have children. I just couldn't see the use of bringing kids into this polluted world. But in the revolution marriage is different—it's a real humbling thing. It is up to God when you get married and who you will marry."[29]

For many young women, this return to traditional roles came as a relief, as a Children of God member in Texas complained to Rogers:

> What I saw was today's quote-unquote free love was the biggest bondage I've ever seen. You know, you have to go to bed with everybody you go out with. And if you don't. . . . Everyone has completely forgotten the person, the soul. It's all body; it's all flesh. It got to the point in my life where I was just thinking one more pill or one more night with a guy would be the answer. You know, like I'd find the answer and I'd find the love. And no matter how many pills I took, no matter how many guys I slept with, I didn't find it. . . . And now by God's grace I am going to serve him with my whole heart for my whole life. And wow! I am just so happy.

As Beth Bailey demonstrated in her study *Sex in the Heartland*, the "Sexual Revolution" was never a monolithic movement. It took on myriad local forms in thousands of communities across the United States, most having little in common with the celebrated hedonism reported on the East and West Coasts. "The sexual revolution was not a simple, two-sided contest between the proponents of freedom and the forces of repression," Bailey wrote. "Even those who actively supported the 'revolution' had radically different concepts of what it was and what it should accomplish."[30] Some thought free love could help smash the capitalist state, form the basis of a new utopian community, or express a natural alternative to the sirens of materialism and technocracy. Some women came to see eros as an element in their repression by patriarchy, while others celebrated sexual pleasures that had long been ignored or devalued. Gays and lesbians heralded sex as a key element of personal identity. Many men and women came to see sex as one part of a larger remaking of basic assumptions about gender roles. Some but not all of these currents were found in the Jesus Movement, while others played a role by helping define what Jesus People were against: not freedom from traditional sexual codes, but freedom for living out biblical lives inspired by the example of Jesus.

## Let's Get It On

But in the media-fed popular imagination, it was often the escapades of popular artists and entertainers who defined the "sexual revolution." While Al Green worked through the traumatic collision of spirit and flesh in his own life, Marvin Gaye was girding for daunting challenges of his own: a damaging divorce from his wife Anna, the sister of Berry Gordy, who was the founder of Motown and the man who controlled Gaye's career. Cocaine was tightening its grip on Gaye, which was part of the reason why enormous sums of money passed through his accounts without leaving an appreciable trace. The singer was strapped for cash. And he had fallen desperately in love with a high school girl from Los Angeles who had moved in with him and started having his children. As was usually the case with Gaye, there was an element of spiritual turbulence to all of this as he struggled through and against his Pentecostal upbringing. *Rolling Stone* titled its April 1974 profile of the singer "The Spirit, the Flesh and Marvin Gaye."

Gaye and Janis Hunter first laid eyes on each other, the (true) story goes, in March 1973, when Gaye was in the Motown studio in Los Angeles. The song he was recording at that moment was "Let's Get It On," an ode to sexual pleasure that would set the tone for the last ten years of his life. A passionate seduction song, Gaye audibly kicked up his powers of persuasion when he caught sight of the seventeen-year-old beauty, who was the daughter of an Irish American mother and jazz musician Slim Gaillard, best known for "Flat Foot Floogie." Janis had come in with her mom, a friend of the man who was collaborating with Gaye on his new album. By all accounts, the two were instantly and mutually smitten. As the session ended, Gaye turned to friends and remarked, "That's the finest woman I've ever seen."

He recognized that age might pose an obstacle. "Wasn't that something?" Gaye marveled later. "My wife was seventeen years older than I was and this girl was seventeen years younger. I worried how everyone would react — my family, my friends, my fans. I worried about the law, although Jan's mother, who's a wonderful woman, encouraged the relationship." But the romance developed quickly, becoming "an obsession so deeply sexual and wildly romantic that Marvin would never recover from its impact," according to biographer David Ritz. During the extended periods he spent with Gaye, Ritz introduced him to the love poetry of Dante (Janis Hunter as Beatrice), Andrew Marvell, Thomas Carew, and John Donne. "The obsession would possess him totally," wrote Ritz, "changing his music, altering his life, making all other matters mundane." It was, as June Carter had put it, a "Ring of Fire."[31]

"He was drawn to danger," Hunter explained to journalist Steve Turner. "I was a total babe in the woods. I didn't know what was going on. It was try this, try that. I'm gonna take you here. I'm gonna take you there." Hunter was Gaye's muse as he recorded the rest of the album, which marked a dramatic turn of direction. "He'd just come out of *What's Going On* and was recognized as this guru, this master of thought, this spiritual being, and then he turns up with 'You Sure Love to Ball' and people really didn't understand," Hunter recalled. "A lot of it had to do with us meeting and exploring each other. There's no way of knowing whether that album ever would have come out in the way it did if he and I hadn't had the kind of relationship we had." It worked. Released in the summer of 1973, *Let's Get It On* became the most successful album of Gaye's career, reaching number two in the pop charts as an album and number one as a single.[32]

If *What's Going On* offered a spiritual solution to the social problems America faced in an era of urban unrest, economic malaise, and wartime divisions, *Let's Get It On* offered commentary on emotional and physical love in a time of sexual liberty. But the sex here is, as with Green's greatest hits, anything but casual. Gaye's voice is nearly desperate with longing. "I don't think being religious means you can't have sex," Gaye told Tim Cahill of *Rolling Stone*. "I think that you can do it and still be good. I think it's ridiculous to say you can't be a priest and also screw. People are supposed to say, 'If he's giving up the Supreme Goodie, then he must be a good man.' Why can't a religious man have the Supreme Goodie and be an even greater man? If he is intelligent enough to be a priest, he ought to be intelligent enough to handle the goodies." Part of the point is being clear about what's involved in intimate relationships. "I think sex is sex and love is love," Gaye asserted. "I think they can be and are separated."[33]

Cahill quoted Gaye's father's description of how his son had excelled in Sunday school: "He had a quicker grasp of scripture, and sometimes, as a small boy, he almost sounded like a grown man, a minister." "There are two types of world, the flesh and the spirit," Gaye said in interview with *Ebony* that year. "I think God meant you to be in the world but not of it. For a spiritual man, one woman is enough. But the flesh constantly calls. You work to hold things to a minimum while you build on that spiritual thing. The thing is not to go hog wild."[34]

Was Gaye part of the Jesus Movement? Only a fellow traveler in the loosest sense, he was animated by a spiritual quest that evolved and took many forms. In that way, he was definitely part of the broad sixties cultural front that included the Jesus Movement. Was he a "spiritual man"? The woman who knew him best during these years believed Gaye never abandoned his relationship with Jesus. "He knew that his only salvation was through God," Hunter said. "He knew that he should be a good man but it became increasingly difficult for him to separate the good Marvin from the bad Marvin. In his heart of hearts he knew what was right and what was wrong, but when

Marvin Gaye in concert, 1975 (Image © Neal Preston/CORBIS)

you use cocaine you get taken to a place where you don't need to go, and once you feel that it has conquered your heart and your mind and your soul it's as if you give in."[35] Through the seventies, cocaine figured as a major factor in the lives of popular musicians, including secular artists who converted to Christianity and modified their habits accordingly.

In his book *Crossing and Dwelling*, Thomas Tweed advanced a theory of religion that helps make sense of figures like Gaye. Tweed emphasizes "organic-cultural flows," demonstrating through case studies the myriad ways in which religions provide people with resources to find joy and sustenance through the action of making homes (dwelling) and traversing boundaries (crossing). "Religions move between what is imagined as the most distant horizon and what is imagined as the most intimate domain," he writes. "They bring the gods and earth and transport the faithful to the heavens. . . . As itinerants, the religious never remain anywhere or anytime for long. It is in this sense, I suggest, that religions are flows, translocative and transtemporal crossings."[36] We see these sorts of boundary crossings constantly in the history of popular music, as musicians, instruments, and repertories move back and forth between spaces understood to be properly religious and spaces thought to be profane or worldly. Such crossings can be fruitful and exhilarating. But they could sometimes produce spiritual anomie and take a fearsome psychic toll, as Gaye's tragic final years would demonstrate.

## Chapter 7

# SHOCK ABSORBERS

By 1975 the Jesus Movement had pretty much dropped off the media radar screen. After the Nixon landslide, oil shocks, and Watergate, the hippie spirituality with which the decade began seemed out of a different era. But the audience for Christian rock continued to grow. New festivals of Christian pop music continued to spring up in parts of the country not associated with the celebrated California scene: Jesus '74 in Pennsylvania, Salt '75 in Michigan, Fishnet '75 in Virginia, Jesus '75 Midwest in St. Louis, the Sonshine Festival in Ohio, Lodestone in Vancouver, Road Home Celebration in Colorado, the Jesus Festival of Joy in Wichita, and the Hill Country Faith Festival in Texas. New radio stations dedicated exclusively to Christian rock appeared, first in Orange County, naturally, but also in Houston and Lincoln, Nebraska. And new artists continued to be drawn into the fold of what was still being called Jesus music.[1]

The most celebrated double bill in the history of Jesus music appeared on the scene in 1975: Barry McGuire and the 2nd Chapter of Acts backed by a group that called itself "A Band Called David." At a series of gigs at auditoriums and theaters up and down the state of California, McGuire and the young trio of two sisters and a brother delivered performances that stand as classic statements of the genre. In doing so, they inspired new artists to replenish the talent pool of what was just beginning to become a rapidly expanding niche in American popular music.

Born in 1935, three years after Johnny Cash, Barry McGuire was by then as close to a senior statesman as Jesus music had. He had helped found the New Christy Minstrels and the Mamas and the Papas. He had written and sung "Green, Green," which reached fourteen on the pop charts in 1963. Two years later, he had a number-one solo hit with "Eve of Destruction." He had hung around with the Byrds and Bob Dylan. He had starred in the Broadway cast of *Hair*. Even in the wild cast of a wild show staged in an uninhibited time and place, McGuire stood out. He was the "one real hippie in the cast," according to fellow cast member Lorrie Davis. "He seemed to genuinely love everybody and vice versa. Nobody had a bad word for Barry." One evening during a break, he and a woman from the cast engaged in a vigorous, protracted bout of public sex. "People not only lined up to see the exhibition, but many ran out to get friends, even from other theaters, to come watch," Davis recalled. In the dressing room, McGuire was beloved for his hilariously obscene "cock impressions," which he gave names like "The Shy Turtle," "Half a Grapefruit," and "Al Jolson Singing 'Swanee.'"[2]

During most of the sixties, though, McGuire had been "searching for a deeper meaning to life. I had done years on the road, I'd performed at the White House," he told an interviewer. "I saw all this opulence and wealth. People that were so famous, Elvis Presley, Sammy Davis Jr., people that I knew, some of 'em I performed with. And none of 'em were happy. I felt, why should I spend my life trying to get like them?" Even Frank Sinatra struck him as terribly bored. McGuire pondered Eastern mysticism, rapping late at night with a friend in the Christys, wondering about reincarnation and what happens to the soul. He also plunged into the counterculture, "a real shedding of the old dogma, like boundaries of morality were being broken down and everybody was into the new party mode of just loving on each other."

But the costs were high. "One time I was with a friend of mine who's dead now, and we had this big block of cocaine about the size of a shoe box," he recalled. "And we were slicing off lines and I was just ready to spoon a spoonful into my nose. . . . I looked up, and here's these posters on the wall, this house we were at. And there's Jimi Hendrix and Janis Joplin and Marilyn Monroe and Lenny Bruce and all these posters, and I looked at them with my one eye open and I turned to my friend and I said, maybe this stuff ain't good for us. Like, what are we doing here?"[3] McGuire estimated he lost sixteen personal friends to hippie hedonism.

Barry McGuire in Los Angeles, 1967 (Image © Henry Diltz/CORBIS)

One by one, McGuire discovered the Ten Commandments. The Helter Skelter murders shocked the L.A. music community: "Well, maybe we should have one rule: we shouldn't kill each other." McGuire's prized Italian roadster was stolen and stripped: "Maybe we should have another where we shouldn't steal from each other." A lover left him for another man: "Maybe we shouldn't rip each other off for our old ladies." "Why can't we do these things?" he told an interviewer. "Because you just can't do those things. I didn't know why. So I threw all the rules away, and everybody started dying around me, and I wound up desolate and bankrupt, and I said, oh, that's why. So I adapted that into my life."[4] One thing led to another, and on Father's Day in 1971, McGuire was baptized.

Before and after being born again, McGuire projected charisma. "When Barry stepped out on stage to sing, we were immediately struck by his presence," recalled Melody Green, wife of Keith Green, who would become a Christian rock icon in the late seventies. "At first glance, he looked a little rough around the edges—a big, burly guy with long hair and a bushy beard. He looked like he might ride to church on a Harley Davidson motorcycle or something. But as soon as he spoke, I was amazed at his meekness." McGuire was especially adept at interspersing his songs with short anecdotes and testimony that doubled as Christian witness and song introductions. "He sang and talked about God in a way that we never heard before," Green said of their 1973 encounter. "He made knowing God sound simple. Barry's mannerisms were so warm and easygoing that we were glued to every word he sang or spoke."[5]

All of McGuire's warmth, playfulness, and timing were on display in the summer of 1975 as McGuire played one-nighters across California with 2nd Chapter of Acts. He punctuated his testimony with sound effects and laughed at his own stories. Raised in San Pedro, a beach town in Southern California, he frequently interjected the "mee-ann" of a surfer dude. McGuire told a long story about communing with dolphins—whacking them with a dish towel, actually—while out on a fishing boat as a teenager. "But I remember sitting on the foc'sle of the boat that day watching him swim away, and something deep, deep down in my heart whispered to me: 'See those dolphins, Barry? I made those dolphins just for your pleasure.' And you know, I've heard that voice whispering to me, not often but every once in a while, usually when I'm by myself. And I didn't know it then, but I've come to recognize it as the voice of my Lord, calling to me."[6]

McGuire made it clear that the boomer Christians who came to his concerts had a crucial role to play in human history. "You are a chosen generation," he bellowed in one hard-rocking song. "It's a royal priesthood and a holy nation." Jesus People were called to be shock absorbers, he explained.

I was looking at the body of Christ around the world, and I started seeing that Jesus was the shock absorber. And that us, in him, when we are crucified, with him, we become shock absorbers in this world. And running through our society, man, are incredible shock waves of destruction, and we see them. They come up against us every day. And try and bend us and twist us and destroy us and get us crazy inside. But with Jesus within us, we can open up to that shock because he's received it. And if we don't open up to the shock and let him absorb it through us, well, then, it will bounce off of us with more energy than it had when it hit us and go on to destroy somebody else. That we the body of Christ, man, can absorb the insanity with Jesus within us, allowing him to do it, that's ripping the world to pieces right now. So every time a shock wave hits, know where it's coming from. And you've got two choices. You can either get hard and get mad, like I do

99 percent of the time. Or you can remember where it's coming from and ask Jesus, Lord, allow me to be used to get this out of the world. Shock absorbers. Amen. That's what we are.[7]

*Incredible shock waves of destruction*: many of McGuire's audience would have heard echoes of the hit song "Eve of Destruction," which had topped the charts exactly ten years earlier, before so much had changed in the world. That song had wedded fear of nuclear Armageddon with outrage at war and violence perpetrated on the civil rights movement. "Think of all the hate there is in Red China, then take a look around to Selma, Alabama." "And even the Jordan River has bodies floatin'"—a line that apparently prophesied the Six-Day War two years later. In 1965 McGuire was singing somebody else's song, mining a vein of musical protest that had propelled Dylan to fame. By 1975 McGuire was framing many of the same ideas in the Christian end-times doctrine so pervasive in the Jesus Movement, ideas popularized by Hal Lindsey, Larry Norman, even Johnny Cash. The signs were all around, just as they had been a decade earlier, but their meaning was quite different.

> You can read it in your newspaper and watch it on your color TV
> You know the hand of writing is on the wall, it's for all to see
> There's earthquakes and famines, violence and crimes
> You know the Bible clearly plainly tells us we're living in the end of time.

The mood was hopeful and expectant, not pessimistic. McGuire had coached his audience in the chorus, and they joined in readily: "He's coming back, He's coming back / He's coming back to take his own, gonna take us away now." Another song, "Jesus People," gave the Rapture a whimsical spin. When those strange young Christians come witnessing at your door, McGuire sang, "don't you get uptight, things'll be all right / 'Cause it won't be long till they'll be gone. . . . When it finally happens it's gonna blow their minds / When all us Jesus People fly away-ay-ay-ay."[8]

If McGuire was the grizzled veteran preaching the honest truth, his partners on this tour brought a kind of youthful angelic purity to the same themes. In contrast to his full-throated raspy voice, 2nd Chapter of Acts offered impeccable three-part harmony, soaring crystalline melodies occasionally spiced with the soulful melisma of the trio's youngest member, Matthew. His two sisters, Annie and Nelly, rounded out 2nd Chapter of Acts. Adverse circumstances had brought the three close together. Their parents had died a few years earlier, and Annie and her husband had raised Nelly and Matthew, then young teens. The family had been raised Catholic but were born again under the guidance of Annie's husband, Buck Herring, a disk jockey and band promoter who himself had accepted Jesus when his drug dealer was born again.

McGuire seemed to enjoy telling the story of how he had met these young musicians who were so different from him.

> I'd like to introduce to you, you've probably already noticed them, these three thin people to my right. Not to be confused with the microphone stands [laughter]. This is the 2nd Chapter of Acts. And you know, when I first met them, I went over to see Buck one afternoon about three years ago. . . . And while we were talking, his wife Annie . . . she came into the living room and brought me a nice delicious cup of coffee. And pretty soon Matthew came into the living room chasing a paper airplane. He makes the most incredible planes; they never land, they just keep flying. . . . And I didn't know what to expect, you know, three skinny people and a piano. I thought [in a grumpy voice], well, praise the Lord [laughter]. . . . But you know, when Annie sat down and started to play, and the three of them started to sing, I just felt the spirit of God just fill the whole house, you know, fill me. And I started to receive healing. I started to receive promise and reinforcement from their songs.

McGuire had actually begun working with the young trio shortly after that first meeting. He brought them in as background singers on his first Christian album, *Seeds*, released in 1973 and produced by Buck Herring. That same year, McGuire began touring with 2nd Chapter of Acts. All of them shared the rapturous enthusiasm of new Christians recently born again. The Ward kids had been born in rural North Dakota. In 1963 they moved to Sacramento partly for the sake of their mother's health. She died in 1968; her husband died exactly two years after the day she was buried. Being the youngest, Nelly and Matthew had the choice of living with their aunt and uncle in Sacramento or their sister Annie and brother-in-law Buck in Los Angeles.

They chose Los Angeles. Annie had already been pursuing a career as a singer, first in San Francisco, where she lived on Haight Street, and later in Hollywood. She struggled with drugs and a general lack of self-worth. Buck, her boyfriend, recommended the Gospel. "And the Lord told me," Annie recalled, "you can have everything you've ever wanted, everything: fame, money, everything. Or you can have me. And it was simply that. . . . And I said, Lord, after seeing you, I don't want anything else."[9] She learned how to play the piano and invited her younger siblings to pull up chairs and sing along when they came home from school. Annie, Nelly, and Matthew created and learned new songs at an astounding rate.

There was some friction in the surrogate family, especially between Matthew and the stern, hulking Buck Herring. A staunch Christian, Buck forbade Matthew from listening to secular music, including Motown, his first love. ("Who's the black girl singing that song?" was reportedly the question asked by music executives when first hearing recordings of the trio.) They tangled over other issues as well, including conduct in school. "Buck was a firm believer in corporal punishment ('Spare the rod,' etc.), so when I brought home one of these slips, Buck and I would talk over the offense. Then he would spank me so hard that he burst blood vessels in his hand. He also prayed with me after the disciplining, which I thought was good because it showed that he wasn't just mad but really wanted the best for me."[10]

Being the youngest in a large family, Matthew had been initiated in worldly ways. One of his older brothers "would spin tales of what he had done with his girlfriends, leaving out none of the graphic (actually, pornographic) details," Ward recalled. On a wall in their garage near the washer and dryer were jotted hundreds of girls' names and phone numbers; the brother claimed he'd had sex with all of them. A different brother got Matthew high when he was fifteen, a nerve-wracking experience for the young Christian. "A few years later, by the Grace of God, all but one of my brothers had quit their pot habits and become strong Christians," Ward wrote.[11] By then Ward was born again and touring with his sisters and Buck. For a time, the foursome had attended the First Assembly of God Church in North Hollywood, where Matthew heard people speaking in tongues for the first time. After a year, they switched to the Church on the Way in Van Nuys, then a small congregation (it would grow massively) much like the Evangel Temple that Johnny and June Cash had begun attending at roughly the same time. The Church on the Way also attracted unusual numbers of musicians and actors, including Pat Boone, who had invited the musical family.

Healing and prophecy were integral to this faith. When Buck told the trio that God had given them the name 2nd Chapter of Acts, they "thought it was a horrible name . . . clueless," according to Matthew. "Buck let us vent for a few minutes and then said, 'Well, why don't we all just go to our rooms and read the second chapter of Acts.' To be honest, I didn't know what was in that chapter. So the girls and I went to our rooms. I opened up my Bible and soon found out that a lot happens in Acts 2. First there's Pentecost, then Peter gives a rocking sermon, after which thousands are saved and baptized. And then follows the story of all the believers being together and experiencing many signs and wonders." The siblings decided that Buck had been led to the right name after all.[12]

This tumultuous family history shaped the distinctively tight, nearly other-worldly sound of 2nd Chapter of Acts. Like McGuire, the siblings took turns mixing testimony with music as they introduced their songs in the summer of 1975. Annie Herring talked about her girlhood fascination with Snow White.

> And I used to go out into the woods, and I'd sing the theme song to Snow White [sings]: "Some day my prince will come, some day I'll find my love." And expected, you know, the squirrels to come down and look at me, and the butterflies to fly all around me, you know [laughter]. . . . Finally, my older sister saw that I was in trouble, 'cause she knew, you know: "Annie, I hate to disillusion you, but you can't marry a prince. Because you have to have royal blood to marry a prince." But an incredible thing did happen to me when I was 23 years old. My prince did come. The prince of peace came. And He took away all my sins, and He gave me royal blood. And He is coming for me. And He is going to come on a white horse, with King of Kings and Lord of Lords written on his thigh. And He's coming for us, his bride.

Along with Nelly and Matthew, she broke into song:

> He is coming to take us away
> He is coming it could be today
> Are you watching, are you waiting, are your lamps bright?
> For He's returning.

2nd Chapter of Acts would sing and tour together until 1988, giving them a longevity matched by few groups formed in the Jesus Movement.

### Green, Green

2nd Chapter of Acts were not the only Christian performers inspired by Barry McGuire. He would give some decisive direction to another singer, Keith Green, who would go on to become a legend of the Jesus rock crowd. Even if the era of media attention to the Jesus Movement was long past, much was brewing among a set of spiritually attuned young musicians in Southern California.

Green was an unforgettable person, ebullient and abrasive. "At first I didn't know what to make of him," recalled Matthew Ward. "He was so hyperactive (the pot calling the kettle black?) that in many ways he took the cake for being the 'strange musician' type." Ward worked with Green for a time on an unusual project: a corporate mogul hired the pair to sing backup vocals for his wife in a studio he had built in their Bel Air mansion, and the sessions were then broadcast on local UHF channels. Later, when Green started recording his own music, his producer (who had played drums with Andraé Crouch) invited Ward to sing backup vocals. But Green was not happy with Ward's contributions. "His objections grew so loud that I could hear him in spite of the glass," according to Ward. "He was yelling things like, 'I don't want that kind of crap on my record.' This put a halt to the session."[13]

"I'd never met anyone with as much reckless zeal for the Lord," Ward recalled. "I always thought of him as a bull in a china shop. Keith had a way of challenging everything and everybody. He was truly an evangelist at heart. At one of his early concerts, he gave a most unusual altar call. He'd have everyone stand up, ask the Christians to sit down, then ask those who were left standing why they were standing. He was a kind of a modern-day John the Baptist." Ward was not the only one with a kind of ambivalent awe toward Keith Green. His wife and biographer, Melody Green, admits to similar misgivings about Keith.[14] He perceived the world in absolutes, and people either loved or hated him, sometimes simultaneously. Born in 1953, he was a few years younger than most of the original wave of Jesus People, and it wasn't until 1975 that he became a born-again Christian. By then he had recapped the same sort of spiritual journey that someone like Lonnie Frisbee had undertaken a few years earlier.

From a very early age, Keith Green seemed destined for show business. His grandfather had written music for Warner Brothers and owned an independent record label that signed Hank Williams. His mother turned down a job as Benny Goodman's vocalist to marry his father, a professional baseball player. Growing up in the San Fernando Valley, Green began in Los Angeles–area theater productions at age eight. He also began writing songs, performing some of them at Hollywood's famous Troubadour nightclub. At eleven, he was invited to join ASCAP, the youngest member ever. That distinction got Green national exposure on TV. He appeared on the *Jack Benny Show*, the *Joey Bishop Show*, and *Disney's Wonderful World of Color*; he also signed a contract with Decca, the label that released *Jesus Christ Superstar*.

As child stars often do, Green lost his way for a spell. He began taking drugs and, at fifteen, running away from home. He also started keeping an intimate journal in 1969 that documents a five-year spiritual quest that would take Green through the usual countercultural spiritualities: astrology, tarot cards, the Rosicrucian Order, and the mystery of the pyramids. He read widely from Hermann Hesse, Carl Jung, Castenada, Gibran, Ram Dass, and even the Bible. Nothing provided lasting satisfaction for Green. Meanwhile, he was pursuing a career as a musician/songwriter, making music that reminded people of early Elton John or Billy Joel. His first album, *Revelations*, recorded for Amos Records, featured songs about peace and brotherhood, but it flopped. As he approached age twenty, Green felt washed-up.

Jesus was growing on Keith Green, however. He was a third-generation Christian Scientist on his mother's side, but he had Jewish background as well and knew little about Christianity. Around Christmastime in 1972, he announced in his journal, "Jesus, you are hereby officially welcomed into me. Now only action will reveal your effect on me." He bought an old cross worn by a monk in Ecuador, which became his talisman. He was wearing it when he met Melody Steiner early in 1973 and announced, "Jesus is my master." At that point, she considered herself Jewish. Melody had grown up in Venice Beach and Santa Monica, and after her parents divorced when she was twelve, she began smoking, drinking, and dating a sixteen-year-old with a car. High school was "one big blur of parties and skipping school." Nominally Jewish through her mother, Melody dabbled for a time in a Japanese Buddhist sect called Nichiren Shoshu, even traveling to Japan as part of a singing group called the Sweetie Seven that performed for adherents in a Tokyo arena. But the trip left Melody disenchanted with Buddhism.

During 1973 Keith and Melody stumbled toward marriage and a deeper sense of Christian commitment. They moved in together in May, but Keith was beginning to have doubts about sex outside of marriage. He convinced Melody that they should sleep together but remain celibate until their wedding. They were married on Christmas Day in the Little Brown Church on Coldwater Canyon Boulevard, a church sometimes attended by Larry Norman, Randy Stonehill, and other Jesus rockers. The newlyweds were affected by the string of Jesus movies then playing in the theaters. They got to know Norman's friend Ted Neeley, who had played Jesus in the *Superstar* movie and numerous stage productions, and invited him over for supper.

"I'm making hamburgers for Jesus," Melody thought with amazement. "Teddy was full of stories about some things that had happened while filming in Israel," she recalled. "It seemed there was some real supernatural activity during the crucifixion scene. Keith and I were all ears. That crucifixion scene, in particular, really touched me. It didn't look like Jesus did anything to deserve what happened." Later, Neeley invited Keith to play in a band that backed him on NBC's *Midnight Special*. Despite Keith's strong statements about Jesus, he and Melody felt hampered in their journey. For one thing, the

Jesus Freaks they met left them cold. "You couldn't have a normal conversation with her," explained Melody of a young convert Keith had met a few years earlier in Seattle. "She'd say things like, 'Oh we're out of milk, praise God,' or 'It's a beautiful day, praise the Lord.' Every other sentence was punctuated with some religious exclamation. It gave me the creeps." For Keith, the objections were more theological. "We went to a 'Jesus Freak' coffee house and they tried to rip on me about believing the whole Bible, word for word, even the part that says God kills my brother, and I just don't believe that," he wrote in his journal. "Not my wonderful Father!"[15]

Green continued to struggle with the idea that Jesus was God, demanding explanations from Christians he knew. The other obstacle was the couple's continuing use of drugs. "Despite our heady, spiritual dialogues, we were once again falling back into the same old sloppy habits to deaden the pain of Keith's lack of success—not to mention our inner emptiness," Melody recalled. "Still Stoned," Keith wrote disgustedly in his journal in July 1974. Another entry read: "Took a downer, snorted coke—not good enough—smoked dope till the cows crowed."[16]

Only in 1975 would Keith Green sink fully into his new identity as a born-again Christian. A couple of turning points happened when he was performing his music. For years, a small club on Ventura Boulevard in the San Fernando Valley had been Green's musical hangout, a home away from home. The Bla Bla Café was dark and narrow, with a small bar and a one-man kitchen; none of the furnishings matched. "When packed, the Bla could hold about sixty-five people, seated on chrome-and-vinyl chairs—the kind you'd find around a Formica table in someone's kitchen in the 1950s," wrote Melody. Playing a one-nighter in early February, Green felt himself touched by God. He described the evening in his journal: "Got stoned again. . . . Had religious experience while playing 'Jericho.' Decided to immediately stop smoking. God entered my life again. . . . Out of the gloomy despair of a dope-clouded mind came to the call to New Life—the Christian calling again."[17]

Later in the year, Green played a benefit for a Christian theater group in a Beverly Hills venue called the Daisy, attended by luminaries of the Southern California Jesus scene: Pat Boone, Julie Harris, Jerry Houser, Larry Norman, Dale Evans, and Randy Stonehill. The audience was electrified, and some were brought to tears, by his performance of "Prodigal Son Suite." Green, who had been considering abandoning his music to turn to full-time ministry, was convinced that God "gave me back my music while I was playing tonight."[18] By the end of the year, he was being invited for the first time to give concerts in churches across Southern California.

Meanwhile, the Greens had begun attending Bible study classes instead of parties. One took place in a tiny house up in the Hollywood Hills hosted by a show-business couple named the Cramers. "They had a goat tied up on their front porch, and in their loft they had a monkey in a large circus cage that chattered through our Bible studies," Melody remembered. "One 'regular' there had starred in a movie with Liza Minnelli, and he was now a Christian recording artist. And Leo, their next-door neighbor who had a drinking problem, was there whenever he was 'dry.' It was *almost* a typical Hollywood crowd—only it was different." One time a "new Christian" they'd discussed the Bible with came tearing out of Leo's house and charged buck naked into the swimming pool, embarrassing Keith and Melody in front of a young woman they had recently converted. "It was apparent now that the attitude of many Christians was pretty lax," Melody wrote. "Keith fell into a real depression of what we were seeing."[19]

More satisfying was the Bible study known as Vineyard Christian Fellowship and led by a pleasant, blond-haired young man named Kenn Gulliksen. The group met in a nice home in posh Coldwater Canyon. Around thirty-five young Christians crowded into the home, sitting on couches and the carpeted floor. Gulliksen had started out on the pastoral staff at Calvary Chapel under Chuck Smith and had worked with Lonnie Frisbee. He was a fellow musician and songwriter who'd worked with the Maranatha! groups. His gentle manner put the Greens at ease, and he led the group in simple songs that Keith and Melody had never heard before. He also led conversational, down-to-earth prayers and devotions that focused on ordinary things, like a tiff he'd had with his wife.

"I'd never heard anybody talk like that before," Melody realized. "It just sounded so down to earth. He made Jesus sound like his best friend or something. It didn't seem abstract or mystical at all." She looked over at Keith, who had "that intent look on his face, the one where his eyes got deep and penetrating. He was totally absorbed." After speaking for forty minutes, Gulliksen invited people to accept Jesus; Keith did, but Melody held back.[20] Later, the couple was baptized Calvary-style at a beach near Sunset Boulevard. Gulliksen's Bible study would continue to attract musical types from around Los Angeles for years, including the reluctant superstar from Minnesota known as Bob Dylan. The Vineyard would grow into a highly successful association of churches, with congregations around the world.

According to Bill Dwyer, a young Vineyard pastor who moved to Los Angeles from El Paso in 1973, the influence of Christian pop music on the Los Angeles Bible study scene was pervasive.

Terry Talbot, Debby Boone, Henry Cutrona, Brian McKee, and many other established artists were right in the middle of the Vineyard. Kenn was a musician and composer and really connected with artists, even if he wasn't a rock and roller. They attracted even more musicians, like Keith Green, Donn Thomas, Marty Goetz, Tata Vega, and many drummers, guitarists, etc. We even had a cluster of jazz musicians who were New York Jews who had moved to L.A. Arnold Fishkind, Shorty Rogers, and a few others were pretty well known in their part of the industry. . . . As the years went on, we would go through phases of wanting to be more sophisticated. I recall one home meeting at Larry Norman's where, after one time of worship, he declared, "If we are going to sing these stupid songs I'm not coming" and then stormed into his bedroom. We had just sung, "He is Lord of the sky, He is Lord of the sea" to the tune of "It's a Small World."[21]

Gulliksen's Bible study actually drew on two groups that had already started meeting, one in Chuck Girard's house and one in Larry Norman's apartment at Doheny and Sunset. "About forty or fifty [people]," Norman recalled. "It was really packed. Everybody was in tight little balls. . . . People would squeeze in between other people and had to put their arms behind them because their shoulders would get in the way otherwise. It was a lot of friends, it was a lot of musicians and actors."[22] Actors Jerry Houser and Julie Harris were regulars, and Martin Sheen came to a function.

Continued Norman:

It was a happening thing. It was the hippest Bible study there was. And what happened was people started showing up. . . . They'd just come on in and sit down. And I found out later just by chance from one of them that I was on the list as part of a tour. This Canadian travel agent was selling them a ticket. Go to Universal on Tuesday, go to Larry Norman's Bible study on Wednesday, go to Disneyland on Thursday. I thought, that is really smart. Wow! So I felt like the whole concept was starting to get mushy. . . . I just wanted artists that were fierce and on the edge and I wanted to give them a powerful Gospel but it turns out that most artists are mushy.

Keith Green was an exception. Through these Bible studies, Green was quickly meeting the movers and shakers of the California Jesus rock scene. He already knew Larry Norman and Randy Stonehill. Now Green got to know

Andraé Crouch; Chuck Girard of Love Song, the first group to get its start at Calvary Chapel; Phil Keaggy, a guitar virtuoso who had first hooked up with the Jesus Movement through Scott Ross at the Love Inn in upstate New York; and Billy Ray Hearn, who had started the Myrrh label in 1972 and was about to found Sparrow Records. And Keith and Melody finally met the youngsters who made up 2nd Chapter of Acts. The first time Melody Green met Annie Herring, Annie was in an apron washing dishes. Keith was nearby debating Buck Herring about whether it was better to record with "secular" labels in hopes of reaching the unchurched or to sing for the already saved. "I was really in awe of this beautiful woman with the elegant, high cheekbones and dark, dancing eyes," said Melody, "this woman of God, who sang like an angel and did dishes like a normal person! And I was standing in her kitchen. I wasn't sure how to act."[23]

The Greens had been equally starstruck by Barry McGuire when they tracked him down backstage after a performance a couple of years earlier. "There was something about his eyes," Melody explained. "They were like clear peaceful pools. His spirit was far different from his gruff-looking exterior—this was obviously a man who had been transformed. He was married, and he and his wife traveled all over the country telling people about Jesus—often living out of their small vehicle that had a camper shell on it. We were impressed by this 'singing star' who was now following Jesus in such a humble, sacrificial way. After that evening, Keith and I knew Barry McGuire had something we wanted."[24] Now Keith had been invited to sing a duet with McGuire on *Firewind*, an album version of the Christian musical written by two other remarkable siblings in the Jesus music scene, John Michael Talbot and Terry Talbot, founding stars of the country-rock band Mason Proffit.

But Green's identity was shifting; he was no longer a musician who happened to be Christian, he was a Christian evangelist who used music for his ministry. After a long-awaited New York audition for Clive Davis of Arista went poorly, Green felt the door to secular music was irrevocably shut. He witnessed to friends and strangers more aggressively. In true Jesus People fashion, the Greens opened their home to troubled runaways and single mothers in need of a place to sleep and to get refuge from their demons. Before long, their house was filled with troubled kids, and they rented an apartment to live in. Their view of the world was darkening. "We knew now that Satan was a for-real, hardball-playing bad guy, who was determined to capture and destroy every unsuspecting soul he could," Melody wrote. In contrast to the more winsome view of McGuire and 2nd Chapter, they absorbed a bleak view of the end times from *Jesus Is Coming Soon*: "The book said anyone involved in idolatry, fornication or witchcraft, to name a few, would be swept away in the Day of Judgment."[25]

At a concert in Oregon, Green blasted the decline of morality over the last twenty years. "In L.A. right now on the streets, there are rows, and rows, and rows of pornographic newspapers," he thundered. "For fifty cents — right at the eye level of little kids. There's women lying with women right on the front covers. Men lying with men. It's Sodom and Gomorrah time!" Green quoted Jesus to the effect that this was a sure sign of the last days: "Two months ago, there were two crimes never before recorded in the history of Los Angeles crime — two homosexual gang rapes. . . . We're at the doors. The Lord is returning soon."[26]

### Anyone but Jesus

One of the Green's most important mentors in 1975 was an eighty-seven-year-old man named Richard Gene Lowe. He had been a Christian for more than seventy years, and he had a long history with faith healing. In his journal, Green had resolved, "I will not take any steps to cut myself off from Christian Science until I feel sure that its benefits of healing the sick are as plenty in a Christian's life." Lowe helped convinced him that this was in fact possible. Lowe was also Chinese, a fact that gave Green pause when a friend first offered to introduce them.

> Keith's face fell. "Chinese? Forget it!"
>
> "Why?"
>
> "I'm not into eastern religions anymore — all that stuff's occult. Forget it."
>
> "But this guy's a *Christian*," Doug insisted.
>
> "He's probably into some eastern mix of Christianity — with Jesus and Buddha and eastern mysticism all blended together. I don't want anything to do with that stuff."

The two did meet, and Green quickly got over his apprehensions. "Richard Gene Lowe was radiant," Melody wrote. "His happy grin pushed his round cheeks up toward his eyes, making them all crinkled and laughing around the edges. It was almost as if there was some kind of a holy light streaming from this little man. He had something special. It was the kind of inner joy we wanted."[27]

But Green's initial suspicion was typical of many Jesus People, especially those who had dabbled in alternate forms of spirituality. These teachings, from Taoism to tarot cards, represented not an equivalent experience, not even a friendly rival, but the most cunning work of the Great Deceiver himself. Part of accepting the Lord was to wean oneself from spiritual influences not part of familiar styles of evangelical Christianity. Robert Ellwood had identified "multiplicity" as the "basic symbol of evil for the Jesus movement" in his perceptive 1973 study. "The unconverted life is described as confused by countless options, symbols, and alluring paths," he explained. "It is the world of innumerable beckoning experiences, too many for any one person to taste, except perhaps by living for a new one every day—drugs, easy sex, political involvement, overadvertised possessions and products. The world offers ways out of any problems these experiences may create, but only through other confusing pluralisms—any number of schools and techniques of occultism, meditation, enlightenment, and behind them a cosmos animated by a kaleidoscope of Buddhas, Hindu gods, spirits of good and evil."[28]

Jesus People scoffed at comparisons between their Lord and any other. "I'm not gonna think about, I'm not gonna talk about, I'm not gonna sing about anyone but Jesus," Barry McGuire sang during the summer of 1975. "He's my king." He broached the subject of spiritual alternatives in a characteristically whimsical way, comparing the way he thought before and after being born again.

> You know, I used to wonder how anybody could say, you know, that Jesus is the only way. I used to think, you know, what about Buddha, Krishna, Baha'u'llah, all those dudes, you know? They were all talking the same kind of stuff, you know? How can anybody say Jesus is the only way?
>
> But you know, every place I went I kept hearing this name, Jesus Christ. Walking down the street, you know, somebody drops all their books in the mud [splatting sound]: Jesus Christ! [laughter] Right? I asked a buddy of mine one time: Hey man, how come we always say that name Jesus Christ? . . . How come we don't say Hare Krishna or something? Drop a big rock on your toe [groans]. Oh, Buddha! [laughter] You know? Hey even the Jewish people they don't say Abraham and Isaac, right? Jesus Christ! And you know why that is? It's because His is the only name by which man can be saved. And you know, the enemy, Satan, the father of lies, he knows that's true. And he's tried

to make the name of Jesus the most useless, the most valueless word in our language, spoken hundreds of times every day and people don't even know what's coming out of their own mouth. Jesus Christ.[29]

In his own way, Larry Norman was notably cosmopolitan: he lived in England for years and toured the world. But this didn't lead to an appreciation of Eastern spirituality, as Norman explained to an interviewer.

When I was in India, I talked to people about their gods. They have more than 3 million gods. They don't even know who all the gods are. They live in fear. They make sacrifices to the gods they do know about. But it is such a bondage to them. If God is loving and good, then the Hindu gods can't be real, can they? If they are sex-crazed gods, and gods who will kill your children, and gods who venerate cows more than babies, what kind of god? . . . I don't have a negative attitude toward the Hindus. I love them. They are a very gentle people. At least the ones I met. They are very childlike and maybe confused, like children, because of their fear and hope placed in reincarnation and other beliefs.[30]

These attitudes could put Jesus People at odds with many in their cohort — particularly boomer seekers attracted to alternative religious movements. In *American Jesus*, Steven Prothero observes that "the sixties were as spiritual a decade as the United States has ever seen — an Age of Aquarius and of avatars. After the U.S. Congress opened up immigration from Asia in 1965, the country seemed to be flooded with wise men bearing spiritual gifts from the East": Transcendental Meditation, Krishna Consciousness, Tibetan Buddhism, but also Western or syncretic religions like the Unification Church, Scientology, Wicca, Neo-Paganism, and various New Age possibilities. As Stephen A. Kent has shown, these alternative religions had particular appeal for former political activists disillusioned by infighting in their organizations and the apparent failure of the antiwar movement. Only by changing individuals from within, former New Left leaders like Rennie Davis decided, could society be transformed.[31] Since very few Jesus People had emerged from the New Left, there were already deep differences between these cohorts, even if they shared a general goal of spiritual transformation of individuals.

These skeptical or hostile attitudes toward alternative spirituality among Jesus Movement musicians contrasted in striking ways with mainstream artists who held more eclectic views. Earth, Wind & Fire's 1975 album, *That's the Way of the World*, went platinum two months after its release and reached number one on both pop and R & B charts, finally bringing the kind of massive commercial success Maurice White had been working towards since 1970. For years, their songs and concerts had been drenched in gospel spirituality, with messages of redemption through spiritual enlightenment. Their albums included songs packed with devotional, nearly biblical language. *Last Days and Time* had "They Don't See," a lament for people who lost their faith, turned their back on God, and ruined their lives: "They don't see what you are to me / guiding light for all to see." On *Head to the Sky*, it was the title track: "You need faith to understand, so we're saying for you to hear / Keep your head in faith's atmosphere." *Open Our Eyes* had two deeply spiritual tracks: "Devotion" and "Open Our Eyes." The latter begins with pealing church bells: "Grant us thy lovin' peace, and let all dissension cease / Let our faith each day increase / And master—Lord please—open our eyes, open our eyes."[32]

*That's the Way of the World*, EWF's first blockbuster success, was shot through with messages of spiritual uplift and redemption. In "All about Love," White gives a flat-out pastoral meditation. About halfway through the song, he calls the audience to attention. "Now, I want you to stop whatever you're doing," he says with casual authority. "Just stop. Cause I'm gonna rap to you." In a few pithy sentences delivered in a streetwise manner, White addresses beauty, the tension between the inner and outer self, and the need to create beauty where it doesn't exist. "You know, for instance, we study all kinds of sciences, astrology, mysticism, world religions, so forth, you dig? And like, coming from a hip place, all these things help because if you're inside your inner self. Have mercy!"

The album's tour de force, though, is the final song, a brilliant showcase titled "See the Light." The song begins with turbulent jazz and disturbing images—"sky of gases" and "troubles everywhere, more than I can bear." The song moves into a radiant, virtual pastoral prayer of reassurance and redemption, delivered in Philip Bailey's stunning falsetto. "Give me strength, when temptation calls," Bailey supplicates. "Lift me up when life's battles make me fall." He asks the "dear Lord" for shelter "from the evil and the wrong" so he'll have the necessary strength to answer "when you call." In the next verse, Bailey petitions: "Master, then when my final song is sung / With your mercy, I pray that you'll say well done.[33]

But the band's mission went beyond writing uplifting, redemptive songs. "You can ask any of the cats in the band, all of our messages are about love," insisted guitarist Al McKay. "We got this far on faith, and it's the only thing that we know. . . . It's kind of like we were hand-picked and put together. That's why we always call our band the Creator's band, because he brought us together." Asked how the group differed from other popular funk bands of the day, like the Ohio Players or Kool and the Gang, White replied that "we are different because we all have different messages. Our thing is a thing for people in relationship to the Creator; other groups have other things they want to say." Success had not gone to their heads, he claimed, because of the band's goals. "We came out here to try to render a service to Mankind, not to be stars," insisted White. "We are actually being used as tools by the Creator. If I'm gonna try and help people then I have to remain the same, so I'll always be old country Maurice White."[34]

Reporters noticed that EWF in fact practiced what it preached: no smoking of any kind backstage, no alcohol, just Baskin-Robbins milkshakes. Before going on, band members formed a prayer circle to focus their concentration. And the band could affect the audience like Christian revivalists. "This band has a very positive effect on people," said White. "It's weird, man, but I feel we were . . . elected to do this by a higher force. . . . I've had dudes, some of them addicts, thank the band with tears in their eyes for helping them get through." Bailey added: "We've had some incredible stories about people who have totally changed their direction in life because they felt that Earth, Wind & Fire's music made them think—people who were drug addicts, people on the brink of suicide. It brought them emotionally and psychologically to a point of considering life more seriously."[35]

The band actually modeled the black church at their concerts. "Anybody here know anything about the church?" White asked the audience one night at the Los Angeles Forum as the band launched into their song, "That's The Way of the World." "Philip and I, we remember the choir members marching down the aisle, and we were deeply impressed by that. First you had to have the right *attitude*. Let us show you." A writer for *Rolling Stone* watched the two singers "stroking hand over hand and strutting gracefully in tandem, like slow motion boxers at the arc of their pounce" as they made their way "merrily and coolly" across the stage. "I was jolted," the reporter confessed, "not by what I'd seen, but by what had happened around me: large parts of the crowd rose to their feet in a spontaneous flash, and offered an uncontrived roar of recognition. I, having grown up in a church known for its reserve and for its *whiteness*, had never before witnessed firsthand this kind of invocation. Gospel music, I figured, cut deep."[36]

But Earth, Wind & Fire was not Andraé Crouch and the Disciples, let alone Barry McGuire and the 2nd Chapter of Acts. For starters, the band's name was based on the elements of White's sign, Sagittarius. The band's eclectic spirituality set them well beyond the pale of the Jesus Movement; preaching a message of love, spiritual uplift, and cosmic harmony was a far cry from winning souls for Jesus. White had no interest in locking his listeners into "a specific solution. I'm not trying to tell people to go to church, but at least I want to leave that open." His own spiritual path had led him to believe that all religions were ultimately one, deploying different symbols but pointing toward the same underlying reality. "I am not a man of any denomination, because there are too many things about each one that I believe and disbelieve," he said. "So, I've found that the best thing for me is to try to love and understand life. I would say that I'm a student of life. That's about the best I can describe it."[37]

White denied that he chanted or followed a guru: "I have adopted a little from each religion that I thought applied to me, but I can't adopt any single religion because there are good things about all of them and I try to adopt those for myself. I know a lot of people are chanting and it's probably good for them, but I don't feel I have to do that to get what I want. I meditate and it's a good thing for me, but I'm not the kind of person to imitate what a lot of other people are doing. The other guys in the group are all the same and we have a love for each other that is important in helping us create." While touring Asia in the midsixties as a drummer with jazz pianist Ramsey Lewis, White had taken an interest in Asian religion and martial arts. "I started studying Buddhism under an old master in Japan," he said. "I would just talk about things, and he'd give me books to read."[38] A more powerful influence, though, was the jazz saxophonist John Coltrane, whom White played with for a time when regular drummer Elvin Jones was sick.

Coltrane himself had made a long spiritual odyssey from his Methodist upbringing in North Carolina through drug addiction and a "spiritual awakening" in 1957. By the time of his death ten years later, Coltrane was being heralded as a kind of jazz saint, serving as an inspiration to musicians ranging from Roger McGuinn, Jerry Garcia, and Ray Manzarek to Steve Reich and Philip Glass. "I never forget enlightening words because enlightening words don't come too often," said White in 1975. "When you get them you should utilize them. He was responsible for encouraging the concept I had in mind. I consider him the major spiritual force of his time, and he is still a force." What he learned from Coltrane, among other things, was that all forms of music could contain a valid spiritual message, not just gospel music. "I thought of the jazz and blues as get-down music," said White, "and I could never put the two together, as if we couldn't deal with spirituality while having a good time. Coltrane didn't say much, but when he did, I heard him. Later on, after I started to develop music with spirituality in mind, I realized that all of our musical forms are headed toward a oneness."

Though his acolytes would later found a church in his honor in San Francisco, Coltrane was by no means an orthodox Christian, and the musicians most strongly influenced by Coltrane turned not to Christianity but to Asian religions. Most of the rising stars of the seventies jazz world had played together in bands led by Miles Davis a few years earlier and were turning in a dedicated way to spirituality. The first was guitarist John McLaughlin, founder of the Mahavishnu Orchestra, who became a disciple of Indian guru Sri Chinmoy in 1970 and spent years in intensive study of Indian music. Pianist Herbie Hancock had begun practicing Nichiren Shoshu Buddhism (the same sect that Melody Green joined) in 1973, the same year he released his breakthrough fusion album, *Headhunters*. Pianist Chick Corea and other members of his important fusion band, Return to Forever, turned to the teachings of L. Ron Hubbard and became practicing Scientologists.[39]

These two important strains of baby boomer religion—the evangelical Christian message and the more eclectic Asian one—came face to face in 1975 when Earth, Wind & Fire opened for Santana during a six-week tour of Europe. By this time, through the influence of fellow guitar masters Larry Coryell and John McLaughlin (himself a Coltrane devotee), Santana had become a devotee of Indian guru Sri Chinmoy. Now christened Devadip, Santana dressed in white and played mostly acoustic songs influenced by Indian music. "We meditate, we pray, there are certain types of food, certain types of people we hang around," he explained in 1974. "After a while you listen to certain types of music. . . . You begin to demand a lot more." Rock and blues now made him yawn. "It's very temporary and comes from a lower consciousness. Whereas music from India and music from John Coltrane, I can go to sleep to it and have some incredible dreams and wake up and have some beautiful actions." No one was more fulsome in his praise of Coltrane than Santana. "I haven't heard anything higher than 'The Father and the Son and the Holy Ghost' from the *Meditations* album," he said. "I would often play it at four in the morning, the traditional time for meditation. . . . I could hear the Supreme One playing music through John Coltrane's mind."[40]

Santana's lead singer, though, had recently become a Christian. Riding a transatlantic jet to Europe with Santana band members on one side of the aisle and EWF on the other, Leon Patillo felt a tailor-made opportunity to proselytize for Jesus. Holding a Bible, he perched on an armrest to talk to fellow musicians, who themselves had come prepared with a Bible and books about Buddhism and other beliefs. "It almost felt like the disciples because one of the guys was named Andrew and the other was named Philip," Patillo joked later. "I thought, if this is not a setup . . ." After the bands were on the road for six weeks, it was reported that "Philip Bailey and several other members of Earth, Wind & Fire made full-on commitments to Christ." Like the proverbial prophet who failed to reach his own people, Patillo's efforts were less successful in his own band. "I was fired as soon as we got off the tour, because people were becoming Christian and nobody was becoming Buddhist," he claimed. "Carlos thought it was the best power play, since it was his ball and he could take it and go home. They said they were not satisfied with me as lead vocalist."[41]

Meanwhile, Bailey was facing his own sort of fallout. He thought about leaving EWF but then decided that God did not want him to. Bailey was convinced that his calling was to be an entertainer, not a musical evangelist like Keith Green or Andraé Crouch. But he was criticized by other Christians. "Instead of people just saying, 'Praise God, a brother saved! I hope everybody gets saved!' it's 'How dare he stay in the band?' But Earth, Wind & Fire has never promoted any type of drugs, any kind of illicit sex. They've always been a very positive band." Some believers were offended by the band's use of mystical symbols on album covers. "Man, people are stupid," Bailey responded. "That just gets on my nerves. You ask people who become saved, 'Now, do you work for an all-Christian company? Do you only deal with Christian people?' 'Well, no.' Well, shut up." He added, "It's different if somebody has to promote something that's not them. But we weren't promoting the signs and things that were on the record. That was just something that Maurice put on the cover." When Bailey went on to record Christian albums for Myrhh, listeners wrote in to register their outrage about his secular recordings: "How dare you promote an artist who promotes promiscuity!" read one.[42]

Evangelical music fans could be uncompromising. Even 2nd Chapter of Acts, whose credentials in the Jesus Movement seemed beyond question, faced flak from evangelical Christian churches that regarded them as emissaries from a tongues-speaking cult. "This fearful goofiness always upset me," Ward wrote, "and it made me conclude that Christians — at least Western Christians — are the most narrow-minded people on the planet. And that's an opinion I still pretty much hold."[43]

But no musician experienced the volatile, judgmental nature of the Christian rock flock more dramatically than Randy Matthews, the Jesus Freak who recommended warm dill pickles as cheap road food because they simultaneously fill you up and deaden your appetite. Matthews was already a rising star in Christian rock, born into a musical family with good connections to the gospel music industry. His father, Monty, had helped found Elvis Presley's first back-up group, the Jordanaires, and recorded with a gospel quartet. After high school, Randy Matthews sang in a quartet called the Revelations while he studied at Ozark Bible College and Cincinnati Bible Seminary, where he became a Street Christian. In 1971 he joined forces with Arthur Blessitt of the Sunset Strip, carrying crosses and banners around downtown Cincinnati to publicize the need for ministry to young people in the city; shortly afterward, the Jesus House was established.

He also recorded his first album, *Wish We'd All Been Ready*, borrowing the song and title from Larry Norman. It was a folkish album recorded at Word Records under the supervision of Billy Ray Hearn, a compatriot of Ralph Carmichael who would become a major producer in the early contemporary Christian music scene. For his follow-up recording, Matthews persuaded Hearn to push Word to create a subsidiary label to allow for somewhat more adventuresome music, resulting in the formation of Myrrh Records with Hearn as president. The stage properly set, Matthews's third album, *Son of Dust*, completed the tilt from the more staid folk sound to a "gospel rock" sound. One of its songs, "Didn't He," was unveiled to great acclaim at Explo '72 and became a signature song for Matthews.

The stage seemed set for Matthews to eclipse Larry Norman as the superstar of the Jesus rock scene when he took the stage at Jesus '74. Matthews was poised for crossover success, slated to open that fall for ZZ Top and Lynyrd Skynyrd. In preparation, Matthews and his band had begun playing at bars to acclimatize themselves to more worldly audiences. Matthews himself "grew his hair waist-long, sported a thick untrimmed beard, put on an earring, and donned his 'cosmic cowboy suit,'" according to Paul Baker, signaling a full embrace of the counterculture. The actual setting for the concert was bucolic, a patch of farmland in Mercer, Pennsylvania. A similar festival the previous summer had brought together a reunion of musicians from Dallas's Explo '72: Andraé Crouch and the Disciples, Randy Stonehill, and Danny Lee and the Children of Truth, in addition to Matthews. "Through makeshift entrance gates set up in a field passed festival-goers in automobiles, trucks, vans, Winnebagos, on motorcycles, and even on horseback," recalled Baker of the three-day festival. "There were numerous hitchhikers, too. From all over America and from overseas people came to join in the fellowship."[44]

For their third song, Matthews and the band launched into "Four Horsemen," an acid-rock version of the hair-raising prophecies of Revelation 6. Fearing what they took to be "demon music," the festival promoters cut the power to the stage. Bedlam ensued. A violent crowd surged forward as Matthews and his bewildered bandmates retreated. "People seemed to turn into mad dogs, foaming at the mouth and biting at me," he recalled. He passed out while trying to climb a fence, waking up later in a hotel room with patches of chest hair missing and his clothing ripped. Despite escaping the angry Jesus mob intact, the damage to his career was permanent. "That one situation wiped out everything for me," he explained. "It wasn't the unplugging, it was what happened after that. People would actually come up to me and say, 'I pray that God takes away your voice, and that you never write another song.' These were some pretty heavy changes, especially for a young guy who had nobody to talk to about what was going down."[45]

Rumors circulated that Matthews had become a drug user, and partly because of his trauma, he graduated from "imbibing and toking" to mescaline and LSD. "It was a period of depression, loneliness, and searching," he recalled. "I was sort of 'de-fellowshipped' from the whole industry, and the only people who would have anything to do with me were rock musicians." His next album, *Eyes to the Sky*, included an account of Jesus '74 called "Pennsylvania Weekend"; its cover depicted Matthews as the prophet Elijah being fed by ravens, banished and persecuted yet protected by God. In 1976 Myrrh completed his contract with a *Best of Randy Matthews* album and dropped him from the label. He toured and recorded only sporadically after that. By the late 1990s, Matthews had opened a shop in Florida selling American Indian–themed art. "Nobody here knows I have made records," he admitted. "I'm not very visible, and I don't mind that a bit."[46]

The Christian fundamentalist old guard had never abandoned their contempt for Christian rock, as scholars Jason Bivins and Eileen Luhr have demonstrated. The most prominent critic was an evangelist named Bob Larson, who wrote a series of vituperative books condemning the concept that Christianity could accommodate to pop music: *Rock & Roll: The Devil's Diversion* (1967); *Rock and the Church* (1971); and *The Day the Music Died* (1973). "I maintain that the use of Christian rock is a blatant compromise so obvious that only those who are spiritually blind by carnality can accept it," he wrote in 1971. Larson doubted that the music really produced the spiritual fruits its proponents credited it with: "Some have speculated that more often than not, conversion to Christ at Christian rock concerts and musicals is not really a born-again experience but an identification with the person of Jesus within the perspective of the 'groovy Christian life.'" Larson and his successors, notably Jeff Godwin, who published a series a screeds on the subject during the eighties and nineties, were especially concerned about rock music as a kind of Trojan horse for occultism and new religious movements. The title of Larson's book from 1972 was telling: *Hippies, Hindus, and Rock & Roll.*[47]

But the people that savaged Matthews in Pennsylvania were not old guard; they were Jesus People attracted by the prospect of three days of Christian rock. Providing some historical perspective, Mark Allan Powell suggests that the Matthews imbroglio followed a pattern of Christian schism that reached back to the early church of Roman times, when believers who embraced the world clashed with sectarian separatists who rejected society. "[T]he event symbolized a division within the Jesus movement analogous to that which developed in the early Christian church: a schism between ultimately ortho-dox world-affirming Christians and ultimately sectarian separatists," writes Powell. "Such divisions have in fact marked the history of Christianity in every time and place with a consistent result: the separatists win many battles, but always lose the war." According to Powell, "Randy Matthews was all but slain on the field of battle. Unlike Bob Dylan [famously heckled at Newport in 1965], he did not recover."[48]

Because the Jesus Movement intentionally embraced American popular culture, especially music, it placed itself in the role of policing the bound-aries of proper Christian behavior against many less-than-acceptable forms of belief and conduct associated with the music. This was a difficult filtering act, made even more challenging by the relative youth of most involved and the lack of seasoned mentors. Spirituality is an intrinsically fluid social prop-erty, never more so than in the wake of the counterculture, when so many assumptions had come unmoored. Jesus People were quite aware of the flood of new religious movements swirling around youth culture in the late sixties and seventies; like Barry McGuire and Keith Green, many had dabbled with those forms of spirituality before turning to Jesus. This experimentation was a signature element of the generational structure of feeling, a defining feature of the massive sixties cultural front that has shaped the spiritual tendencies of boomers from adolescence through middle age.

But to identify a broad-based cultural front in retrospect is not to mini-mize the sharp differences and divisions that characterized the lived experi-ences of youth that came of age during the sixties and seventies. Whether the fear was Eastern religion or garden-variety occultism, the evangelical surge put in motion by the Jesus Movement was about to undergo a fateful change, dramatically increasing its public and political profile.

## Chapter 8

# YEAR OF THE EVANGELICAL

A *Newsweek* cover from October 1976 shows a well-dressed preacher with his back to the camera, his left hand pointed upward with index finger extended, and his right hand resting on the head of a burly-looking young man who looks like he might be a football player. The preacher has mod hair and is wearing a bright-patterned shirt collar spreading wide around his neck. Above his head, in large type, is "Born Again!"; below, simply, "The Evangelicals."

"Year of the Evangelical" — that was the label that stuck to America's bicentennial year, thanks to *Newsweek*. In good newsmagazine fashion, the article explained who evangelicals were, where they lived and came from historically, and their newfound interest in electoral politics. Historians, theologians, and sociologists offered pithy insights from their respective disciplines. A Gallup survey showed startling numbers of Americans bearing all the signs of being full-fledged evangelicals; a third of all Americans claimed to have been born again, while a substantial proportion believed the Bible literally. (It was George Gallup who actually designated the "Year of the Evangelical.") The article skillfully sketched out differences between believers in the North and the South. It described pitched battles being fought over the inerrancy of the Bible, which was emerging as a litmus test of true commitment to the faith. Christians were behaving like entrepreneurs, creating "Christian Yellow Pages" to direct shoppers' dollars to fellow believers. And Bill Bright of Campus Crusade was hard at work, planning to bring a crusade called "Here's Life, America" to 113 cities.

A sidebar presented vivid testimony from several celebrities and prominent figures who had accepted Jesus: Chuck Colson, recently imprisoned for his role in Watergate and author of the best-selling book *Born Again*; Mark O. Hatfield, a liberal Republican senator from Oregon; Jimmy Snow, son of Hank and pastor of the small church Johnny and June Carter Cash attended near Nashville; and former Black Panther Eldridge Cleaver, who had recently returned from years as a fugitive exile and was baptized in the swimming pool at Campus Crusade for Christ in Arrowhead Springs. "I was looking up at the moon and I saw the man in the moon and it was my face," Cleaver recounted. "Then I saw the face was not mine but some of my old heroes. There was Fidel Castro, then there was Mao Tse-tung. . . . While I watched, the face turned to Jesus Christ, and I was very much surprised. . . . I don't know when I had last cried, but I began to cry and I didn't stop. . . . It was like I could not stop crying unless I said the prayer and the Psalm and surrendered something. . . . All I had to do was surrender and go to jail."[1]

Surprisingly, given the historical context *Newsweek* provides, there was no mention of the Jesus Movement that had flared so vividly in the media just years earlier. But another newsmagazine, *U.S. News & World Report*, had picked up that story a few months earlier. The article reported that the "emotional young people of a decade ago are becoming a potent new force in old-line congregations they once condemned as bastions of the 'establishment.'" These new worshippers included both Protestants and Catholics, many Pentecostals, and people attracted by organizations like Campus Crusade and Intervarsity. Most had married, started families, and settled into communities. They might still attend Jesus music festivals, but they were more likely to demand creature comforts and devote time to Bible study and reflection. "Most of our people are looking for the strength of a close-knit family, because so many have suffered from broken homes, drugs, and permissive parents in the past," said a camp-meeting organizer named Harold Zimmerman.[2]

The cooling off of the Jesus Movement was the result of several factors, according to historian Larry Eskridge. The seventies witnessed an inevitable maturing of sixties youth, as they settled into jobs and started families; the Year of the Evangelical was also the year in which the oldest baby boomers turned thirty. This centrifugal tendency was exacerbated by the economic distress of the early seventies, driven by the OPEC oil shocks, which combined inflation, high unemployment, and high interest rates that made survival on the margins more difficult. Jesus communities, which had earlier "served as something akin to a gigantic Jesus People marriage bureau," were especially hard hit, both by the economic downturn and by the tendency of married couples to want independent living arrangements. Another adverse influence was the "Shepherding" movement of the midseventies, which imposed strict "discipling" relationships between elders and young evangelicals that sometimes bordered on abusive. Finally, the seventies saw the rise of new forms of popular music—heavy metal, disco, punk rock—that made Christian rock based on the musical styles of sixties rock 'n' roll seemed passé. In an era of the Sex Pistols and *Saturday Night Fever*, the countercultural style of the Jesus Movement no longer conferred style points on teenagers.[3]

Of course, a turning away from the Jesus Movement style didn't mean that young evangelicals were necessarily losing their faith. "The media may have lost track of the 'Jesus Movement' as it moved from the streets into private homes and church pews," said Zimmerman. "But, believe me, it's stronger than ever. . . . We're reaching so many other Christians now—neighbors, parents, and pastors. What we're building is the backbone of a whole new church."[4] The seventies witnessed a rapidly expanding network of Calvary and Vineyard churches, both of which emerged out of the Southern California Jesus Movement scene and were pastored by former Jesus People. These churches were in many ways institutional outposts of the Jesus Movement, capitalizing on the success of informal worship styles, conversational preaching, and more contemporary styles of worship music.

In an election year that was also America's bicentennial, it was impossible to ignore politics. *Newsweek* uncovered evidence of nascent mobilization by what would eventually be called the Religious Right, including the use of questionnaires used to determine which candidates held biblically "correct" views on issues like abortion and school prayer. But they also detected signs of liberalism among evangelicals: a group called Evangelicals for Social Action, an Evangelical Women's Caucus inclined toward biblically based feminism; college students drawn to Christian liberals like Oregon senator Mark Hatfield; and a new magazine of radical Christian opinion called *Sojourners*. "We think that Christians must count the cost of conversion and recognize that the way of Jesus is a radical alternative to the values of our country," asserted the journal's editor, Jim Wallis, a young firebrand who had organized an antiwar protest at Explo '72. John Styll, a fellow traveler since the early days of Calvary Chapel, doubted whether many Jesus People were politically motivated. Caring for the poor and hungry were the important issues for the early converts; there was certainly no sign of a cohesive political agenda, left or right, though Street Christians inclined toward the former. "I don't think that generation defined itself politically," Styll says now.[5]

Judging from *Newsweek*, the Year of the Evangelical might have been called the Year of the Southern Baptist. It turned out that the nation's largest Protestant denomination was a pretty inclusive tent, including many conservatives but also liberals like Foy Valentine of the Christian Life Commission, who dismissed the category of "evangelical" as a "Yankee word." "We don't share their politics or their fussy fundamentalism," he said, "and we don't want to get involved in their theological witch-hunts." A noted theologian at Southern Methodist University described Southern Baptists as "culturally isolated," "theologically unsophisticated," spiritually arrogant, and unable to relate to Catholics, Jews, or seculars—all of whom they consigned to hell. "They want a society ruled by those who know what the Word of God is," the theologian explained. "The technical name for that is 'theocracy,' and their Napoleon, whether he likes it or not, is Jimmy Carter."[6]

Carter, of course, was the cynosure of Year of the Evangelical hype. The article's lead paragraph drew readers to the basement of the Plains Baptist Church, where Carter's cousin Hugh was seen leading a men's Sunday School class, where Jimmy "boyishly" raised his hand to answer questions. When the *Newsweek* issue appeared, Carter was poised to be elected as the first openly evangelical-born president. What's less remembered now is that president Gerald Ford, an Episcopalian, was also positioning himself as a devout believer, courting endorsements from national groups and claiming that he read the Bible daily and prayed often in the Oval Office. He was also a member of the now-infamous shadowy organization of Beltway movers and shakers known as the Fellowship. Regardless of who won on Election Day, it appeared to evangelicals that God had blessed the election. "This is the first time in 200 years that the leading Presidential candidates have made a public professional of their faith," said a spokesman for the Full Gospel Business Men's Fellowship.[7]

Despite the fears of the Methodist theologian, Jimmy Carter was an unlikely candidate to be a Napoleon for any Baptist theocracy. The father of three baby boomers, Carter's own cultural and political beliefs had been shaped by the sixties, especially the civil rights movement. As governor of Georgia from 1971 to 1975, he was part of a new breed of moderate Democrats. He refused to join the White Citizens Council, voted to admit blacks to the Plains Baptist Church, and became the first governor from the Deep South to publicly condemn segregation and appoint many African Americans to state offices. Campaigning as a dark horse for the presidency, Carter positioned himself as a mix of liberal and conservative — not splitting the difference, but selective. "On human rights, civil rights, environmental quality, I consider myself to be very liberal," he explained. "On the management of government, on openness of government, on strengthening individual liberties and local levels of government, I consider myself a conservative. And I don't see that the two attitudes are incompatible."[8]

Though Carter was an Annapolis graduate, navy man, and devout Southern Baptist, the counterculture had rubbed off on him as well. He attributed it to the influence of his sons, Jack, Chip, and Jeff — prime boomers born between 1947 and 1952. This was intriguing to the journalist who interviewed him for *Playboy*, Robert Scheer, who questioned his friendship with gonzo journalist Hunter S. Thompson. "I'm not a packaged article," Carter shot back, "that you can put in a little box and say, 'Here's a Southern Baptist, an ignorant Georgia peanut farmer who doesn't have the right to enjoy music, who has no flexibility in his mind, who can't understand the sensitivities of an interpersonal relationship. He's gotta be predictable. He's gotta be for Calley and for the [Vietnam] war. He's gotta be a liar. He's gotta be a racist.'"[9]

Carter emphasized that he was not a hidebound fundamentalist but an ordinary human being with a range of ideas and friendships. He was particularly drawn to musicians: Otis Redding, whom he got to know through Capricorn Records, as well as Chubby Jackson and Tom T. Hall. Based in Macon, Georgia, Capricorn held a series of successful fund-raisers for a cash-poor Carter during the Democratic primaries, featuring the Amazing Rhythm Aces, the Marshall Tucker Band, the Allman Brothers, and Charlie Daniels.[10]

The Georgia governor reserved his greatest admiration for Bob Dylan. He admitted that his son's musical tastes had influenced his own, and he saw how Dylan had affected their attitudes, along with many of their peers, on social justice and war. They were ideas that affected Carter's own emerging politics in Georgia. At a 1974 University of Georgia Law Day address, the governor paid tribute to Dylan, "a friend of mine," along with the theologian Reinhold Niebuhr, for shaping his views on justice. "After listening to his records about 'The Ballad of Hattie Carol' [sic] and 'Like a Rolling Stone' and 'The Times They Are a-Changing' [sic], I've learned to appreciate the dynamism of change in modern society. I grew up as a landowner's son. But I don't think I ever realized the proper interrelationship between the landowner and those who worked on a farm until I heard Dylan's record, 'I Ain't Gonna Work on Maggie's Farm No More'" [sic]. Carter might have gotten the titles slightly wrong, but his admiration appears to have been genuine. The speech turned out to be a defining moment for him, impressing Hunter S. Thompson, who called it "a king hell bastard of a speech. . . . I have never heard a sustained piece of political oratory that impressed me more."[11]

Carter's interest in Dylan began when his son Chip took a vacation from the family peanut farm and made a pilgrimage to see Dylan in Woodstock, where he lived in seclusion after his motorcycle accident. "Apparently, Dylan came to the door with two of his kids and shook hands with Chip," Carter told Scheer. "By the time Chip got to the nearest phone, a couple of miles away, and called us at home, he was nearly incoherent. Rosalyn couldn't understand what Chip was talking about, so she screamed, 'Jimmy, come here quick! Something's happened to Chip!' We finally deciphered that he had shaken Dylan's hand and was just, you know, very carried away with it."[12]

In 1974 Carter had the chance to invite Dylan to the governor's mansion. Touring with the Band, Dylan was skeptical but went anyway. Carter found him quirky but agreeable. "He never initiates conversation, but he'll answer a question if you ask him," he said. "I asked him if he wanted a drink, but he only wanted orange juice and would only eat the vegetables." The two discussed music, "changing times and pent-up emotions in young people," according to Carter. "He said he didn't have any inclination to change the world, that he wasn't crusading and that his personal feelings were apparently compatible with the yearnings of an entire generation. We also discussed Israel, which he had a strong interest in." Carter would go on to quote Dylan in his acceptance speech for the presidential nomination at Madison Square Garden. "I had never had more faith in America than I do today," he said near the close. "We have an America that, in Bob Dylan's phrase, is busy being born, not busy dying."[13]

Carter's expansive recollections about Dylan appeared in *Playboy*, itself a fact of some significance. Up until then, no candidate had spoken nearly so candidly about personal matters for a national publication; the tenor of presidential politics was changed. Carter was definitely down-home. Scheer was nonplussed to learn that he did his own sewing, mending a ripped jacket on a plane and using his teeth to bite off the thread. Carter admitted that he prayed frequently, as often as twenty-five times a day. One sister was a faith healer, the other a "McGovern Democrat" who rode a Harley.

"I've looked on a lot of women with lust" remain Carter's most famous words from the *Playboy* interview; "I've committed adultery in my heart many times." Carter went on to offer an explanation consistent with his evangelical beliefs. "This is something God recognizes I will do — and I have done it — and God forgives me for it," he said. "But that doesn't mean that I con-

Bob Dylan and the Band in 1974, the year Dylan met Jimmy Carter
(Image © Bettmann/CORBIS)

demn someone who not only looks on a woman with lust but who leaves his wife and shacks up with somebody out of wedlock." Carter was adamant about his understanding of the Christian Gospel: to avoid pride and self-righteousness, to recognize that all people sin and fall short of the glory of God but that divine forgiveness is freely given through God's grace. "The thing that's drummed into us all the time is not to be proud," he said, "not to be better than anyone else, not to look down on people but to make ourselves acceptable in God's eyes through our own actions and recognize the simple truth that we're saved by grace."[14]

Knowing that some voters were concerned about his potential to yoke religion and politics, Carter emphasized the independent spirit of his faith community. "Every Baptist church is individual and autonomous," he stressed. "We don't accept domination of our church from the Southern Baptist convention. The reason the Baptist Church was formed in this country was because of our belief in absolute and total separation of church and state."[15]

Considering how "family values" issues would be injected into U.S. elections by the end of the seventies and for decades afterward, it's worth noting how a progressive but by no means unique Southern Baptist like Carter parsed issues like abortion and homosexuality in 1976. "I think abortion is wrong," he told Scheer, "and I will do everything I can as President to minimize the need for abortions—within the framework of the decision of the Supreme Court, which I can't change." He admitted preferring Georgia's more conservative approach, adding that "the Supreme Court ruling suits me all right."[16]

Detecting ambivalence, Scheer asked what he should tell a woman concerned about abortion. "If a woman's major purpose in life is to have unrestricted abortions, then she ought not to vote for me," Carter replied. "But she wouldn't have anyone to vote for." This was an issue that spooked Carter during his long campaign and would become a political liability in the years to come. Regarding homosexuality, Carter said he had known gays in Plains, even church members, but didn't recall any animosity or harassment. "The issue of homosexuality always makes me nervous," he conceded. "I don't have any, you know, personal knowledge about homosexuality and I guess being a Baptist, that would contribute to a sense of being uneasy."[17]

Carter stressed that as governor of Georgia, he had reduced penalties for victimless crimes like marijuana and alcoholism. "You can't legislate morality," he opined, while adding that states had the authority to regulate conduct in these areas and that moral standards as a whole were socially useful. Pressed on this paradox, Carter responded: "I believe people should honor civil laws. If there is a conflict between God's laws and civil law, we should honor God's law. But we should be willing to accept civil punishment. Most of Christ's original followers were killed because of their belief in Christ; they violated the civil law in following God's law."[18]

Carter agreed to the *Playboy* interview partly to reassure liberal voters, but it would cost him support among evangelicals. Many were put off by Carter's use of vernacular terms like "screw" and "shack up"—even if he was innocent of these transgressions himself—and by his willingness to talk to a skin magazine in the first place. No less a luminary than the Reverend Wallie Amos Criswell, pastor of the world's largest Southern Baptist church (and mentor to super pastor Rick Warren), publicly endorsed President Ford over Carter, a fellow Baptist. "I am highly offended by this," he said of the *Playboy* interview. "I think he's mixed up in his moral values, and I think the entire church membership will feel the same way. The whole thing is highly distasteful." *Newsweek* ran a photo of Criswell and Ford together after the endorsement, the Dallas pastor pumping his fist in enthusiasm. Other evangelicals had qualms about the peanut farmer from Georgia, including Harold Lindsell, editor of the influential evangelical weekly *Christianity Today*, who repeatedly raised doubt from the pulpit about Carter's born-again bona fides. So did fellow Southern Baptist Jerry Falwell.

To be sure, non-Christians had their own grounds for disliking the Carter that emerged from the interview, as his extreme sincerity shaded into what campaign manager Hamilton Jordan referred to as the "weirdo factor." And President Ford had his own public-relations challenges with cultural conservatives, mainly caused by the liberal positions publicly held by his wife, Betty, who supported the *Roe v. Wade* decision liberalizing abortion and campaigned for passage of the Equal Rights Amendment. The First Lady raised eyebrows (and drew record mail to the White House) when she professed in an interview for *60 Minutes* that she wouldn't be surprised if her sixteen-year-old daughter was having a love affair.[19]

Carter had apparently grasped the Zeitgeist of the midseventies in a nation reeling from a series of national traumas and a sense that its glory days were receding. "Somehow the notion of a man grounded in solid family and religious values gave a certain amount of confidence that this was the kind of person who could do the healing the American people expected in the wake of Watergate," said Carter adviser Stuart Eizenstat. "Jimmy Carter perceived this mood in the country before some of us who were more public policy–oriented did." Press secretary Jody Powell added: "For a lot of people, the idea that this was a man of religious faith gave them some measure of hope that he meant what he said, that he would do what he said, that he would abide by the law, that he would behave in a way that was moral and decent and just. That is one of the things religion is supposed to do for us."[20]

Not surprisingly, Johnny Cash was a strong admirer of Carter in those years. Jimmy and June were cousins, and Cash first met Carter when he was running for governor and pasting up his own campaign flyers in Lafayette, Georgia. Carter came over to chat and made a good impression, so Cash invited him onstage that night at a concert, where the candidate seemed to go over well with Cash's fans. Carter, Cash, Jimmy's brother Billy, and songwriter Tom T. Hall all became friends. "Whenever [Carter] came to Nashville he'd stay with Tom T. and Dixie, and June and I would go over there for dinner if we weren't on the road," Cash wrote. "So he was family by blood, and just about family by heart." Visiting the White House after the election, Cash found Carter "the busiest president I've known," racing the Cashes around to introduce them at a series of meetings that left the First Couple of Country needing a nap.[21]

The Man in Black was himself training for the ministry in those years. Amid his busy schedule of tours and appearances, Cash took correspondence courses on the Bible, eventually earning an associate degree from the Christian International School of Theology. He was also writing a novel, *Man in White*, about the Apostle Paul; the book was published in 1986. It read almost like an autobiography, with Cash's "identification with Paul so strong that the connection cropped up on virtually every page. Secondary characters resembled people in his own life, such as June and Jack, and the plot line tracked his own life's path."[22]

Cash embraced some fairly orthodox views during the Year of the Evangelical. He blasted liberal churches that seemed to reduce Christ to a "mere prophet or a philosophizing do-gooder," not the son of God. "I have more tolerance for people of other religions who traditionally reject the divinity of Jesus," Cash wrote in 1975, "than I do for those people who claim to be Christians, yet disclaim and deny His virgin birth, His resurrection, or any of His miracles." Encouraged by his mother, Cash made appearances with fire-breathing Texas evangelist James Robison. He wondered why men like Robison were so bitterly criticized, regarded by non-Christians "as some kind of freaks." Robison's message was harder-edged than, say, Billy Graham's, whom Cash had been drawn to at the peak of his commercial success a few year earlier. "These men, these preachers whose voices touched millions — they look strange, sound strange to the world out there because they have seen farther from the top of the mountain," Cash decided.[23]

## His Eye Is on the Sparrow

A few days before the Year of the Evangelical officially began, middle-of-the-road superstar B. J. Thomas embarked on his final, greatest bender. Fueled by a mixture of cocaine, speed, and marijuana, he claims to have stayed awake for eleven straight days before collapsing. When he woke up, he began chain-smoking joints, hoping somehow to relax enough to sleep. "I had a very real sense that the next cocaine binge would be my last," he recalled in a memoir. "My professional life was over. No gigs were planned; everything was off. People were saying, 'Don't book him — he's flipped out.' Absolutely no one would book a drug addict."[24]

Thomas's career had followed what was beginning to feel like a familiar trajectory. He had something of a Johnny Cash vibe about him. Thomas had grown up near Houston and began developing his reputation in high school as lead vocalist for a band called the Triumphs. After cutting some regional hits in the midsixties, Thomas was invited to join the Dick Clark road show and opened for James Brown. He began edging higher in the pop charts. A 1966 cover of Hank Williams's "I'm So Lonesome I Could Cry" became his first million seller. "Hooked on a Feeling" reached number five in 1968, his second million seller. "Eyes of a New York Woman" reached the Top 10 in

December 1968, when Thomas and Gloria got married. Then came his monster hit, "Raindrops Keep Falling on My Head," which spent four weeks at number one in 1969 and was featured in the box-office smash *Butch Cassidy and the Sundance Kid*. In 1971 Thomas again found commercial success with the gospel song "Mighty Clouds of Joy" and auditioned for the part of Jesus in the movie version of *Superstar*. In 1975 "(Hey, Won't You Play) Another Somebody Done Somebody Wrong Song" topped the charts.

Meanwhile, Thomas's personal life began to unravel in a most spectacular fashion, combining the excesses of Johnny Cash and Marvin Gaye. Like Cash, Thomas gobbled amphetamines and Valium by the handful, trashed hotel rooms, and started fights, nearly dying on multiple occasions; like Gaye, he snorted fortunes of cocaine. (In addition, Thomas's wife, Gloria—like Gaye's second wife, Janis—was seventeen when they met; the two marriages came to bear a strong resemblance). As Thomas has described, his excesses during the early seventies held their own with any in the rock world. "I was so high in New Mexico one night that my ears rang and I could hear my heart pounding and even the blood rushing through my veins," he remembered of one stretch. "Antagonistic voices argued in my head and I couldn't get away from them. When I saw Indians galloping through the walls after me, I made the band pack up and head to another hotel at two in the morning."[25]

By the early seventies, Thomas's habits kept him from working for significant periods of time. He was up to two ounces of cocaine a week, he estimated. "I know that sounds like a lot," he admitted, "but I was so into it that a gram snorted up one nostril wouldn't even wake me up. I had to snort six or seven grams up each side to get a hit. Two ounces in seven days? Often." The cost ran over $4,000 a week. In 1975, Thomas claimed, "we spilled more coke across this country than most junkies will use in a lifetime." His sidemen "tried to stay up with me, but they couldn't. Nobody could. . . . It's a wonder I'm still alive, considering how many times my bodily functions quit and someone had to revive me."[26]

He also skirmished endlessly with Gloria, who had given birth to their daughter, Paige, early in 1970. The family bounced around the country in search of an environment that would stabilize their turbulent relationship, moving from Memphis to Manhattan to Connecticut. Gloria separately made her way to Fort Worth, and Thomas went to Los Angeles. Like June Carter during her years with Cash a decade earlier, Gloria alternately fought to save Thomas's life and separated to escape his abuse. "Isn't that some picture?— June Carter rasslin' that big hunk of a guy?" Thomas wrote. "I'm bigger than Gloria too, but she punched me out once. Gave me a black eye and really got my attention. Unfortunately, when I hit her it got my attention too. I slugged her once during 1974 and broke her nose and wrenched her neck."[27] The couple repeatedly separated, missed each other, reunited for a day or two, fought, and separated again. Thomas stopped sending Gloria checks, and she ran up household bills she couldn't pay. He had someone drive away with her Mercedes one night, leaving her without a vehicle.

Feeling abandoned with a young child, waiting for a divorce, and cut off from Thomas's income, Gloria was also on the verge. Exhausted and depressed, she was befriended by an evangelical couple, a rodeo worker and his wife who lent her a car and helped around the house. They patiently evangelized her, asking Gloria to accept Jesus, answering her questions, and praying for her. After months of conversation and soul-searching, she drove home from the couple's house determined to change her life. After praying, she felt a transformation. "I could feel the room literally filling up," she wrote later. "My shoulders quit aching and seemed to rise three inches. I gave God the future, the drugs, the fear, the depression, my heart, my pain, my loneliness, everything." Afterward, she stood grinning, "loving God so much I couldn't think of anything else."[28]

A few days later, as Thomas was beginning his weeks-long binge on the West Coast, Gloria told Thomas that she and Paige had been born again and invited him home. He agreed to a visit. According to Gloria, her new friends at church were praying for Thomas to have no peace until he returned to his family. Gloria brought her husband to the couple's house, where a skeptical Thomas became involved in a discussion of scripture. The rodeo worker prayed that Thomas be freed of demonic forces and then encouraged him to utter his own prayer. "I began a twenty-minute prayer that was the most sincere thing I had ever done in my life," Thomas wrote. "And I know the Holy Spirit authored it, because it was so precise and perfect. . . . I got straight with the Lord everything I could think of, and the bridge between ten years of hell and a right relationship with God was just twenty minutes—the most unforgettable twenty minutes of my life. When I looked up after saying amen, it was midnight, January 28, 1976. The memory of seeing that second hand sweep by the 12 will never leave me."[29] It was the Year of the Evangelical.

Thomas's dramatic conversion was cause for celebration among the musical vestiges of the Jesus Movement. "The first really big one was B. J. Thomas," remembered John Styll, referring to mainstream musicians turning publicly to Jesus. "That was 1976. He came out with a Christian album called *Home Where I Belong*. That was a pretty big deal in the Christian music world. That was a very big deal." Released by Word Records, which offered Thomas a contract after one of their representatives heard him give testimony during a concert at Six Flags Over Texas amusement park, *Home Where I Belong* went platinum and became the best-selling album of his career. "B. J. was only a medium-sized fish in the secular pop ocean," points out Mark Allan Powell, "but he was a whale in the Christian pond—a pool that suddenly did not appear as tiny as everyone had always thought."[30]

By 1976 it was becoming clear that the Christian music industry was changing dramatically in ways that would shape evangelical culture through the succeeding decades. John Styll described the evolution of the music from small-time acts to big-budget, commercial productions.

> I would say the first era from sometime in the sixties with youth musicals up through '74 was like the first phase of the beginnings of it. You had things like the All Saved Freak Band, and out of California you had Agape, which is hard rock. . . . Very counterculture. . . . I think 1974 is when 2nd Chapter of Acts' first album came out, and Barry McGuire came out with an album. . . . Michael Omartian came out with *White Horse*, which was on ABC Records, which was a landmark record. The Richie Furay Band, another secular artist, came out with a very well-produced album, being on a pop label. But that was a new era of music with a Christian message but produced at a much higher level than the earlier stuff. Much higher budgets, much better production value, much more commercial appeal. And it started to turn into a real business.[31]

No musician better exemplified this newfound professionalism than Omartian, who led a music team called Armageddon Experience for Campus Crusade for Christ before moving to Los Angeles; he was an original member of the group that came to be called Loggins & Messina. Rivaling Billy Preston, Omartian went on to contribute ace studio work to artists ranging from Steely Dan, Billy Joel, Glen Campbell, and Eric Clapton to Michael Jackson, B. B. King, the Four Tops, and the Fifth Dimension (this in addition to his work on Christian rock albums by Barry McGuire, 2nd Chapter of Acts, Phil Keaggy, and many others). Omartian's accomplishments as a producer are equally impressive. During the seventies, he produced Top 10 hits based on television shows, such as "Theme from S.W.A.T." (which went to number one in 1975), "Baretta's Theme (Keep Your Eye on the Sparrow)," and "Theme from Happy Days." And he produced chart-busting albums for Christopher Cross (for which Omartian won a producing Grammy in 1980), Donna Summer (who had been born again and attended the same church as Omartian, the Church on the Way in Van Nuys), and even Rod Stewart, who reportedly was reading Pat Boone's spiritual autobiography during the making of *Camouflage* (1984). "Rod and I had many opportunities throughout the project to talk about the Lord," Omartian recalled. "There were two Christians in his band who drew strength from our conversations."[32]

On the business side, Sparrow Records signaled Christian rock's new aspirations. Sparrow was founded by Billy Ray Hearn, already the most savvy operator in Jesus music, whose roots extended back to the very first Christian youth musical, *Good News*, which premiered in 1965. "I came from the church as a minister of music in Georgia to Word to head the music promotion department and print music publishing," he told an interviewer. "I came to Word to help Ralph [Carmichael] and Kurt [Kaiser] be in touch with the churches. I had been involved with the Baptists in a musical called *Good News*, so when they wrote *Tell It Like It Is*, I promoted it. That's what I really came to do. But in 1970 and '71 we started discovering a lot of young writers and artists, so by '72 they let me start a label just for contemporary music and I named it Myrrh. Within a year or two it was a major part of Word's sales."[33] Hearn recruited Jesus Movement artists like McGuire, 2nd Chapter of Acts, Randy Matthews, and Petra. When B. J. Thomas hit bottom and was born again, it was Myrrh that brought out *Home Where I Belong*, his first gospel album targeted for a Christian audience.

Record sales were starting to soar, and Jesus music was becoming increasingly integrated as an industry. Myrrh distributed recordings for Larry Norman's Solid Rock label, as well as New Song, Good News, Messianic, and Seed, all independent Christian rock labels. Word (the Waco-based parent company of Myrhh), Light Records (which recorded Andraé Crouch and the Disciples), Lamb & Lion, and New Pax records saw a shift from 5 percent of contemporary Christian music in 1975 to 60 percent three years later. In 1975, when Word was bought by ABC, Hearn began thinking about launching a new company of his own. Sparrow was a small "boutique" label, but its roster included several of the big names in Christian rock, many of whom followed Hearn from Myrrh: McGuire; Annie Herring; Keith Green; John and Terry Talbot; and, before long, the 2nd Chapter of Acts. Other artists signed were BeBe & CeCe Winans, Steven Curtis Chapman, and Steve Taylor.

Christian radio was also experiencing a boom in the midseventies. It had been around for decades, of course, but most Christian radio was heavy on preaching, and its music was targeted toward older listeners, not boomers. In the summer of 1967, Scott Ross—the hotshot New York deejay who hung with rock stars, married one of the Ronettes, and became a born-again Christian—met an ambitious Christian media whiz named Pat Robertson at a Full Gospel Business Men's Fellowship meeting in Baltimore. (Like Campus Crusade, the group played an important role in introducing promising Jesus People to older evangelicals willing to provide financial backing.) The two regarded each other warily across a wide generation gap. "This guy, I was sure, would be an ultra-conservative southern super-dude," Ross decided. "I could just see his chalked face if some long-haired people from the rock culture showed up at his sanctified station." Robertson was likewise taken aback by Ross's long hair and mustache, admitting it "blew my mind" that Ross had partied with the Rolling Stones and Beatles. "Despite the fact that he was dressed in a wild psychedelic shirt with tight pants and boots," he said, "I liked the sparkle in his eyes and the contagious smile he flashed through his mustache."[34]

The two ambitious Christians decided they could work together. Ross and his wife, Nedra, moved to CBN headquarters in Portsmouth, Virginia, where he piloted a radio program aimed at young Christians. Ross struggled to find decent music to play; Robertson suggested Ralph Carmichael. When Ross played anything further out, "the call buttons on the phone lit up like a computer panel" with complaints from concerned Virginia parents. "A little later, the studio door burst open," according to Ross, "and a red-faced, furious guy rushed in and jerked my power-supply cords out of the wall. 'You . . . you . . . if you play any more of that sin music may God strike you dead!' We finally got the guy out of the studio, but when Pat heard about it he made the decision: 'No more Peter, Paul & Mary.'"[35]

Robertson also allowed the deejay to try his ideas on the struggling TV station. "One of Scott's first brainstorms was to go out and bring in a shaggy rock combo from the drug scene in Virginia Beach and put them on TV," Robertson wrote. "His plan was to allow these dirty, long-haired musicians to appear in the studio and have the camera pan their sad faces one by one as they played. Then Scott would come on and say, 'Does God love these people?' Then they would hit the music loud and heavy, and Scott would keep breaking in with the gospel message, speaking to the kids in language they could understand." At first the CBN staff bridled, especially when the musicians were observed "taking dope" in the studio before the broadcast. Eventually the staff were won over, but another problem proved insuperable: Ross's marriage to a woman of color. CBN could accept it, but the couple's landlord asked them to leave.

Providentially, it would seem, a tantalizing opportunity presented itself to the fledgling network. Robertson heard about a string of five interconnected

Class B FM stations for sale in upstate New York, headquartered in Ithaca but able to reach listeners from Toronto and Pennsylvania and across New York to New England. Robertson persuaded to phone company that owned them to part with the stations, valued at $600,000, in exchange for a tax deduction. Ross was dispatched to take charge of programming (in the marginally more racially tolerant environs of rural New York). "Instead of the usual back-to-back preaching of most Christian radio stations," Ross envisaged, "ours would have varied programming. . . . In between good records, people would call in to talk about their problems; I knew from my experience in Portsmouth that there was no better setting for a natural lead-in to Jesus. The show would be reaching into bars and automobiles and dorms and drug-scene parties: the 'marketplace' where my kind of people hung out, hungry and thirsty for something they couldn't define."[36] Ross began broadcasting in January 1969. Within a year, the "Scott Ross Show" was carried by sixteen stations.

At the same time, Ross organized the influential Jesus commune Love Inn in Freeville, which adopted Robertson's Pentecostal tenets: an expectation that the supernatural intervenes on a regular basis in the form of prophecies, miraculous healings, and speaking in tongues; a propensity to pray aggressively and often, both individually and collectively; a willingness to make what would normally seem like reckless decisions based on the conviction that God will provide; a constant struggle to overcome personal desires and submit to divine direction; and a conviction that setbacks of any sort—no matter how ordinary—were the direct work of Satan, and, conversely, that all successes were signs of God's blessing.

As Ross's show spread, youth-oriented Christian radio began cropping up elsewhere in the country. In Florida, Paul Baker had started a Christian rock show called A Joyful Noise in 1970 that was carried by stations in cities ranging from Oklahoma City and Denver to Nashville and Richmond. In 1974 John Styll had begun broadcasting a one-hour Jesus music program called Hour of Praise on KGER, a traditional religious station in Orange County, California, that carried mostly preaching. The following year, a mainstream rock station in Santa Ana switched to Christian rock, even broadcasting concerts from Calvary Chapel. The switch to an all-music format was the key change. Also in 1975, KFMK in Houston and KBHL in Lincoln, Nebraska, brought contemporary-sounding Christian music to the airwaves—not as syndicated programs but as more-or-less full-time offerings.

In 1976 Rick Tarrant was a disk jockey at WHBQ, a Top 40 Memphis radio station that in 1954 had been the first station to play a song by Elvis Presley.

As a young man, he had been drawn to the church, but only for the chance to sit next to his girlfriend. He remembered playing organ on "Natural High," one of the Ralph Carmichael Christian youth musicals, using Leslie speakers with rotating horns. The production was organized by his girlfriend's Presbyterian church but was actually staged at Tarrant's high school, which allowed an altar call following the performance. He thought about becoming Christian but resisted for a time. At age twenty-one, partly due to the influence of Hal Lindsey's *The Late Great Planet Earth*, Tarrant was born again.

By then he was an up-and-coming Memphis deejay. "When I became a believer, I became a little more concerned about what the message of the music was," Tarrant said. "Being a DJ, you heard everything that was popular in Top 40 at the time. A lot of it was less than edifying, shall we say. So if you were trying to lead a life that was encouraging more of a moral behavior, yet the music you were listening to was encouraging more of an immoral behavior, there was a conflict there. So I found myself searching for music that wasn't such a contradiction to the life I was trying to lead." But on the little gospel stations, "about the most contemporary thing you could hear was a song by Danny Thomas. It was a little bit of a challenge there, musically. I would even find myself singing to the songs that I played, making up my own lyrics, you know, trying to tune out the lyrics and make it my own."[37]

Tarrant remembered being at parties in Memphis where stories were told of B. J. Thomas's drug-fueled antics.

Then I see this gospel album that he released, and it's still got the pop rhythms and contemporary sounds from pop music culture. Maybe he was one of the first ones that introduced me [to the fact] that there was real music that still had the message about Christ that wasn't such a contradiction to me. . . . Then I began to hear other artists, and other doors began to open, and ultimately I kind of thought, you know, the rest of the world needs to hear this stuff, 'cause they're not hearing it.

Our big dream back then was boy, if we could just get a station to play all Christian music without interjecting these little gospel shows, the Jimmy Swaggart show or these preaching shows. 'Cause it was preaching shows that made the money for the radio stations. Music brought no revenue in. Of course, us being young and naïve, we didn't care about the business, we were passionate and on fire, you know? In time it did become profitable because if you played all music, you could garner a larger audience; and if you could garner a larger audience, then you could sell advertising, and the business model would come along.

Both recording and radio were becoming larger, more consolidated, and more corporate. "Early on it was Word records, which was just a little record company," Tarrant continued, "and so was the Benson record label, and Sparrow records, and Starsong records were just little bootstrap operations. People who were just passionate about this music and wanted to see it get out there. . . . In time—it really started happening in the nineties, although back in the eighties ABC Corporation bought Word records—we started seeing these secular conglomerates buying up the record labels. I guess if you dangle enough cash in front of the owners, it's kind of hard to turn it down."

## Just Go Have a Talk with God

Released less than a month before the 1976 presidential election, Stevie Wonder's magnum opus, *Songs in the Key of Life*, debuted at number one and stayed there until the end of the year; it also spawned two number-one singles. Two years in the making—a long wait in those years when Wonder generally produced at least an album each year—the record spilled beyond even a double album, requiring a 45-sized supplement to contain all its music. Musically and lyrically, *Songs* was as richly variegated as any record Wonder ever made, blending funk, jazz, gospel, rock, and Latin sounds in a remarkable tapestry that both captured the African American experience and expanded its scope to a universal plane. It was recorded by a stable group of musicians, something Wonder hadn't had since working with the Motown house band. Some of the music was created during marathon sessions running forty-eight hours straight, during which Wonder would forget to eat.

In the tradition of earlier African American spiritual seekers, Wonder's beliefs remained incorrigibly eclectic. As Craig Werner observed about the song "Pastime Paradise," "the combination of the choirs from the Hare Krishna Temple and the West Angeles Church of God redefines Wonder's spiritual tradition as surely as Ellington's *Far East Suite* or John Coltrane's meditations on the relationship between Hindu, Islamic, and black Baptist spirituality in *Ascension* and *A Love Supreme*." Like many jazz artists before him, Wonder developed a diasporic connection to Africa, making his first pilgrimage in 1975 and toying for a while with the thought of retiring from music to work with handicapped children in Ghana. He was in Nigeria when he won his Grammy for *Songs in the Key of Life*, which he accepted via remote feed.[38]

But there was an unmistakable evangelical texture to the album, even if Wonder would never be confused with an orthodox Christian. His spiritual outlook and musical range had deepened over the series of solo albums that began in 1971 with *Music of My Mind* and *Talking Book*. This may have had something to do with Wonder's near-fatal car accident in North Carolina in the summer of 1973, through which he felt God was sending him a message to change his life. *Fulfillingness' First Finale*, for example, the album that preceded *Songs*, contained the song "Heaven Is 10 Zillion Light Years Away."

Why does God seem so far away, the singer's friends want to know, while evil and hate seem always close at hand? The world seems shot through with sin, particularly in the form of racism and inequality. "And I say it's taken him so long / 'Cause we've got so far to come," the singer responds. People need to open themselves, to let God's love shine in their soul, or remain trapped by their "evil souls": "For those who don't believe will never see the light." Calling on the Pentecostal tradition, Wonder exhorts his listeners to open their hearts so they can "Feel his spirit, you can feel his spirit." They will learn, like the singer, that "He lives inside of me."[39]

*Songs in the Key of Life* begins on a prayerful note, with "Love's in Need of Love Today." But the evangelical tone is strongest on "Have a Talk with God." Wrapped in a sinuous funk vamp, the song addresses those who have given up on life, who find their load too hard to bear. Since God "lives within," he's always available, anytime and anywhere. People face their hardships alone, "Forgetting all about the One who never lets you down." God has the answer to "every problem"; he bestows "peace of mind"; he's "always around"; he's even "the only free psychiatrist that's known throughout the world."[40]

Unlike Wonder, whose Christianity would always come with an overlay of New Age beliefs, Al Green was hearing a more orthodox call. During his convalescence from the burning grits incident, Green prayed, read the Bible, and spent time with his spiritual friend, Laura. He returned to the Hi Records studios to record his eighth album, *Al Green Is Love*, which included the number-one, Grammy-nominated single "L-O-V-E." But the doubts Green had experienced earlier about success as a secular star were returning. His drummer and dear friend Al Jackson, who had made his name with Booker T and the MGs, had been brutally murdered in his Memphis home. Disco was in the ascendance, and the city's musical scene was changing. Stax Records closed its doors early in 1976, and the Memphis Horns were often out of town on other jobs.

Willie Mitchell, the producer who had helped engineer the sound that made Green a superstar, balked at making gospel records. True, Green had written a gospel song called "Jesus Is Waiting" for *Call Me*, his 1973 gold album; but, as Mitchell explained, it was one thing for a singer to record music that referenced God and sounded gospel and quite another for that singer to be born again and passionate about his music's overtly Christian lyrics. And Green apparently "still hadn't sorted out in my mind and heart that age-old dilemma that puts a poor man between singing for God and singing for the devil, and was convinced that somehow, some way, I could have my success and still serve the Lord."[41]

So Green invested half a million dollars in his own recording studio, hired a new band, and decided to produce his next album. He also came up with a game plan for diversifying: he created a new line of beauty products called Al Green International Hair. "I had always believed in looking my best," he reasoned, "so it seemed only natural to encourage others to let their own God-given beauty shine." And he wrote and recorded *The Belle Album*, whose single "Belle" made it to the Top 10. The song included a telltale line: "Belle, it's you that I want, but it's Him that I need." As Green explained, it was a swan song to the one-night stands that had been a feature of his superstar years. "I loved those women, loved their softness and sweetness and the way they gave themselves away for the chance to be lost and found in love," he wrote. "But those days — and those ways — were past me now. God had called me to a higher place, turned me away from earthly to heavenly love, and while it hurt to say it, I had to leave the sensual for the spiritual."[42]

Green's boldest move of all was to buy his own church and begin preaching. There was an eerie irony to this career move. The woman who scalded Green with grits before taking her life had prophesied that the soul singer would one day be a great evangelist. "You're going to stand in front of great congregations," she told him. "And you're going to preach wonderful sermons that will turn the hearts of many." In his autobiography, Green gives an account of being led by God past the white gates of Graceland to an obscure little church called the Full Gospel Tabernacle, located in a quiet neighborhood called Whitehaven, where he stood full of reverence, bathed in memories of childhood worship.

But in an interview with filmmaker Robert Mugge, Green offered a more prosaic account.

I said, man, this is too fast, this is too much happening here. One year I'm a rock star, the next year I'm a gospel preacher. This is . . .

I don't understand. Anyway, it was bugging me so bad I found this
church down here [Memphis]. So I was going to buy it. And the guy
says, "Well I don't know if we want to sell it or not." So I had them
find a church—just find a church, man, because my head is going on.
So when we found the church on Hale Road, I says, buy it. You know
how I wrote the check? Out of a little book I had in my pocket. Just
a little pad book. Not even a real . . . book. I wrote the check right
on that for the whole building. And signed it, threw it at him. 'Cause
see now, Sunday I'm preaching—that's all. You know, 'cause see,
man, three years of . . . hey, man, please just give me some rest! Went
home, slept like a baby, preached my first sermon about two weeks
later. And that started that.[43]

The sanctuary was modest—a low-slung brick building, blond wood
paneling, red carpet, a brick wall at the back of the sanctuary, and a large
faux scroll behind the pulpit with the message, "LET GOD BE MAGNIFIED."
A plaque at the entrance read:

FULL GOSPEL TABERNACLE
DEDICATED TO THE GLORY OF GOD
DECEMBER 19, 1976
REV. AL GREEN, PASTOR

David Less, a reporter from *Down Beat*, recorded the following scene early in
Green's pastorate. A French crew happened to be on hand filming a service
for French national television.

A young girl in the choir stands clapping and dancing and suddenly
falls to the floor with a violent jerking motion. Another choir member
quite routinely goes over the check on her and once convinced of the
younger girl's safety, re-takes her seat. The audience is a sea of hands
with scattered women leaping to dance, trance-like, up and down the
aisles. In the middle of all this is Reverend Al Green. Tall and mus-
cular, wearing a white three-piece suit and waving a handkerchief, it
seems inconceivable that this bespectacled young man who looks like
an accountant will within a matter of minutes take complete control of the congregation. To this spectator the service is like a roller
coaster ride. The Frenchmen appear totally befuddled.[44]

While Green was anointed by the spirit, Marvin Gaye lurched in the other
direction, deeper into those fleshpots from which Green was trying to dis-

tance himself. After the huge success of *Let's Get It On* and the packed concert tour that followed, Gaye's use of cocaine was spiraling. His obsessive love affair with Janis Hunter continued to deepen: she gave birth to a girl in September 1974 and a boy the following November. His wife of twelve years, Anna Gordy, sister of the Motown founder, filed for divorce in 1975. Gaye had embraced New Age spirituality at its most eclectic and had taken to wearing a large brass pyramid on his head. "He was into biofeedback, visualization, pyramids, vegetarianism, and everything else that was going on," according to Hunter.[45]

Meanwhile, Gaye was at work on his next album. Most of the album had already been written, arranged, and recorded by Leon Ware, an old friend from Detroit. But Gaye seized the chance to add his own multitracked vocals. Ware and Gaye worked on the album for fourteen months in a new studio bought for Gaye by Motown. The studio was located on Sunset Boulevard on a block thick with prostitutes, a neighborhood that inspired Donna Summer's disco hits "Bad Girls" and "Sunset People." Gaye and his entourage essentially lived in the studio, which had a secure loft bedroom with a large Jacuzzi and king-sized waterbed. Gaye's work habits were casual; he played basketball nearly every day and recorded his vocals while reclining on a sofa or sitting at the mixing board. "It was an amazing period," recalled Ware, who was with Gaye constantly during the making of the album. "There was definitely something godly about Marvin. He had this incredible magnetism. We all felt that, and we knew that to work for him meant serving him at this pleasure."[46]

The album that emerged from what Ritz called a "Kubla Khan" atmosphere was *I Want You*. Released in March 1976, the album went platinum and reached the top of the R & B charts and number four in the pop charts. Sonically seasoned with orgasmic pants and moans, the album included songs like "Feel All My Love Inside" and "Since I Had You." "The message of the album was — make love to everyone you see," according to Ware, who wrote most of it. But others interpreted the album as actually a long love poem to Hunter, who was often in the studio during the making of the album. "I proposed to Jan on that record," Gaye told Ritz. "A lot of people didn't hear it, but it's there. Of course I couldn't marry her then, and I changed my mind a million times before I finally did, but I wanted to, I needed to, I had to. With all the freakery I did during those sessions, all those crazy parties, Janis never left my mind."[47]

Hunter was aware of her importance as Gaye's muse. "After we met, the emphasis of his work shifted away from the social awareness of *What's Going On* and focused on sex," she told Turner. "He went from *Let's Get It On* to *I*

*Want You* to 'Sexual Healing' to a song that was originally called 'Sanctified Pussy.' I think that was his way of confronting the feelings he held inside about sex and sin because he knew what was right and wrong." In March 1977 Gaye's divorce became final, and he married Janis in October. But the arrangement brought little peace to either Gaye or Hunter. Already guilt ridden about corrupting Janis with cocaine and kinky sex, Gaye encouraged her to have affairs. "I taught her—I forced her—to torture me," he admitted. "It began beautifully, but then it quickly became brutal. . . . The more I lived with Jan, the more I loved her, the more I made her miserable."[48]

Like Barry McGuire, Johnny Cash, B. J. Thomas, Al Green, and many other stars before him, Marvin Gaye seemed poised for a dramatic conversion. But unlike the others, he was not born again. Gaye remained an unsaved seeker, uncommitted either to Jesus or to any particular faith tradition. In this way, he was like the majority of popular musicians of the seventies, many of whom were sorely tested by cocaine but did not turn to Christianity. But even if Gaye's ending turned out differently, his private life had a recognizable trajectory, a structure of feeling that made him a recognizable emblem of the sixties cultural front. At the same time, as the seventies wore on, musical stars of the Jesus Movement like Randy Matthews revealed themselves vulnerable to the sort of sexual and mind-altering temptations that beset their more secular counterparts. These issues were not unique to boomer musicians, of course, although cocaine seemed to exert a particular grip on artists of the era. And the personal narratives of temptation, straying, and redemption were particularly well developed and recognized within the culture of American evangelicals.

The baby boomers—famous or not, born again or otherwise—were finally growing up, and not especially gracefully. The Year of the Evangelical also happened to be the year in which the first boomers turned thirty. "Many Rebels of the 1960's Depressed as They Near 30," proclaimed a front-page article published in the *New York Times* a few months before *Newsweek*'s declaration. The story reported that sixties youth were "experiencing a generational malaise of haunting frustrations, anxiety and depression" as they approached thirty with few of their youthful hopes realized and no clear path into what represented success in the adult world. Based on dozens of interviews with mental-health specialists in fourteen cities around the country, the reporter found increased levels of suicide, alcoholism, and requests for psychiatric help by baby boomers, in addition to "a boom in the popularity of certain charismatic religious movements, astrology, and pop psychology cults that reflect part of this generation's search for contentment."[49] The conditions were ripe for some sort of spiritual revival.

Chapter 9

# CRISES OF CONFIDENCE

On 20 January 1977, Jimmy Carter stood in front of the Capitol to give his brief, eight-minute inaugural address. "He hath showed thee, O man, what is good," he said, quoting the Old Testament prophet Micah, "and what doth the Lord require of thee, but to do justly and to love mercy, and to walk humbly with thy God." Then he and Rosalyn set off down Pennsylvania Avenue on foot to the White House, establishing a precedent. His first meeting in the Oval Office was with Max Cleland, a former Georgia state senator and paraplegic Vietnam vet who, as a U.S. senator, would be smeared many years later by Karl Rove's campaign operation. Carter's first official action was an executive order granting amnesty to Vietnam draft evaders. He signaled the end of Nixon's imperial presidency with a flurry of symbolic gestures: carrying his own suit bag; enrolling daughter Amy in D.C. public schools; selling the presidential yacht; scaling back the playing of "Hail to the Chief"; reducing perks and pay for the White House staff; and eventually turning down federal thermostats to save energy.[1]

Few twentieth-century presidents had signaled such dramatic changes in presidential style and image. With a humble, pious, music-loving Southern Baptist in the White House, Jesus music had a sympathetic ear at the highest echelons. In fact, Christian rock was steadily becoming a commercial force.

B. J. Thomas's first gospel album, *Home Where I Belong*, released by Myrrh in 1977, was a massive success. Debby Boone, daughter of Pat, who had mentored (and baptized in his swimming pool) so many musical Jesus People over the years, had a huge hit with "You Light up My Life," which topped the charts for ten weeks in 1977 and won the singer widespread TV coverage, including *The Tonight Show*. "The power of the Holy Spirit will come across and it will do the work!" she proclaimed. "I don't try to hide it, but I don't try to force it either."[2]

After building his reputation in the Los Angeles–area Jesus scene, where he met Barry McGuire and 2nd Chapter of Acts, Keith Green achieved some stardom in 1977. Green had also met Billy Ray Hearn and encouraged him to come to a live show. Early in 1977, Hearn signed Green to a contract with his new record company, Sparrow. Bill Maxwell, an experienced producer and drummer for Andraé Crouch, was brought in to produce the session. By summer, the album, titled *For Him Who Has Ears to Hear* (a riff on a passage from the beginning of the book of Revelation) was shipped to Christian bookstores and quickly became the best-selling debut album in the history of Christian rock, moving over 300,000 copies. By the end of year, Green was flooded by requests for concert bookings from around the country.

Behind the scenes, there were other signs that Jesus music was continuing to expand its commercial reach. Capitalizing on the new market for Christian music, Myrrh launched a promotional blitz ("The music is today, the message is forever"), festooning Christian bookstores with posters, free records, and special displays. "The $75,000 campaign was run with all the noise and glamour of a movie premiere in Hollywood," recalled Paul Baker. He also noticed a marked improvement in the production quality of Christian rock albums, owing mainly to increased recording budgets. By the end of the following year, Baker had completed the first book devoted to Jesus music, borrowing his title from Larry Norman (who had cribbed it for a song title from Martin Luther): *Why Should the Devil Have All the Good Music?* Another milestone was the founding of a magazine called *Contemporary Christian Music* (later shortened to *CCM*), the first lasting publication devoted to Jesus music. Its publisher and editor was John Styll, who had grown up in Orange County, hung out with the Calvary Chapel crowd, and started a Christian rock radio program in 1975.[3]

Politically, a high-water mark for Jesus music came on a September afternoon at the White House, when Carter invited a number of performers to a three-hour "Old Fashioned Gospel Singin'" on the White House grounds.

Welcoming his guests, Carter explained the tradition of the "fifth Sunday": the occasional extra Sabbath, "particularly in the summer and fall," Carter remembered, "when people would get together for an all-day singing, and dinner on the grounds, and great local and even distant gospel groups would come, quartets and others, as a time to bridge the gap between churches and between denominations, between communities, and let people reach down, into down-to-earth singing and kind of lift the spirit up to heaven." Carter was referring to fasola singing, in which participants would sing in four parts from the *Sacred Harp* or some other nineteenth-century songbook that used "shaped notes" rather than conventional notation to designate pitches. As a young couple, the Carters had enjoyed those all-day sings when he returned to Plains from the navy. "We've been down to Bonifay, Florida, where they have twenty-four-hour sings, and we apologize for cutting this one short," Carter said, drawing laughter. He emphasized that gospel was both black and white: "It's a music of pain, a music of longing, a music of searching, a music of hope, and a music of faith."[4]

The White House gospel gathering felt a little like an Explo '72 reunion: Barry McGuire was there, as was Reba Rambo, who had toured with Andraé Crouch and the Disciples, and a vocal group from Northern California called the Archers, who had some number-one hits on Christian radio. All had performed at Godstock. To his surprise, Larry Norman had been invited, despite some opposition within the Gospel Music Association.

> I was at the White House and I was warned, don't sing anything political. It was a picnic. He wanted people to experience a southern picnic, church style, with southern fried chicken, potatoes. He had beautiful little paper plates. And members of Congress were there, those who showed up. . . . Carter was sitting on a blanket, and I was sitting next to him. And I got up and I sang, "I was born and raised an orphan . . ." That's political, that whole song is. And afterwards some people were really upset with me. Carter didn't want to make a big deal about it. Had his legs on the blanket, and he just went like [gestures], excellent, excellent, that's great that you sang that song. "The Great American Novel": it's very political but it's not partisan at all. And so he did that—like, don't worry about what people are saying.
>
> Afterwards we were talking, and I said, "Have you heard Bob Dylan's *Slow Train Coming*?" He said, "No, I haven't and I'd like to." And I said, "I will send you a copy of it." He said, "Good, I'll put it in my presidential library." And I said, "If it's okay I'll send you a copy of

Andraé Crouch and the Disciples performing for President Jimmy Carter
(Photo courtesy of David Di Sabatino)

one of my records. It's called *Only Visiting This Planet.*" He said, "Yeah, what a great title. Please send that to me." . . . I got a nice note from him. And Gretchen Poston, his social secretary, sent me some presidential cuff links.[5]

Norman said he lingered around the White House taking photographs, including one of Carter running around the Rose Garden in "little shorts and a skimpy T-shirt." Someone suggested that Norman should sell the photo to the *National Inquirer.* "He is such a godly man, I have no question about it," Norman said. "And he accomplishes so much. He's a whirlwind."

By the time of the White House gospel picnic, Norman needed a boost as much as the president did. Musically, the late seventies marked the end of Norman's most productive period. He had recorded his trilogy of albums: *Only Visiting This Planet* (1972) and *So Long Ago the Garden* (1973), both for MGM, and *In Another Land* (1976), said to be the biggest commercial success of his career. In 1976 he founded Solid Rock Records and began producing records for a number of Christian rockers, including Randy Stonehill, Daniel Amos, Tom Howard, and Mark Heard. The label was distributed by Word, which had itself been acquired by ABC, so the prospects for Norman's venture seemed good. In 1977 he recorded what some consider his most musically compelling—and certainly his hardest-rocking—album.

*Something New under the Son* is also the album that expresses most clearly the African American influence that Norman claimed was formative to his style. The cover shows him dressed in black, his long blond hair illuminated by the sun as he emerges from an inner-city "Record & Afro Shop." He looks toward his right, moving through a posse of streetwise young black men done up in classic seventies form with Afros. One stands barefoot in cutoff shorts, while another wears dirty beige painter's pants. It's hard to tell whether the pale singer thinks he belongs or is leaving in a hurry, although he is striding confidently toward the camera. The first four songs exude a strong blues feeling: "Hard Luck Bad News," "Feeling So Bad," "I Feel Like Dying," and "Born to Be Unlucky." Whereas Norman could often sound something like Neil Young, the album finds him with the raspy voice of Mick Jagger with overtones of Jim Croce.[6]

Norman was about to experience a full dose of the blues. For starters, his marriage was crumbling. His wife, Pamela, had grown up Baptist in Minnesota, worked as a stewardess for Northwest Orient, and lived the "fast life of the jet set" with the Johnny Winter band, the Rolling Stones, and Fleetwood Mac before becoming a born-again Christian in St. Paul. "Some of my greatest thrills were when pilots and stewardesses would come to Christ, and we would read the Bible and pray together on layovers," she recalled. "They nicknamed me 'Missionary Stew.'" Hearing about the Southern California scene, she traveled out to see for herself, living in Jesus communes and witnessing on Hollywood Boulevard. She first laid eyes on Larry Norman at a Jesus Festival at the Hollywood Palladium then met him at another Christian festival on a beach. "Suddenly I looked up and saw the blonde singer I had heard at the Palladium," she said. "Without stopping to think about it, I went up to him and said, 'Hi, I know you.' But when our eyes met, my mind went blank. 'What's your name again?' I knew at that moment that God had chosen Larry Norman to be my husband. And so did he. We were married on December 28, 1971."[7]

The marriage was troubled from the beginning, according to Larry Norman. The two didn't know each other very well, he realized. He told CCM magazine that Pamela had announced to him that their marriage was over just two weeks after the wedding. In other interviews, Norman claimed that his wife had ongoing drug problems he wasn't aware of, that she married Norman hoping that his connections would get her a break in Hollywood as an actress, that her interest in modeling got her involved in a "jet set crowd and ended up in compromising situations," and that she began having affairs. "I was so emotionally damaged for so many years because of a chaotic marriage that I couldn't even smile on stage," he said later. "I could preach and I could sing, but I couldn't emotionally open myself to the audience because I was so numb. I was cold because I was dead." Others familiar with the breakup remember it very differently. According to Pamela, his musical protégé Randy Stonehill, and other associates, Norman began an open affair with Stonehill's wife, Sarah, whom he had dated prior to his marriage. In any event, the Normans separated in 1978 and were legally divorced two years later.[8]

Norman claimed he wrestled mightily with the moral and theological implications of divorce, as evangelicals had been long taught to do. He resisted for years because he thought it would prevent him from going to heaven. Some of the Bible's least equivocal statements about moral conduct leave no doubt that divorce is a serious sin. Jesus himself makes the point clearly several times — "I tell you that anyone who divorces his wife, except for sexual immorality, and marries another woman commits adultery" — as does Paul: "A husband must not divorce his wife." Among evangelicals, attitudes toward divorce started softening during the 1970s, partly as a result of rising divorce rates among born-again Christians. "During the 1970s, by my count, *Christianity Today* ran eight articles and editorials decrying the growing rate of divorce among evangelicals," writes historian Randall Balmer. "By the 1980s, however, after Ronald Reagan's election, those denunciations ceased almost entirely as evangelical condemnations shifted to other, more elusive targets: abortion and, eventually, homosexuality."[9]

The year he and Pamela separated, Norman suffered a mysterious accident that would haunt him for years. A United Airlines 747 in which he was flying made a hard landing. The entire overhead compartment, complete with luggage, came crashing down on Norman, reportedly damaging his head, neck, and spine. "And I should have been dead," he said. "I put my head down just enough so I didn't get my head crushed. But I had brain damage for twelve years. I couldn't write, make albums; I was helpless, couldn't find my way home." It took years for Norman to get a diagnosis: "a bi-polar trauma," he explained, "which means the accident caused an interruption in the information from one side of my brain to the other. . . . The neurons spark but sometimes don't make a connection." He never got compensation from the airline. "I didn't sue them because I didn't want to go to hell," he explained as being his reasoning at the time. "I probably would have gotten five million. Who knows? I don't want to go to hell. If you sue anybody you're going to hell. If you get divorced you're going to hell. Great! So now I'm going to hell."[10]

Randy Stonehill, early 1970s (Photo courtesy of David Di Sabatino)

To cap it off, Norman's independent record company began to disintegrate. "I couldn't run Solid Rock Records anymore because of my mental condition due to the accident," he said. "I couldn't concentrate. I couldn't finish anybody's album. I couldn't get any work done in the office, it was just real hard." In addition, there were personality clashes and business disagreements among Norman and some of the Solid Rock artists, in particular Stonehill, Tom Howard, and the members of Daniel Amos. "There was a lot of personal strife in everybody's life," Norman explained. "My wife had decided she wanted to marry somebody else and all of the artists at the same time were leaving their wives, and I just thought this was appropriate time for introspection. I didn't want to be up on stage and having kids come back afterwards and ask me why everyone was getting divorced." Norman's account of his failed marriage and record label caused further controversy, with several parties disputing his version of events; the upshot was some long-running feuds.[11]

It was during this dark period that Norman moved to England. He had acquired a reputation as a capricious maverick with an oversized ego and poor social skills. His best albums were banned from Christian radio and bookstores. He was dogged by persistent, sometimes outlandish rumors. "I was accused of having left my wife and becoming a homosexual," he said in 1980. "Some rumors said I had become a heroin addict. I was accused of having left Jesus and become a Satanist. Different rumors said I was living in a cave in Greece, and studying the Koran. An alternate one had me living in the hills of Hollywood like a hermit, studying the Koran. I had supposedly run away to live in New York, run away to live in Africa." A woman in a restaurant asked Norman if it was true he'd become a porn star. A journalist asked if it was true he'd sued his mother. A minister in Australia told his youth group that Norman had appeared as a nude centerfold in *Cosmopolitan*. His friend André Crouch, no stranger himself to slings and arrows, suggested he write a song about the charges. "Man, I always hear rumors about you," Crouch told Norman. "For a white boy, you sure get in a lot of trouble."[12]

## For Those Tears I Died

The various breakups of Larry Norman and his Solid Rock circle were not the only divorces to roil the world of Jesus music in the late seventies. The first marital failure to draw attention was that of John Michael Talbot. Along with his brother Terry, Talbot was a founding member of Mason Profitt and a rising star of the secular country rock scene before having a profound Christian conversion experience in a Holiday Inn in 1971. Talbot had met his wife, Nancy, when he was sixteen and touring the country with Mason Profitt; she was a nineteen-year-old groupie. They wed when his father threatened to "call in the law" on his underage son. Within two years after his born-again experience, Talbot found it impossible to continue the life of an aspiring rock star and left Mason Profitt, pursuing a mercurial spiritual journey that included a phase as a "walking, talking Jesus freak" who came on "like a Bible thumper" and railed at old friends for their worldly lifestyles. Meanwhile, the couple continued to drift apart, despite their best efforts to salvage the marriage. Openly consumed by guilt, Talbot received the support of most of the Jesus music community, with the exception of Keith Green, who told Talbot that he must repent or be damned. Talbot became a Franciscan monk, embraced celibacy as penance for his divorce, founded a small monastic community in Arkansas, and eventually resumed a career in Christian music.[13]

In some ways, the most startling marital-musical parting took place among Children of the Day, a group that had coalesced in 1969 from the purest strains of the Orange County Jesus Movement scene. The combo began with sixteen-year-old Marsha Carter, who accepted Jesus at a beach church service, and her younger sister, Wendy, whom Marsha convinced to accept Jesus. The young Street Christian also converted her friend Peter Jacobs, who led a successful jazz combo, and another member of that band, Russ Stevens, who married Marsha three years later. The high school kids formed a vocal group in which they played guitars and stand-up bass, naming it after a passage in Paul's letter to the Thessalonians that warns of Jesus returning like a thief in the night: "But ye, brethren, are not in darkness, that that day should overtake you as a thief. Ye are all the children of light, and the children of the day."

The quartet had a Peter, Paul & Mary, folk-rock style, but they also sang madrigal-style pieces with a baroque flavor. Calvary Chapel was their spiritual base, and Calvary's newly founded Maranatha! label quickly recorded them, bringing out their first album, *Come to the Waters*, in 1971; pastor Chuck Smith reportedly put up the $900 cost of making the record. Buck Herring was the engineer for the session at a Hollywood recording studio, whose piano had been broken the day before by none other than Larry Norman.[14]

The album's last track, "For Those Tears I Died," would become the group's trademark song. That same song appeared on *Everlastin' Living Jesus Music Concert*, the pathbreaking Maranatha! compilation that first brought Jesus music to a record-playing audience outside Orange County, from where it entered the canon of the Jesus Movement. It was written by Carter when she was sixteen for a school project and to share her new faith with her younger

Children of the Day, early 1970s (Photo courtesy of Marsha Stevens-Pino)

sister. The Carter girls had been brought up in a mainline church but had a troubled home life. "Let's just say that when you grow up with an alcoholic in the house," Marsha said, "you learn that night is a time to hide." The song's lyrics reflect wonder regarding salvation ("But, Jesus, why me?," a phrase Kris Kristofferson would use a couple of years later), praise, and thankfulness. The chorus sounds a note of divine solidarity amid human vulnerability, inviting listeners to "Come to the waters" where their thirst would be satisfied by a reassuring Jesus: "I've felt every tear-drop when in darkness you cried / And I strove to remind you that for those tears I died." The song "expresses adolescent piety better than any other Christian song ever written," writes Mark Allan Powell "and yet [it] does so in language that evokes imagery of baptism and liberation that even theologically mature adults (who may or not care for the sentimental qualities) can appreciate."[15]

The four group members enrolled at Azusa Pacific University, where they toured with the choir. And they continued to record albums. *With All Our Love*, released in 1973, featured two love songs written by Marsha and Russ Stevens to each other for their 1972 wedding, shortly after the recording of *Come to the Waters*. "What I see and what I love is Jesus using you," Marsha sang in "Russ's Song." "You're a gift from heaven above / You were meant for me and I was meant for you," Russ replied in his song. Peter Jacobs had also gotten married and included a romantic song for his wife. The group recorded two albums in 1975, including an album of Christmas music, the first done in the world of Jesus music. Their last two albums, *Never Felt So Free* (1977) and *Butterfly* (1979), were released by Word.

Children of the Day's most important long-term legacy, though, was probably a Maranatha! release from 1974 called *The Praise Album*. Along with other Calvary musicians, the four pioneered what Powell judges to be "the most significant liturgical innovation of the twentieth century—the use of simple praise choruses that seemed to combine Eastern religious mantras with Madison Avenue advertising jingles to produce an either infectious or annoying (depending on perspective) style that would come to dominate information worship services around the world." Jacobs arranged the strings, a crucial ingredient in the new worship sound. The first album was followed by *Praise 2*, *Praise 3*, and more from Maranatha! Other companies have followed suit. The popularity of praise music, which grew directly out of songs from the Jesus Movement, has been a key factor in the expansion of evangelical Christianity since the seventies, a development that has reshaped Protestant worship and, by extension, America's cultural-political landscape.[16]

After seven years of marriage and two children, though, the Stevenses were coming unglued. "We were focused on Jesus coming back," Marsha explained. "We were not focused on our relationships. We had no idea that relationships were work and that we were supposed to be working on them." The emphasis was on saving souls while there was still time, not negotiating family relationships for the long haul. With a congregation of 20,000, Calvary Chapel had only one staff member assigned for counseling, according to Stevens, and he would only address the husband. "You could be there as the wife but he would only interact and speak with the husband, and your husband had to speak to you," she recalled. "It was very bizarre. And you were only with somebody because it was the one [who] God told you to marry. It wasn't that you developed a relationship or had anything strong to stand on. . . . By that time we were getting older and having to deal with real relationships, having to deal with our children, and we were completely unequipped. I mean, we had no idea. Like every age of innocence, it had its down side—innocence ends and you've got to keep on dealing with life."[17]

"You need to find someone else," Russ Stevens eventually told his wife.

"You know," Marsha replied, "I think it might be a woman."

Following the couple's breakup and Marsha's pronouncement that she was a lesbian, the backlash from Christians was quick and strong, if not as physically traumatic as it was for Randy Matthews after the "demon music" attack on him at the Pennsylvania Jesus festival. "The Christian community excised me from its life," she remembered. Members of her church demanded she take down a "Jesus is Lord" sign over her door. Her songs, including the widely published "For Those Tears I Died," were torn out of hymnals and sometimes mailed to her. Maranatha! tried to withhold her royalties, citing a "backslider clause" in her contract. Congenital heart disease claimed the life of her lover's daughter, which Christians took as a sign of divine judgment, predicting that Stevens's children would face a similar fate. "It became a favorite sermon illustration repeated up and down the West Coast," according to Stevens. "God killed our baby because we loved each other."[18] With her musical career temporarily derailed, she supported herself working as a registered nurse.

Perhaps surprisingly, Stevens refused to abandon her faith. "The church didn't want me," she admitted, "but I just loved Jesus too much to stay away."[19] Years later, she founded a company called Born Again Lesbian Music (BALM) that began releasing a flurry of her records in the nineties. But she disappeared virtually without a trace from Christian bookstores, radio, and the print media that had sprung up to communicate news of the burgeoning Christian music industry to its audience.

A similar fate overtook Lonnie Frisbee, the charismatic hippie who joined forces with Chuck Smith to bring the Jesus Movement to national prominence. Frisbee, already a fervent Christian, had married Connie in 1968, about the time he started his work at Calvary Chapel in Costa Mesa. Stevens remembered Frisbee's unique role in the community during that era.

Lonnie was ubiquitous. He was there at every service, he was there at every event, he was there at every baptism. People talk now as though you might not have known him if you were there. That's just not true. He was absolutely everywhere. He was the one a lot of us went to when we had contemporary questions. Like how come we don't believe in free love anymore? If God is love, why don't we believe in free love, meaning sleep with everybody that we like? Chuck would give you more of the pat answers that you grew up with: "Well, men give love to get sex and women give sex to get love," and he'd give you more of those. But Lonnie would just sit down and tear through the scriptures with you on it: "Let's figure out what sex is really for, what it's designed for. And are we using it for what it's designed for?

And what happens to you and to the other person? And what's really loving?" . . . You're not going to ask Chuck, "How far can I go with my girlfriend?" But you would ask Lonnie.[20]

Tensions between Smith and Frisbee mounted over the years, mainly because Smith was uneasy about Frisbee's Pentecostal leanings that stressed physical manifestations of the Spirit, such as tongues and healing. Frisbee's marriage had also suffered because of the intense pace of his ministry. Frisbee joined the staff for a time at another church, returning to Calvary four years later; again, he didn't last long. He was drawn next to a Calvary satellite church in Yorba Linda, California, pastored by a man named John Wimber. This church would develop late in the seventies into a rapidly growing church association called the Vineyard, which won over some Calvary Chapel congregations that had connections to the musician-friendly Bible studies led by Kenn Gulliksen, Larry Norman, and Chuck Girard. In 1980 Frisbee became an invaluable asset to Wimber, who was more open than Smith to "signs and wonders" as manifestations of the supernatural. Again, though, Frisbee was let go by the church as its membership was multiplying.

Frisbee, it turned out, was gay and had known it for many years, since before he became a Christian. Prior to his marriage in 1968, he had confessed it to Connie, but he claimed he had been "saved out of" the lifestyle. Many of his friends believed that he was no longer a "practicing" homosexual, even if he occasionally backslid; others felt it was a lifelong orientation even if he didn't always act on it. "I think that's one area of his life that was never broken, he was never free of it," Gulliksen told David Di Sabatino in an interview. "And it remained hidden away and would manifest itself very secretly, very privately."[21] When his "open secret" became too widely known, the powerful evangelical leaders that appreciated his charismatic spiritual gifts cut him loose for fear of having their reputations tarnished.

Like Marsha Stevens in the annals of contemporary Christian music, Frisbee was airbrushed out of the official histories of both Calvary Chapel and the Vineyard. But unlike Stevens, Frisbee felt used and betrayed by the ordeal. "Lonnie's bitterness, I think he was entitled to it, if I can say that anyone's entitled to bitterness," opined Chuck Smith Jr. in an interview. "I think that both my dad and John [Wimber] were like father figures to him, but fathers who rejected him. And that had to be extremely painful for Lonnie. I think it's part of the tragedy of his life."[22] Frisbee died of AIDS in 1993.

Despite the turbulence surrounding a few admittedly significant members of the Calvary Chapel circle, no group showed more clearly the disarray caused by crosscurrents of sex, piety, and music among the vestiges of the Jesus Movement than the Children of God. What had begun as a particularly straitlaced group in 1969 was by 1974 being directed by its leader, "Moses" Berg, in the direction of sexual libertinism that would embroil the group in international scandal by the end of the decade. Miriam Williams was a dreamy, small-time rebel teenager from Lancaster, Pennsylvania, who joined the Children of God in 1971 after a brief, frightening drift through New York City. Earlier, she had been impressed by the young evangelicals she saw in the NBC documentary "The Ultimate Trip." Music was part of the draw. "For idealists who were disillusioned with the sex, drugs, and rock and roll that hippiedom offered, the fresh and hopeful sounds of the group's music was a definite attraction," she wrote. "Mo's early disciples each played a musical instrument, usually guitar, and many were accomplished musicians and songwriters before they became his disciples."[23]

Renamed Jeshanah, Williams married a fellow member the next year, a drummer in Jeremy Spencer's band whom she calls Cal. The marriage was arranged and, while Williams reports that she never loved him, Cal's status as a musician opened doors for the couple across the United States and Europe. The first move was from the compound in Ellenville, New York, to Boston, where the band was working on a record for Columbia, for which they'd been offered $50,000. Released as *Jeremy and the Children* in 1973, the record sold poorly and the group relocated to Europe. Spencer again assembled a Children of God band in Paris and brought in Cal and Miriam. The band did much better in France, where they expanded into a larger "Show Group" that included Williams on backup vocals. They took the name Les Enfants de Dieu; Williams described the band as a "clean-cut singing group comparable to the *Sound of Music* family."[24] Two of their singles were hits with French teenagers, and the group was invited to perform on radio and television and eventually to tour France, Spain, Holland, Belgium, Germany, and England in 1976.

In the meantime, Williams and other members were expected to bring in donations, which she did through musical "busking" at outdoor cafés and in the Metro, where they had considerable success. The group began opening weekend discos — called Poor Boy Clubs — in European cities to attract young people who might be converted, and Williams became a go-go dancer while her husband played drums. Gradually, the tactics became more sexual. Berg had issued a letter titled "Flirty Little Fish" in 1974, and over the next several years, he released a constant stream of letters that encouraged all manner of sexual practices: open "sharing" in marriages, including threesomes; "flirty fishing" to recruit converts through sex; and sexual intimacies in the presence of children.

After relocating with a few fellow members to Monte Carlo, Williams found herself devoting more and more of her time and energy to flirty fishing but continued to sing in restaurants and private parties, while also trying to raise her son. The lines between entertaining, proselytizing, and prostitution became increasingly blurred as Williams and her comrades circulated among the European jet set, which she said included some of the wealthiest men in the world. Her already strained marriage finally collapsed. "For many years, I did not feel physical pleasure during sex or even desire while flirting," she recalled. "I took on the role of a vestal virgin offering my body as God's gift of love, a perverse combination of the purity of sacred devotion and the intimacy of marriage bonds." Only years later was Williams finally able to break her connection to the Children of God.[25]

## Clouds of Doubt

The timing of the messy scandals and meltdowns ruffling the world of late-seventies Jesus music was almost providential. At least they paralleled the rising prominence of concern over family values in the country at large. These issues had galvanized many of Jimmy Carter's core evangelical voters in 1976, who were alarmed by what they considered moral decline: divorce, unwed mothers, abortion, sexual promiscuity, drug use, secular humanism, and all-round hedonism. "The American family is in trouble," Carter said in a stump speech. "I have campaigned all over America, and everywhere I go, I find people deeply concerned about the loss of stability and the loss of values in our lives. The root of this problem is the steady erosion and weakening of our families."[26] Though Carter had wooed and won these voters effectively in 1976 by pitching himself as one of them, it proved much harder to hold onto them as the commander in chief of a left-leaning Democratic Party and Congress chafing to finish the Great Society aspirations of the sixties. Ironically, Carter would be driven from office partly as a result of the perception that he was too liberal and not authentically Christian—unborn again, some critics said.

As a candidate, Carter had played up his religious faith, calling it "the most important thing in my life." "I'll be a better president because of my deep religious convictions," he announced during the campaign. Interviewed by Pat Robertson on CBN, Carter pledged to help bring secular law in harmony with "God's laws" and to defer to the latter.[27] Making no promises, Carter also agreed to consider a list of evangelical candidates for positions in his administration. But as he had stressed to *Playboy*, the bedrock of his Southern Baptist faith was a commitment to religious liberty and a clear-cut separation of church and state, an ideal running all the way back to Roger Williams, the Puritan dissident who founded Rhode Island. And at the core of Carter's personal piety was the injunction to avoid moral pride and judging others for their sins. In fact, conscious of the suspicion of his faith among much of the Democratic base, once in office Carter felt he had to bend over backwards to soft-pedal the expression of his Southern Baptist views in policy decisions. For example, he was criticized for hosting in the White House a meeting with leaders of the Southern Baptist Convention to discuss global missions. He seemed to learn the lesson that he needed to be more politic about avoiding the appearance of conflict of interest.

This was something that newly energized evangelical activists had a hard time accepting (and would continue to have a hard time accepting from subsequent presidents, Republican or Democratic). Christian conservatives had also counted on him to appoint some fellow evangelicals to high positions in his administration, and again they were disappointed. Hamilton Jordan and Jody Powell were not what they had in mind. Carter did appoint a devout Catholic, Joseph Califano, to head the Department of Health, Education and Welfare. But most Carter appointees were decidedly liberal, especially among his mid-level staff, whom Attorney General Griffin Bell once described as the "McGovern-Kennedy-Nader government-in-waiting." Ironically, the White House staff members most likely to interact with activists concerned about family values were the ones who seemed most out of step. For example, after Carter made anti-abortion statements in a press conference, presidential assistant Margaret "Midge" Costanza, a staunch pro-choice feminist, organized a protest meeting of forty administration staffers.[28]

By the 1978 midterm elections, the leadership of Carter's own Southern Baptists was starting to turn against him. Alarmed by the possible impact of defections, a few of his confidants called for a presidential liaison to work with evangelicals. A Southern Baptist pastor from Georgia named Robert Maddox volunteered his services to the new administration, but his offer wasn't accepted until after irreparable damage had already been done. When Carter invited the president of the Southern Baptist Convention to the Oval Office for a cordial visit, the preacher flatly declared, "I hope you will give up your secular humanism and return back to Christianity." Attending a meeting of Baptist ministers from Georgia, columnist Bob Novak heard a consistent message from the preachers: "I was part of Carter's team in 1976. I delivered my congregation for Carter. I urged them all to vote for Carter because I thought he was a moral individual. I found out otherwise, and I'm angry." Novak decided at that point that "Jimmy Carter's goose was cooked."[29]

During the summer and fall of 1979, Maddox wrote increasingly frantic memos urging Carter to meet with televangelists. The president finally met with Jerry Falwell, Jim Bakker, and Oral Roberts, but the meeting backfired badly. Afterward, Christian author and evangelist Tim LaHaye prayed: "God, we have got to get this man out of the White House and get someone in here who will be aggressive about bringing back traditional moral values." Falwell spread word that Carter had admitted to having "practicing homosexuals" on his White House staff. The exchange between Falwell and Carter was proven to have been wholly fabricated, but Carter's reputation among evangelicals was already shredded. Robertson, who had campaigned for Carter in 1976 and invited him on the *700 Club* after the election, felt betrayed. "I sensed something was wrong when I interviewed him for our show," he said. "There was this wonderful exterior charm to him. But underneath, terrible coldness. It was frightening."[30]

The alliance between activist clergy like Jerry Falwell, Republican political operatives like Paul Weyrich, and conservative lawmakers like Jesse Helms that defined the Religious Right coalesced during the Carter years. Focus on the Family was founded in 1977 in Arcadia, California, from where it would relocate to Pomona and, ultimately, its sprawling Colorado Springs compound. Another powerful group, Christian Voice, was founded in 1978 by Dr. Robert Grant. Religious Roundtable was organized the following year by Ed McAteer. Plans for yet another group were hatched at a Holiday Inn in Lynchburg, Virginia, at a meeting attended by Falwell, Weyrich, McAteer, and others in May 1979; the next month, the Moral Majority was officially inaugurated with a Washington headquarters.[31]

That summer, a who's who gathering of evangelicals huddled in a hotel near the Dallas–Fort Worth airport. Bill Bright hatched the idea with Billy Graham and invited James Robison, Pat Robertson, Rex Humbard, and several prominent Southern Baptist pastors who would go on to lead the denomination following that year's fundamentalist takeover. The evangelists went around the room confessing their despair for the future of the Republic. "I believe God has shown me that unless we have a change in America, we have a thousand days as a free nation . . . three years," said Graham. "I do not believe we'll survive more than three years as a free nation," agreed Bright, who at the time of Explo '72 had set the target of 1980 for "saturating" the world with the Gospel. "I believe the same thing," said Robertson. "I'll die to save this country," added Robison. "Whatever it takes. We can't lose this country."[32] None of these figures were alumni of the Jesus Movement, exactly, but Graham, Bright, and Robertson had all cultivated it. Their message found a receptive audience among the young evangelicals who had recently transitioned into adulthood and were flocking to churches whose pastors, theology, and worship style had been shaped by the Jesus People.

## A New Gog

By now it was becoming a familiar pattern: a troubled pop star, a beach in Southern California, a born-again experience. This one was off Malibu two days before Christmas. The artist was Cat Stevens, whose tenth album had been released earlier that year, going gold within a month and reaching the Top 10 in the pop charts. But it was not Jesus whom Stevens accepted as his lord and savior; it was Allah.

Stevens was British, born Steven Georgiou and raised Greek Orthodox, the son of a Swedish mother and a Greek father who was a restaurant owner in London. Under the name Steve Adams, he started writing and performing songs while a student at Hammersmith College. Discovered by a record producer in 1966, Stevens was signed by Decca on the strength of a demo he had written called "I Love My Dog." Several of his singles ascended high on the charts and were covered by other artists. Now named Cat Stevens, his debut album, *Matthew and Son*, was released in 1967 and made the Top 10. But the next year, Stevens contracted tuberculosis and, after some disappointing record sales, left Decca.

Stevens began writing more introspective songs along the lines of Bob Dylan and was signed by Island Records in 1970. His third album contained the single "Lady D'Arbanville," which was inspired by a girlfriend, actress Patti D'Arbanville. Stevens was poised for major success, which arrived in 1971. His fourth album, *Tea for the Tillerman*, exploded on the charts, buoyed by the success of a single called "Wild World." Two more hit singles appeared that year—"Moonshadow" and "Peace Train"—followed that fall by yet another album, *Teaser and the Firecat*, which shipped gold, almost reached number one in the U.S. charts, and did nearly as well in Britain. The album contained Stevens's cover of an old hymn, "Morning Has Broken," which became a Top 10 pop hit and reached number one in the easy-listening charts. This was the year the Jesus Movement was making national news, and lots of musicians not known for Christian piety were having hits with Jesus songs.

Stevens contributed songs to the black comedy *Harold and Maude* (1972) and continued releasing albums that went gold or platinum and yielded hits on both sides of the Atlantic. But the stress of stardom began to wear on him. He moved to Brazil for a time (ostensibly for tax reasons), reduced his concert appearances, and declined interviews.

Struggling in the surf off Malibu in December 1977, Stevens found himself starting to drown. Realizing how close he was to death, Stevens made a promise to God: if God spared him, he would change his life. "I had to deflate myself," he explained. "I had to come back to life."[33] He became a Muslim and took the name Yusuf Islam. His eleventh and final album of new material, *Back to Earth*, came out the following December. He retired from popular music, moved to London, sold his possessions, and opened a Muslim school. Yusuf Islam entered an arranged marriage (his wife chosen by his mother between two candidates) and proceeded to have five children. A decade later, he denounced novelist Salman Rushdie and appeared to endorse a fatwa leveled against Rushdie by Ayatollah Khomeini. In response, classic-rock stations stopped playing his music, and his albums were incinerated in bonfires—much like Beatles records after John Lennon boasted that the group was bigger than Jesus.

Cat Stevens wasn't the first British pop star to be born again. Cliff Richard, England's first rock star, had set the precedent in 1966, announcing his conversion onstage at a Billy Graham rally in London. Jeremy Spencer of Fleetwood Mac had wandered into a Children of God commune in Los Angeles in 1971. He was preceded by the band's cofounder, Peter Green, a Jew who first embraced Jesus in 1969 before becoming a pious eccentric who reportedly gave away his fortune to Save the Children. That same year, Eric Clapton, touring with Blind Faith, revealed that he had become a born-again Christian and contributed a song, "Presence of the Lord," to the album the group released that year. Nor was Stevens the first United States–based musician to convert to Islam. Several notable jazz musicians had become Muslims in the decades after World War II, including drummers Art Blakey and Kenny Clarke, saxophonist Yusef Lateef, and pianists Ahmad Jamal and McCoy Tyner. But Islam was an unexpected choice for a mellow-sounding singer-songwriter like Stevens, whose boomer musical peers were mostly embracing, if not Christianity, then quasi-Asian or New Age spirituality.

Islam was, of course, increasingly on the minds of Americans as the nightmares of Vietnam were replaced by fresh worries. For many Americans, oil shortages and the rise of OPEC created a loose association between ruthless Middle Eastern sheiks, anti-Israel politics, and the mundane pain of increasingly expensive, difficult-to-obtain gasoline in a nation of car dependents. For evangelicals who embraced the end-times prophecy popularized most successfully by Hal Lindsey, Islam had loomed as a major interest and concern for a long time. During the Middle Ages, a belief that Muslims were minions of the Antichrist helped fuel the Crusades, with Europeans pursuing the futile dream of driving Saladin from Jerusalem and redeeming the Holy Land for the church. (The pope and, predictably, the Jews were also suspected of being the Antichrist or in his league.)

By the twentieth century, especially with the rise of the Soviet Union as a superpower and global rival, proponents of end-times prophecy put godless Soviets ahead of Islamic Turks as the most probable candidates for the biblical Gog, the mysterious power that would invade Israel from the north and set in motion the events leading to the Rapture, Tribulation, Second Coming, and end of human history. But the two threats were not mutually exclusive; the Arab nations were expected to be part of Gog's alliance. And many Americans easily conflated Arab culture and politics with Islam (the same error that would lead them to forget that the Ottoman Turks were not Arab). As historian Melani McAlister notes, "What had been understood, albeit incorrectly, as 'the Arab world' in the 1960s and 1970s became, again, incorrectly, 'the Islamic world' in the 1980s."[34]

Prophecy belief, with its tendentious and often fantastical readings of Ezekiel, Daniel, and Revelation, had permeated the Jesus Movement and its musicians since the early days. Chuck Smith of Calvary Chapel, for example, remained a leading exponent of end-times belief during the seventies and beyond. Though Jesus People didn't dwell on the Soviets, it was impossible for them not to absorb some of the anti-Soviet bias of popularizers like Lindsey, a rabid opponent of Communism in all forms. But this animus was joined to another visceral intellectual and emotional reaction: support for Israel. The establishment of the state of Israel in May 1948 was celebrated by prophecy believers as the first of three conditions stipulated in the Bible for the Second Coming of Christ. The second condition was met in June 1967 during the Six-Day War, when Israel recaptured the Old City of Jerusalem. "The hands on Israel's prophecy clock leaped forward on June 8, 1967," LaHaye put it in his prophecy treatise *The Beginning of the End* (1972).[35] All that remained to be fulfilled, according to most prophecy believers, was the rebuilding of the Jewish Temple in Jerusalem, which had been razed by Roman occupiers in 70 C.E.

Here again, Islam appeared as an obstacle to, if not an enemy of, God's inexorable plan for human history. For on the so-called Temple Mount site, where Israel's Temple must be rebuilt, are two mosques, one dating from the seventh century (the Dome of the Rock) and the other from the eighth (Al Aksa Mosque). According to prophecy, Christian history could not take its providential course without the cooperation of Israel, which must restore itself and expand, and the Jewish people, who must ultimately convert to Christianity; Muslims appeared to stand in the way of Israel's sacred destiny and thus of God's will. Of course, that could all be changed with a well-placed earthquake, bomb, or surface-to-surface missile that would obliterate the Dome of the Rock and clear the way for rebuilding the Temple.

With these concerns in mind, Carl Henry, a leading evangelical intellectual and editor of *Christianity Today*, announced the convening of an international conference on biblical prophecy held in Jerusalem. Israel's government strongly supported the 1971 parley, providing the meeting hall and sending Prime Minister David Ben-Gurion to welcome the conferees, which included 1,500 delegates from thirty-two nations. Future antigay crusader Anita Bryant was there to provide music, along with Met opera singer Jerome Hines and the Azusa Pacific University choir (in which Children of the Day had sung). Baptist luminary reverend Wallie Amos Criswell attended, as did future Reagan surgeon general C. Everett Koop. Also present were officials from Inter-Varsity Christian Fellowship and Youth for Christ (the outfit for which the young Larry Norman almost worked) and scholars from Dallas Theological Seminary, the intellectual epicenter of U.S. prophecy belief.

Marsha Stevens and the other members of Children of the Day were invited. As full-fledged Jesus People, they felt a slight distance from their peers. "The people that were there from our perspective were very clean-cut, grew-up-in-church kind of people," Stevens said. "We had already sowed our wild oats, so we were genuinely there to worship and to learn. Some of the people who actually grew up in church were the ones that might have been buying hashish on the corner. They were away from home for the first time and maybe getting in trouble they shouldn't have been in. But we'd been there, done that; we had no interest in it anymore. So we actually ended up hanging out more with the adults and the teachers and the preachers because that's where we wanted to be."[36]

Stevens and her bandmates were told to be careful not to proselytize to Jews, but they weren't quite sure what that meant. "So we just went out into the city of Jerusalem," she recalled, "and had an incredible time and took our guitars and sang to the taxi drivers" and relaxed in the publike taverns where Israeli families and children gathered. "We hung out there and sang Jewish songs that we knew and sang our songs. It was just incredible. So that by the time we got to the conference on prophecy it was even more alive to us, because we could put faces to all those places' names. . . . It made it so concrete."

Stevens said they sometimes found themselves in long, cordial discussions with Hasidic and Orthodox Jews.

> Now I look back—what were they thinking, talking to eighteen-year-olds? But we really loved the Word. We had people who talked to us for hours. I could picture now what happened when Jesus was twelve. People just enthralled with the idea that maybe Christianity isn't a different religion. It's that whole deal of, when Messiah comes, I'm going to say, "Is this the first time—or the second?" . . . People were amazingly open. There's a lot of people who prayed with us. But it's hard to tell because of course more than Judaism is Zionism. Over and over and over again, we heard: we just want you to love Israel like we do. So sometimes it was even hard to tell whether they were just going along 'cause they just want you to love Israel.

An end-times prophecy mindset permeated the Jesus Movement of the early seventies; linked to a staunchly anti-Soviet and pro-Israel foreign policy, it was a major article of faith among the televangelists who birthed the Religious Right. One was LaHaye, who, in addition to publishing his best-selling prophecy book *The Beginning of the End*, was an original board member of the Moral Majority and founder of the American Coalition for Traditional Values. Another was Pat Robertson, who broke ground for a new building for CBN on 5 June 1967, the day Israel went to war with its Arab neighbors (a fact that wasn't lost on Robertson). Israel's victory that year, he wrote later, was a sure sign that the Antichrist would begin gathering his forces for the final showdown with the Lord; he predicted that the world would be "in flames" before the end of 1982.[37]

No one in the Religious Right made his support for Israel more unmistakable than Jerry Falwell. "Theologically," he insisted, "any Christian has to support Israel, simply because Jesus said to. . . . If we fail to protect Israel, we will cease to be important to God." Referring to the founding of Israel, Falwell proclaimed that next to Christ's ascension to heaven, "the most important date we should remember is May 14, 1948." Along with Chuck Smith, Oral Roberts, and other prominent ministers, Falwell led several tours of the Holy Land, where he was treated royally by the Likud government and briefed by high-level government officials. "For the Christian, political involvement on this issue is not only a right, but a responsibility," he said. "We can and must be involved in guiding America towards a biblical position regarding her stand on Israel." And Falwell took a dim view of current U.S. policy in the Middle East. "In spite of the rosy and utterly unrealistic expectations by our government," he announced at the time of the Camp David accords between Israel and Egypt, "this treaty will not be a lasting treaty. . . . You and I know that there's not going to be any real peace in the Middle East until the Lord Jesus sits down upon the throne of David in Jerusalem."[38]

As Falwell's dismissive comment indicates, one prominent American evangelical assuredly didn't belong in the end-times prophecy club: Jimmy Carter. Though most Southern Baptists were prophecy believers, Carter was not one of them. In fact, he and his policies gave prophecy adherents grounds for serious concern. In 1973, when he was governor of Georgia and just beginning his long campaign for the presidency, Carter had been invited to join the Trilateral Commission, which was started the previous year by David Rockefeller and Columbia professor and future Carter national security adviser Zbigniew Brzezinski. The elite group, which brought together powerful individuals from banking, business, government, academia, and the media, was a bête noire of prophecy popularizers. Hal Lindsey himself charged that the Trilateral Commission had indoctrinated Carter and used its connections to the national news media to propel him to the White House. The secretive cabal, which operated with no public involvement or debate, was, according to Lindsey, "setting the stage for the political-economic one-world system the Bible predicts for the last days."[39]

Carter's peacemaking proclivities themselves were suspect. In end-times prophecy, there was no evading the apocalyptic showdown with Gog and the Antichrist. Christians simply had to make sure their souls were saved, prepare for the Rapture, and brace themselves for the sequence of disasters that would precede (and accelerate during) the Tribulation. To work for détente with the Soviets, or to defuse the hair-trigger tension in the Middle East between Israel, its Arab neighbors, and the Palestinian population that believed itself occupied by an imperial power, was to interfere in the unfolding of divine providence. Peacemaking was worse than futile; the Antichrist would initially appear as a peacemaker. Because of his shuttle diplomacy under Nixon, Secretary of State Henry Kissinger was short-listed by some writers as the Antichrist, alongside Carter's Camp David partner Anwar el-Sadat of Egypt, Moshe Dayan, and the pope (and eventually Mikhail Gorbachev and Saddam Hussein).[40] The point for end-times prophecy was not to help win security for the Jews (by which they actually meant citizens of Israel, who were the ones that mattered in terms of prophecy); the point was to convert them. Jews would be fiercely persecuted during the Tribulation, but many would finally accept Christ as the Messiah and enter a glorious eternal future with Jesus after his Second Coming.

As the 1980 election year approached, nearly everyone in the United States had reason to be angry with the Baptist in the White House. Oil was in short supply again, and lines at gas stations stretched intolerably in many areas of the country fortunate enough to have stations open for business. Double-digit inflation coupled with high interest rates, unemployment, and a bearish stock market caused general dismay verging on bitterness. The Cold War had taken an alarming turn with the Soviet invasion of Afghanistan, and cuts in federal social services and domestic spending antagonized the Democratic base in Congress. So-called family values had become a kind of seamless garment of political grievance directed against its most prominent Democratic target. The administration's policy in the Middle East provided yet another last straw.

In July 1979 Carter withdrew to Camp David to reflect on how to reassure the American people. Over the next eight days, he held discussions with nearly 150 people, including religious leaders, economists, labor leaders, and businesspeople, as well as politicians from all levels of government. He also met and took comments from small groups of citizens in private homes in Pennsylvania and West Virginia. Finally, on Sunday night, 15 July, like Moses after his encounter with God on Mount Sinai, Carter delivered a jeremiad — a ritual evocation of sinfulness and collective repentance — that identified the real crisis facing the nation as a spiritual one rather than a material one caused by the shortage of fossil fuel. With the nation at a turning point, it was "time to stop cursing and start praying." Carter diagnosed a "crisis of the American spirit," reflected in the loss of a sense of meaning and purpose, a quest for instant gratification and material abundance, an excessive spirit of negative freedom, and "self-indulgence and consumption." He called on Americans to "join hands" in a "common faith" on a national mission that, with God's help, "cannot fail."[41]

To vice president Walter Mondale, who had doubts about the politics of Carter's approach, the president came across like the famous American preacher Jonathan Edwards, rebuking the American people "like sinners in the hands of an angry God." But the entire exercise was very Baptist, totally consistent with Carter's bedrock beliefs. Good leadership depended on the trust of the people, which had to be constantly renewed. Like a fallen sinner, Carter personally modeled the stages of evangelical conversion: conviction of sin, retreat, meditation, a decision to commit, and a public announcement of rebirth. The speech itself was initially well received, but Carter's follow-up decision to ask for his entire Cabinet and White House staff to resign was not. Somehow he kept the ship of state afloat, even though it was listing badly.[42] A new historical bloc was being born, one that would deal a decisive blow to the few lingering alliances remaining from the sixties cultural front. A Religious Right was starting to beat the New Left at its own game, using methods developed by sixties activists. As much as any other faction, evangelicals were both agents and subjects of the social transformation.

## Chapter 10

# LAST DAYS

As Carter stumbled and the Religious Right began to muster its newly energized forces, remnants of the Jesus Movement found its new Promised Land.
While prophecy-minded evangelicals like Hal Lindsey and Jerry Falwell may
have been cheering Israel's burgeoning settlements in Palestine as necessary
fulfillment of scripture, a small but determined band of Jesus People, mainly
California transplants, had begun clustering about eighty miles east of Dallas,
creating their own New Jerusalem near the little town of Lindale, Texas.

On her first trip to East Texas, Melody Green remembered being struck
by the "huge vistas of open, green fields" as she and Keith made their first
pilgrimage to East Texas. "There were enough truck-stop diners, backyard
oil pumps, and herds of cattle to remind us every mile we drove that we were
in the Lone Star State," she wrote. "When we turned off into Lindale, we
were amazed that Texas was so lush. There were big beautiful oaks hung with
clumps of mistletoe. There were piney woods and many little lakes. There
wasn't a tumbleweed in sight!"[1] But there were plenty of evangelicals. A few
Christian organizations had their headquarters there: Youth with a Mission,
Calvary Commission, the Agape Force (which ran a discipleship school and
had a special interest in music ministry), and World Challenge. The colony
included Christian musicians such as Barry McGuire and Dallas Holm and

his band, Praise; 2nd Chapter of Acts moved in later. David Ravenhill, a transplanted British evangelist and theologian who had made a big impact on Green, also took up residence there.

Lindale's best-known Christian evangelist was a Pentecostal preacher named David Wilkerson, who had become famous for his ministry in New York City and the book he wrote about it, *The Cross and the Switchblade* (later made into a movie starring Pat Boone). Wilkerson had founded Teen Challenge, the ministry that Andraé Crouch had joined in the midsixties, working in Los Angeles's Teen Challenge Center and forming a group called the Addicts Choir that toured and recorded before his career with the Disciples took off. Wilkerson wrote a series of fiery books that castigated America's moral failings and looked forward to "going home to Jesus" amid that "sudden fiery holocaust" that would end the world at Armageddon. Wilkerson was not one to pull his punches. "God is going to judge America," he thundered in one of his books, "for its violence, its crimes, its backslidings, its murdering of millions of babies, its flaunting of homosexuality and sadomasochism, its corruption, its drunkenness and drug abuse, its form of godliness without power, its lukewarmness toward Christ, its rampant divorce and adultery, its lewd pornography, its child molestation, its cheatings, its robbings, its dirty movies, and its occult practices."[2]

After Teen Challenge, Wilkerson had founded World Challenge, whose Lindale headquarters Keith and Melody Green were now seeing for the first time. "As we drove through the iron gates of David Wilkerson's Twin Oaks ranch, we were *very* impressed," Melody recalled. "Nestled on a few hundred acres of lush green pastures, with three lakes, there were over twenty ministry houses, several offices, and even a gymnasium." Wilkerson greeted them warmly in his office. "He was tall and thin, and his glasses had dark-to-light shading, which gave him a hip big city look."[3]

Following the visit, the Greens drove around in search of an old friend from their Hollywood hippie days. Coming across a picturesque field with a waterwheel and a log ranch house, Keith declared: "Lord Jesus, that property needs to be used for you. We claim it for your kingdom." It turned out that it belonged to their friend and wasn't for sale. Eventually, after some prayer, the friend changed his mind and decided to sell the land. Late in the summer of 1979, after a typically hair-raising scramble to get together the financing for the property, Keith and Melody, their two kids, and a group of twenty pioneers from Last Days Ministries set out on a 1,500-mile trek to Lindale. It was a season that felt like the Last Days. Jimmy Carter had given his crisis-of-confidence speech in July, before firing his cabinet; in November, American hostages were seized in Iran. A few weeks later, Carter opened his White House to the gospel artists, including Larry Norman.

East Texas took some adjustment for the crew from Los Angeles. They were used to having the run of seven houses, so privacy was an issue. "Fourteen single girls—two with babies—all shared a large bedroom at one end of the house," Melody Green described. "Right next to them, Keith and I shared our bedroom with Josiah and his crib. The single guys lived at the other end of the house, while the other married couple and their children shared 'The Fish Room'—a small enclosed den with a huge built-in aquarium. It was a cozy beginning, to say the least." Keith Green wanted Last Days to live off the land, so they acquired about a hundred head of cattle and a bunch of chickens. One of the bulls died after surgery, so the community went to work butchering, washing, and freezing slabs of beef. Then the chickens got a bad throat infection, and Green decided to slaughter the lot of them before they starved to death. For fun, he brought a horse into the kitchen, causing a huge mess. And he captured a tarantula in a jar. Deciding the arachnid posed a threat to the children, Green decided to microwave it—to the horror of most of the women. "Luckily the jar had a cover on it," Melody wrote.[4]

The mercurial Green continued to surprise those around him with the intensity of his spiritual evolution. In 1977 he and Melody had begun taking in young people—runaways, single moms, people trying to kick drugs—in need of a place to stay, and by the end of 1977, spilling out of a three-room house with one bedroom, they rented a second house for singles to live in. This was the beginning of Last Days Ministries, which incorporated in 1978, the same year Green's Sparrow debut album, *For Those Who Have Ears to Hear*, went to number one on the Christian music charts. There were also stirrings of concern about abortion, an issue of great concern to the nascent Religious Right but which hadn't yet entered into Christian rock. At Keith's request, Melody took the lead on this, writing an antiabortion article for the Last Days newsletter titled "Children, Things We Throw Away?," which was reprinted as a tract and circulated by the millions.

Jesus Movement deejay Jerry Bryant knew Green well in those days.

I guess Keith was as close to a brother as I'll ever have. [The Greens] didn't just sit on it like we do today. They just got up and started putting it to action. I mean, Keith started a community for one reason. He read in the Bible where you're supposed to minister to the poor and the orphans and the needy. Oh, okay, so that means we have to open our homes. So the first thing he did was take my wife. Took her in with her daughter—her husband had abandoned her about eight years earlier—just make her part of the family. She was discipled by them for about three and a half years. And during that time every Jesus Freak you can imagine came through Last Days.[5]

After months of typically persistent matchmaking, Green succeeded in getting the pair together, and they married shortly afterward. As was often the case in Jesus communes, the marriage was seen as divinely ordained.

By the time Bryant got to Woodland Hills, California, where Last Days had relocated, the community had grown to seventy members living in seven houses. Bryant set up a recording studio in a chicken shed that he soundproofed by covering it with empty egg cartons; there, he created a syndicated Christian rock radio show that went out to 100 stations around the country. He remembered Green leading worship after the community meal, getting out his guitar for songs before embarking on high-octane Bible teaching. "He was an expository teacher before I knew what that word meant," said Bryant. "He'd take a verse and just get incredible revelation on it and just sit there and talk about it for about thirty-five or forty minutes. And you'd just be sitting there with your mouth wide open going, Oh, yeah, I want to know this kind of God. This is awesome that He loves us this way."[6]

About this time, Keith Green was deeply affected by two books he read: *Why Revival Tarries* by Leonard Ravenhill, the older British evangelist who had settled in Lindale; and *Revival Lectures* by Charles Finney, a pioneering nineteenth-century American evangelist who invented many of the techniques used by later revivalists like Dwight Moody, Billy Sunday, and Billy Graham. (More than twenty years earlier, Finney's writings had made a huge impact on a young Pat Robertson, who was up in the woods of Connecticut on a spiritual retreat when his group stumbled on a stone monument marking Finney's birthplace. "It was as though we were on holy ground, and we kicked off our shoes and began laughing and praising God," Robertson wrote. "I knew the Holy Spirit had allowed us to come to this place for a sign. He was about to pour Himself out on us even as He did on Finney."[7]) Green was especially moved by a chapter in Finney's book called "Breaking up the Fallow Ground" and its discussion of how sins of omission were just as bad as sins of commission.

"It just pierced Keith to the very core and he just got on his face, locked himself up in an RV and prayed," Bryant remembered. "He came to the conclusion that he wasn't saved. And so he got saved again. And then he went like a wild animal after each one of us to get us saved. And we closed the community down for one solid week."[8]

Hard as Green drove himself and his Last Days community, he didn't candy coat the jolting messages he delivered to the large audiences that now turned out to see him perform music and preach. His follow-up album for Sparrow, *No Compromise*, described Green's emerging theology perfectly; it also rose to number one on the Christian music charts. He left his audiences sobbing, crying out, choking prayers for mercy and deliverance. "Do you know who the Christian idols are?" he challenged a large audience at a Christian music festival in Oregon. "I happen to be one of them. So is Andraé Crouch, Evie and B. J. Thomas. You can even idolize your pastor. . . . Remember that applause you gave me when I walked out? I didn't hear you applaud the Lord like that anytime today. . . . We're more excited about a 2nd Chapter of Acts concert than we are about the Second Coming! SIN!"[9]

For Green, it was no longer enough to bring about piecemeal conversions through altar calls; he wanted to trigger a full-scale revival of the sort Finney described. Green decided to bring his message to the congenial precincts of Oral Roberts University in Tulsa. When the university cancelled the event, Green showed up anyway with twenty-five members of Last Days. Preaching at Tulsa Christian Fellowship, the oldest charismatic gathering in the city, he attacked Christian hypocrisy. "You don't like it, do you," he asked the congregation. "You come to hear a concert, and you're getting cornered. The Christian walk is a bunch of squirming flesh getting nailed down to a cross. 'Hey man, I want a padded cross. You know, a Posture-Pedic Cross with nice springs in it. Something comfortable.' The Gospel is a no compromise, absolute sell-out for Jesus, one hundred percent walk!" He went on to assail the worshippers as a "brood of vipers and snakes! . . . Who call yourselves Christians and half-heartedly serve Him!"[10]

While the Last Days contingent was still in Tulsa, Oral Roberts reversed its decision and decided to let Green use its 11,500-seat Mabee Center for at least three nights of revival and to allow an altar call. Green preached hard against worldliness — sexual sins, drinking, and dope. He compared sin to venereal disease, fun to get but ultimately deadly, like "long-acting cyanide." "There is sexual immorality on this campus," he asserted. "And there is *homosexuality* on this campus." "There is *sin* in the camp! Oral Roberts has a dream, and it's of the Lord. His dream is to send out men and women of God from this campus all over the face of the earth. And every sin in your life produces a curse, because sin brings a curse. And I'm telling you, according to this principle, if there is sin in the camp — there's a curse upon the whole school." When a "clean-cut, neatly dressed young guy" went forward to publicly confess homosexual activity, a university pastor intervened, requesting no more sharing of personal sins in the amphitheater. Immediately, Green felt the energy of the revival dissipate. "What did I do wrong?" he sobbed afterward. "How did I grieve the Holy Spirit?"[11] The university politely requested that Green discontinue his revival.

As Green ascended to stardom, the Christian rock business was becoming appreciably larger and more commercially savvy, and Green did not spare it from his prophetic fervor. "Keith was really radical," said Bill Dwyer, a Vineyard pastor who knew Green. "He basically thought everyone was a whore." After much prayer, Green decided that Christian musicians should not demand payment for proclaiming the Gospel. He lobbied fellow evangelical artists to consider not selling tickets for their concerts. "The ticket prices for concerts are a nail in Jesus's hand," he told the Fellowship of Contemporary Christian Ministries, an industry group. "Unbelievers aren't going to pay to hear about Jesus because deep in their hearts they know [they] shouldn't have to. The Gospel is free!"[12]

Green resolved to distribute his next album to anyone who requested it for whatever they could afford to pay. He met with Sparrow president Billy Ray Hearn and asked to be released from the contract he had just signed so that he could start his own company and follow through on his plan to distribute the Gospel freely; Green had to mortgage one of his houses to press the record. The album that resulted, *So You Wanna Go Back to Egypt*, came out in May 1980, not long after Last Days relocated to Texas; one of its tracks, "Pledge My Head to Heaven," features an eleven-bar harmonica solo by Bob Dylan.

Green and Dylan had met through the Vineyard Fellowship, where Green had been ordained and sometimes served as music director. Dylan was writing songs for his first gospel album, *Slow Train Coming*, and he showed them to Keith and Melody. He came over for dinner, and they visited him at his Santa Monica offices. Melody remembered Dylan being enthusiastic and full of questions.

> Keith loved him deeply and they talked a lot. Once, however, Keith felt he went too far in trying to make a point. Later, in his journal, he wrote with regret, "Tried to be the Holy Spirit to Bob Dylan today."
>
> One night, we took Bob over to Buck and Annie's house along with Bill Maxwell. We listened to one of 2nd Chapter's new albums and

some rough mixes of Bob's latest album, *Saved*. Bob would tell us that he loved to pick up hitchhikers in his beat-up old car and talk to them about the Lord—without letting them know who he was. He said he was trying to read several chapters of the Bible a day. One of the things Keith counseled Bob to do was to try and get some time off the road so he could rest and study. He did attend a Bible school at the Vineyard for a while, but it seemed impossible for him to get much time "off." Nevertheless, Keith and Bob had kept in contact after we moved to Texas, and when Keith asked him to play on this album, we were thrilled that he said yes.[13]

## Slow Train Coming

In the fall of 1978, word began leaking out that Bob Dylan was born again. He was living in Los Angeles, licking his wounds after a rough few years that included a bitter divorce and a spectacularly failed film project. By then, Dylan had already transformed himself many times, from scruffy folk singer to psychedelic hipster to country crooner and family man to rock icon for aging boomers to ringleader of a traveling variety show. A motorcycle accident in 1966 slowed him down for a time, and he turned inward to a young family. After a fallow period and some knocking around, Dylan entered a period of intense artistic ferment in 1974: his first tour in eight years and the recording of his acclaimed *Blood on the Tracks* album, followed by the 1975 release of *The Basement Tapes* and the opening of the Rolling Thunder Revue tour. He had toured the world in 1978. Now he seemed to have become a Jesus Freak. Christian rock had landed its biggest trophy yet.

Dylan, of course, was Jewish; his fondness for biblical language and Christian music can't be taken as evidence of his personal piety. For several years, Dylan denied having fixed commitments to any organized religion. "I don't have much of a Jewish background," he told *Playboy* in 1978 shortly before his conversion. "I'm not a patriot to any creed. I believe in all of them and none of them. A devout Christian or Moslem can be just as effective as a devout Jew." But he had responded powerfully to black gospel music since before he was a teenager. Dylan's first public performance was in a school production of the *Black Hills Passion Play of South Dakota*. From the beginning of his folk-singing career, he wrote and covered songs drenched in biblical language, like Woody Guthrie's "Jesus Christ" and the traditional "Jesus Met the Woman at the Well." Dylan's debut album contained several songs drawn from gospel sources, including lines like "Jesus gonna make my dyin' bed" and "My heart stopped beatin' and my hands turned cold / Now I believe what the Bible told." His 1962 song "Long Ago, Far Away" began and ended with allusions to the crucifixion of Christ.[14]

Dylan's interest in the Bible was not purely literary; Paul Stookey of Peter, Paul and Mary wrote that Dylan had encouraged him to read the Bible in 1967, and Dylan's mother reported around that time that he kept the Bible on a stand in the center of his study and referred to it often.[15] Meanwhile, a cult had taken shape around the singer himself. Dylan was lionized both politically and musically—politically, for his music's pro–civil rights and antiwar messages ("The Lonesome Death of Hattie Carroll," "The Death of Emmett Till," "Only a Pawn in Their Game," "Masters of War," "Talkin' World War III Blues"); and musically, for his contributions to the folk revival, for being the heir apparent to Woody Guthrie and Pete Seeger.

But Dylan quickly tired of the prophetic role. It wasn't easy to be the voice of his generation and also keep the flame of authentic American vernacular music. By the midsixties he had rejected both roles, claiming he'd been misunderstood from the start. "I never did renounce a role in politics, because I never played one in politics," he said years later. "It would be comical for me to think that I played a role."[16] The 1964 song "It Ain't Me, Babe" may have been addressed to a lover, but it could also be heard as defiantly telling off his many political and musical followers. (One line asserts: "Someone to die for you and more / But it ain't me, babe.") "My Back Pages," written the same year, scorns causes and ideology as futile, somehow both superannuated and sophomoric.

John Lennon could raise a media tempest by suggesting that the Beatles were bigger than Christ, but the thought of such a comparison made Dylan cringe. It was true, he recalled, that he'd been labeled "Legend, Icon, Enigma (Buddha in European Clothes was my favorite)—stuff like that, but that was all right. These titles were placid and harmless, threadbare, easy to get around with them. Prophet, Messiah, Savior—those are tough ones."[17]

Ironically, his disavowal of these roles placed Dylan even more squarely in the mold of the Jesus that had captivated boomer evangelicals. The figure of Jesus has acted as a Rorschach test throughout American history, a screen on which Americans have projected their fondest cultural values.[18] Most visibly in *Jesus Christ Superstar*, the sixties cultural front had created a Messiah very much in the image of Bob Dylan. He was young, shaggy, given to esoteric sayings and cryptic outbursts, unmistakably Jewish and sympathetic to the downtrodden. This Jesus had very little use for established religion and conventional politics, either of the ruling class or the militant opposition. He was streetwise enough to hang with young rebels, yet virile enough to attract women. It was no stretch to imagine this Jesus leading a gang of flower children in lower Manhattan, as he does in *Godspell*. Clearly, he was a reluctant rebel, a diffident prophet, an antihero, someone who dutifully shouldered but frequently resented the demands being made upon him both by his inner circle and by the larger community of newfound followers. This was a Jesus one could imagine singing "It Ain't Me, Babe" to Mary Magdalene but just as easily to Simon Zealotes, leader of the radical Jewish revolutionaries who, in *Superstar*, sought to recruit Christ to their cause.

Dylan's conversion to evangelical Christianity in 1978 may have taken many of his fans by surprise, but he had been moving in that direction for a decade. Well before he turned thirty, Dylan had become a strong proponent of what was coming to be called family values. "From '66 on, I was trying to raise a family, and that was contrary to the whole epidemic of the '60s," he told an interviewer in 1989. "Most people were running away from home and trying to get away from their parents. That was never intentional on my part, trying to run away from anything. My family was more important to me than any kind of generational '60s thing. Still is. To find some meaning in the '60s for me is real far-fetched."[19] The Woodstock festival "was the sum total of all this bullshit," he said a few years later. "And it seemed to have something to do with me, this Woodstock Nation, and everything it represented."[20]

In the early seventies, hounded in both Manhattan and rural Woodstock by cultish fans and relentless Dylanologists, Dylan and his young family had fled the East Coast for Los Angeles, eventually landing in a Malibu beach house (near where Cat Stevens nearly drowned and accepted Allah). He published a book of poems titled *Tarantula*, acted in a Sam Peckinpah movie with Kris Kristofferson (for which he wrote the soundtrack and its signature song, "Knocking on Heaven's Door"), and released *Planet Waves*, an album that reached number one in the charts. Always restless, Dylan, backed by the Band, embarked in 1974 on his first tour since his motorcycle accident; it went on to be one of the most successful rock 'n' roll tours in history.

That same year, the young Calvary Chapel minister Kenn Gulliksen was called to ministry in Los Angeles. Raised Lutheran, Gulliksen had begun speaking in tongues as a teenager. After a stint in Alaska with the Air Force, he was caught up in the Calvary Chapel scene, ordained as a pastor in 1971, and sent to El Paso, Texas, to plant a new youth-oriented church dubbed the Jesus Chapel. Showcasing Maranatha! bands who would drive over a thousand miles from Orange County, the musical services attracted hundreds of worshippers on Friday nights with a mix of Jesus music, worship, and preaching by the artists; parents of the worshippers would wait outside. Jesus Chapel proved especially attractive to mainline Episcopalians from across town. "One night, eighty of them showed up, including the rector," according to Gulliksen. "We prayed for them and they all were filled with the Holy Spirit; many of them spoke in tongues, including the rector." The group was inspired to begin their own charismatic church. "Kenn was a natural church-planter and had the most charming personality of anyone I have ever known, and besides that, he was very funny," explained Carol Wimber, wife of John Wimber, who a few years later took over leadership of the Vineyard.[21]

Returning to Southern California in 1974, Gulliksen felt called to minister specifically to the L.A. entertainment scene. Bible study groups began meeting in the homes of two Christian rockers, Chuck Girard and Larry Norman. "It was a very non-formal, very casual and very alive kind of place," recalled one participant. "It was also filled with people from the arts community." After several years of experience with successful church planting, Gulliksen was confident that his outreach to artists would succeed. "I also knew how to teach the Bible by then," he explained. "I played guitar and sat on a stool and led some worship and taught the Bible, answered questions in homes, and at the end invited anyone who wanted to receive Christ to come for prayer, which they did in droves. So we kept having to move from place to place to place to place."[22] It was at one of these Bible studies that Keith Green experienced his definitive Christian conversion.

The Vineyard was experimenting with different ways to use Jesus music in their meetings, motivating people to actively participate rather than sit back and let the music wash over them. "As far as worship went, we were the only church in the area who was doing simple choruses: 'Thy Loving Kindness,' 'Thou O Lord Art a Shield about Me,' 'Father I Adore You,' etc.," explained Bill Dwyer, who was born again in 1971 while stationed in El Paso with the U.S. Army. He got involved in the Jesus Chapel and moved from El Paso to Los Angeles with Gulliksen; he was on the staff of the Vineyard church where Dylan became a Christian. "It was almost always led by a solo guitar player and was very powerful in that it was driven by the congregational vocals. With so many music types, the harmonies were incredible. You could 'feel the brush of angel's wings.'"[23]

Not all of these experiments worked. An early attempt to create what would later be called a praise band "turned out to be a big flop," according to Dwyer.

People really wanted the intimacy and the sound of congregational voices to dominate, not a band. . . . We went through periods of having fairly weak worship leaders, but it was not a huge crisis because it was congregationally driven worship. Also, it was commonplace for Kenn to invite an artist to sing either after worship or at the end of the service, sometimes impromptu. I recall one Sunday, he simply asked Debby Boone if she would sing "You Light up My Life." Another when he asked Tata Vega to close with an impromptu version of the Lord's Prayer. Tata had just gotten saved and she stood up and said something like, "This is a real heavy song. You can't be singin' this song on Sunday morning if you got laid last night." It caught us a little off guard, but we loved it. That was the Vineyard; spiritual but not religious.[24]

Even before he found the Vineyard, Dylan was increasingly surrounded by born-again musicians. The freewheeling, medicine-show style of the Rolling Thunder Revue had been an intense, quasi-spiritual experience for many participants. The roistering entourage included Dylan, his wife Sara, their young children, Dylan's mother, Joan Baez, Roger McGuinn, Ramblin' Jack Elliot, Scarlet Rivera, Ronnie Hawkins, Bob Neuwirth, Ronee Blakley, Mick Ronson, David Blue, and Allen Ginsberg. Dylan was in peak form, full of improvisational energy, and other members of the tour felt themselves in the presence of genius. The hallmark of the tour was theatrical spontaneity; performers wore costumes, masks, and face paint and didn't always know where they would be playing the next night. At first, there was no advance publicity. Tickets went on sale the day of the performance, advertised on college radio stations and through word of mouth, and the tour deliberately sought out small venues.

That Dylan was meditating on Jesus and Christian themes is obvious from the film he made using the Rolling Thunder entourage as its cast. *Renaldo and Clara* was edited down to four hours from 400 hours of footage shot during the tour. The film—a surreal montage of concert footage; meandering, inconclusive conversations between men and women; trains and buses barreling through frozen landscapes; long-stemmed roses; bored, beautiful, dark-haired women in a bordello doing their nails and chatting—features a surprising number of Christian references and images. There are Bible-waving evangelists, including a pair who hold forth atop of a vw bus parked in front of the federal building on Wall Street where George Washington delivered his first inaugural address; they descend from the bus to do battle with hecklers. There are shots of a cement crucifix and statue of Mary in the Grotto of Our Lady of Lourdes in Lowell, Massachusetts, Jack Kerouac's hometown. Allen Ginsberg and Dylan (playing the character Renaldo) stroll through the grotto examining the sculptures, while Ginsberg narrates the Stations of the Cross in French and English. Another scene takes place in front of the Apollo Theater in Harlem, where a woman from the street begins to recount the prophecy of Daniel, which is central to end-times belief. At one point, we hear Dylan singing a gospel hymn:

Tell me what will you do when Jesus comes.
Will you tear out your hair, will you sit down in your chair?
Tell me what will you do when Jesus comes.

"Jesus is the most identifiable figure in Western culture, and yet he was exploited, used and exploited," Dylan pointed out to a writer for *Rolling Stone* who asked him about the film. "We all have been." Dylan was particularly interested in Jesus as a mortal man and healer who "goes to India, finds out how to be a healer and becomes one. But see, I believe that he overstepped his duties a little bit. He accepted and took on the bad karma of all the people he healed. And he was filled with so much bad karma that the only way out was to burn him up." Later in the same interview, Dylan opined: "People relate to the masochism, to the spikes in his hand, to the blood coming out, to the fact that he was crucified. What would have happened to him if he hadn't been crucified? That's what draws people to him."[25]

Shortly after the Rolling Thunder Revue disbanded, as many as fifteen of its members, including Roger McGuinn, David Mansfield, Steven Soles, and T-Bone Burnett, had born-again experiences and became evangelical Christians. "Beginning in 1976, something happened all across the world," Burnett recalled of that time. "It happened to Bono and The Edge and Larry Mullen in Ireland. . . . and it happened here in Los Angeles: There was a spiritual movement."[26] A copy of C. S. Lewis's *Mere Christianity* circulated among musicians, wives, and girlfriends, winning more converts. At a concert in San Diego in November 1978, someone in the crowd threw Dylan a silver cross, which he picked up. He had endured a punishing year, with poor reviews of *Renaldo and Clara*, his latest album (*Street-Legal*), and even the North American concert tour he was embarked on. And there was lingering damage from his divorce from Sara the previous year, which included an ugly custody battle that left Dylan feeling isolated from his children.

About that time — Dylan wasn't specific about when or where — he had a classic evangelical experience of the sort that was immediately recognizable to any Jesus Freak. "There was a presence in the room that couldn't have been anybody but Jesus," he said. "I truly had a born-again experience, if you want to call it that. . . . Jesus put his hand on me. It was a physical thing. I felt it. I felt it all over me. I felt my whole body tremble. The glory of the Lord knocked me down and picked me up." More specifically, Dylan said, "Jesus did appear to me as King of Kings, and Lord of Lords. . . . I believe every knee shall bow one day, He did die on the cross for all mankind."[27]

Dylan's circle at this point included a girlfriend named Mary Alice Artes, an actress and single mom who lived with her two kids in a house he owned in Brentwood. After attending a meeting of Gulliksen's Vineyard Fellowship, Artes confessed that she "was being kept by a very rich man," recalled Dwyer. "She didn't mention Dylan's name. The pastors told her, 'You need to leave — that's not a faithful way to live.' She said, 'Well, where should I go?' They said, 'You can move in with us.' That's how we did it back then. And so she moved out, and that absolutely blew Dylan's mind. 'What do you mean you're moving out? You're leaving a house in Brentwood with all your expenses paid?'" Jerry Bryant remembered Dylan being "madder than a wet hen" when Artes moved out. "As a result of this experience, he went to at least six weeks of our discipleship school at the Vineyard — I think at the time it was in Reseda — and that's when he was hanging out with Keith [Green]. He and his girlfriend weren't living together anymore."[28]

Artes moved in with Paul and Kathy Emond, both musicians who had recently joined the staff at the Vineyard. "Mary Alice's radical conversion got Bob's attention, and he called the Vineyard to talk," said Dwyer. "I was asked to meet with him, but other than being a huge Dylan fan, I knew I was not the guy for the job. It seemed better to send Larry [Myers] and Paul. It was the right decision, and Larry continued his friendship with Bob and helped him a great deal."[29] Myers had gone to Dallas Theological Seminary, the stomping grounds of Hal Lindsey and end-times prophecy; he was the only Vineyard pastor in the fledgling church who had graduated from seminary, and he had worked as a chaplain at a large hospital in Dallas. Myers was also a talented musician who played mandolin, violin, and rhythm guitar with Love Song founder Chuck Girard. Myers dropped in for several one-on-one sessions with Dylan at his Malibu home, answering many questions about the Bible.

To the best of my ability, I started at the beginning of Genesis and walked through the Old Testament and the New Testament and ended in Revelation. I tried to clearly express what is the historical, orthodox understanding of who Jesus is. It was a quite intelligent conversation with a man who was seriously intent on understanding the Bible. There was no attempt to convince, manipulate, or pressure this man into anything. But in my view, God spoke through His Word, the Bible, to a man who had been seeking for many years. . . . Sometime in the next few days, privately and on his own, Bob accepted Christ and believed that Jesus Christ is indeed the Messiah. After yet more time and further serious deliberation, Bob was baptized.

The two developed a musical relationship as well as a spiritual one. "Bob asked him to come with the band on the road," according to Gulliksen, "so that Larry would be there to lead them in prayer and Bible study, and to minister to him personally. He and Bob became very close and trusted each other. Larry was often the sounding board for Bob to share his lyrics."[30]

Dylan also completed discipleship curriculum held at the Vineyard. The class met from 8:30 to noon in a backroom above a realtor's office on a strip in Reseda. During breaks, Dylan would stand out in the parking lot, smoking and chatting with his girlfriend, dressed in a leather jacket and cap. "He spent four months every day in a classroom and it was out of that came the albums of *Saved* and *Slow Train Coming*," according to Gulliksen. In addition to the Vineyard meetings, Dylan attended Bible study at the home of Al Kasha, an Academy Award–winning writer of musical scores whom Dylan had known from New York since the early 1960s. Kasha was himself a Jew who had also converted in 1978. "Dylan would keep us up until three or four o'clock in the morning asking us all kinds of questions, going from the Old Testament to the New Testament," recalled Kasha. "He would want to see consistencies. He would say, 'Why does Isaiah think differently than Jeremiah but they're all prophetic?' . . . Dylan's investigative mind was trying to see why one Scripture didn't seem consistent to another, but of course, it was consistent."[31]

Jerry Bryant remembered a more characteristically aloof and inscrutable Dylan. "He came over to Last Days community when Keith was in Woodland Hill to write songs with Keith for his album," he said. "So that's where I got to meet him and talk to him. Couldn't get close to him. He was a very distant person, very hurt, very wounded, never could look you hardly in the eye. . . . He expressed himself more through music than anything. He couldn't talk with very many people. I think he really appreciated Keith's radicalness. And yet as two prophets, they probably clashed some too, you know. But he did play harmonica on Keith's one album."[32]

Public worship was a problem because of Dylan's fame. "People would just freak out — 'Ooh, it's Bob Dylan!'" remembered Dwyer. "We were constantly telling them, just leave him alone." The Vineyard folks were celebrity savvy, but many evangelical Christians didn't get it. "Quite honestly, we were shocked by everyone's reaction to Bob," Dwyer said. "Many wanted to use him in ministry or push him to be on the 700 Club. Our values were different. We were just happy this poor guy found Jesus and his life was changed. We wanted to protect him and see him grow." The media exacerbated the problem, according to Gulliksen. "It was absolute craziness because we all of a sudden had thirty or forty media showing up at our services, writing absolutely ludicrous stories," he said. "If Bob wasn't there, they'd make up stories about why he wasn't there. They would talk about us having sections cordoned off just for him."[33]

For Bryant, Dylan's case was symptomatic of how the Jesus Movement often blew its opportunities with well-known musical figures. "Some of the people who came on board at the beginning were Dylan and Kristofferson and Rita Coolidge," he pointed out. "One of the early converts was Eric Clapton. There was no one there to disciple or mentor them. A few people made it, like Kerry Livgren from Kansas. . . . But man, we lost. . . . The church, when they'd see a famous person come to the Lord through the Jesus Movement, they said, 'Come to our church and do a benefit concert, we need to raise some money for this.' And they just got majorly turned off because they were looking for reality; they weren't looking for religion and keeping an institution going. They wanted to have community."[34]

Dylan's seeker conversations continued a few months later at the Muscle Shoals studio in rural Alabama, where Aretha Franklin, among others, had recorded many of the great soul albums of the sixties. Her producer for those sessions, soul veteran Jerry Wexler, was also brought in to produce Dylan's new album. Though Wexler initially rebuffed Dylan's evangelical overtures, telling him "I'm a sixty-two-year-old, card-carrying Jewish atheist," the two evidently joined in spirited discussion of scripture as they worked on the album. Apprehensive of the project at first, Wexler was "knocked out" by Dylan's lyrics. Another music-business veteran, promoter Bill Graham, was similarly impressed when Dylan first brought his gospel songs to the public at San Francisco's Warfield Theater in November 1979, the beginning of a six-month tour that would showcase the new Christian material. "From night to night, the show keeps getting stronger," he observed. "It is awesome. I am a Jew, and I am deeply moved by what this man is doing. It's a very profound public display of personal convictions." (Graham had his limits, though; he once complained to a man passing out Jews for Jesus tracts that Dylan was "pushing this stuff down my throat" and asked how he could get Dylan to quit.)[35]

As in other major turning points in Dylan's career, reactions from audiences and critics to the new gospel material ran the gamut. "If [Dylan] could have found a more antipathetical posture for where the rock scene was at in 1979 than Pentecostal Christian religion I can't imagine what it would be," declared a critic.[36] Performing "with ugly musicians around stadiums of the resentful damned," wrote one biographer, Dylan "was about as hip as General Franco."[37] Some journalists exaggerated the intensity and extent of negative crowd reactions, claiming boos, catcalls, and mass walkouts that hadn't taken place (irking Dylan immensely). Some audiences clearly were more hostile than others. But even for those inclined to give Dylan the benefit of the doubt, the greatest fear was that Dylan was permanently abandoning all of his beloved earlier material for dubious religious reasons. No one knew where this new spiritual direction was taking him.

Larry Norman recalled being at a Dylan concert with Pat Boone (who at one point jokingly offered Norman a joint that was making the rounds) and seeing Dylan really getting "kicked around. Christians were so rude to him. They would yell at him from the audience. He sings all gospel music, but he sings two songs that he wrote before. They're actually about his Jewish quest to see God. But all the Christians know is, that's not on his record! So they're booing him for singing a song that wasn't about Jesus when it was totally germane. And then he was getting it from the non-Christians. They were booing him and yelling out, play 'Lay, Lady, Lay,' play 'Everybody Must Get Stoned.' He just couldn't get any breathing room."[38]

Dylan himself played on this audience ambivalence even as he refused to perform his non-Christian songs. "I told you 'The Times They Are a-Changing,' and they did," he reminded an audience in Albuquerque. "I said the answer was 'Blowing in the Wind,' and it was. I'm telling you now Jesus is coming back, and He is! — And there is no other way of salvation."[39] For once, the diffident spokesman wasn't reluctant to deliver a full-throated prophetic message. For several months, the normally laconic Dylan gave camp meeting–style testimonies at his shows, further angering fans who didn't like the new material and wanted to hear older songs that he was refusing to play. (These sermons were even collected in a curious little volume called Saved! The Gospel Speeches of Bob Dylan, published by Hanuman Books in 1990.)

Like a barnstorming evangelist, Dylan hammered home several themes during his concert testimonies of late 1979 and early 1980. The times were perilous, chaotic, desperate, he pointed out, and the end was rapidly approaching. Yet a better day was coming after Jesus returned, when the lion would lie down with the lamb. Many in his audience were troubled, he pointed out, even considering suicide, while others falsely thought they were just fine. Dylan himself had found the one true solid rock to cling to—Jesus—that he recommended to everyone else. This truth was not something found in churches or conventional religion. He spoke often of Satan as a constant presence in the world, and of demons, the kind that had bedeviled Andraé Crouch. "What a friendly crowd!" he exclaimed in Akron. "I'm not used to friendly crowds. We're used to the Devil's working all kinds of mischief in the crowds we've faced. Just looking out at them demons."[40]

Satan's hand was in everything, even the music that had nourished Dylan. "You know, when I was growing up," he told a crowd in Syracuse, "I used to listen to Hank Williams, Gene Vincent, Little Richard, all those people. I think they formed my style in one way or another. I can't help this type of music I play, this is just the kind of type I've always played. I know what kind of other people are playing this sort of music today, tell me some strange things. And the Devil's takin' rock 'n' roll music and he's used it for his own purposes." He elaborated in Akron: "The Devil's taken rock 'n' roll music and made it *his* music, taken away this free education and made *his* education. Taken away this mess and made *his* mess."[41]

Dylan seemed to realize that he was facing skeptics, and he took the opportunity to remind them of his prophetic authority. "I didn't know a lot of these things forty years ago either," he told a Buffalo audience, "and I don't know why I'm up here telling you this, but I've always told you the truth; I've never told you to vote for nobody, never told you to bow to no guru, never told you to buy no product, never told you what to wear, not how to cut your hair." Preaching the Gospel to rock fans could be thankless, but someone had to do it, and it might as well be someone with a record for telling it like it is. "Anyway, I know not too many people are gonna tell you about Jesus," he admitted in Pittsburgh. "I know Jackson Browne's not gonna do it, 'cause he's running on empty. I know Bruce Springsteen, bless him, is not gonna do it, 'cause he's born to run, and he's *still* running. And Bob Seger's not gonna do it, 'cause he's running against the wind. Somebody's gotta do it!"[42]

Like Keith Green, Larry McGuire, and virtually all Jesus People, Dylan had no sympathy for non-Christian spirituality. "We're not gonna be talking about no mysticism, no meditation, none of them Eastern religions," he told an audience in Hartford. "We're just gonna be talking about Jesus. Demons don't like that name." Confronting a hostile audience in San Francisco ("You all know how to be real rude! You know about the spirit of the Anti-Christ?"), he told a long story about a "certain guru" from Los Angeles who had given Dylan a videotape of himself at a convention of 10,000 followers.

> And what he was doing onstage was, he was sitting there with a load of flowers and things. He sure did look pretty though, sitting up there, kind of like on a throne, y'know? Listening to him talk on that tape, he said what life's about is life's to have fun, and I'm gonna show you how to have fun! And he had a big fire extinguisher and he would spray it out on the people, and they all laughed and had a good time. They took their clothes off. . . . And he said that he was God—he did say that. He said that God's inside him and he is God. And they could think of him as God. I want to tell you this because they say there's many of these people walking around. They may not come out and say they're God, but they're just waiting for the opportunity.[43]

When Dylan performed live, it became clear how significant the vivid visual and sonic presence of the black church was in creating the Christian aura that surrounded him. Like Billy Preston and Andraé Crouch in earlier years, black influences and traditions were a visible sign of the faith. Performing at Toronto's Massey Hall in April 1980, Dylan played only the new Christian songs from beginning to end: "I Believe in You," "When He Returns," "Man Gave Names to All the Animals," "Precious Angel," "Saved," "In the Garden." Behind and to Dylan's left were his five churchy backup singers, all African American—one man and four women dressed in spangled dresses and boots. Dylan introduced "Solid Rock" with a few words of testimony: "I don't know what you got to hold on to. But I've got something called a solid rock to hold on to. That was manifested in the *flesh* [the backup singers respond audibly as to a black preacher], and justified in the *spirit* [response], and seen by *angels* [response], and preached on in the *world* [response]." As the concert neared the end, Dylan offered himself, somewhat stiffly, as a spiritual counselor. "Anyway, I want you people to tell me you'll write to me now," he said gamely. "I want you to write to me now, tell me what you think. Maybe if you got any questions, just write 'em in there, just send 'em in. Prayer requests, questions, any of that."[44]

Introducing the band during the encore, Dylan admitted people were skeptical of his newfound faith. "Somebody's got to have to tell you about Jesus, right?" he asked the audience. "I know sometimes people say to me, Bob, how can you believe that stuff? I was raised in a church. Either Methodist, or Catholic, or Calvinist, or whatever. But there's churches and there's churches. Unless you're in a spiritual church you're in no church at all. It says that the Last Days, God's gonna pour his spirit out on all flesh, and it's happening right now." With the words "Are you ready?," the band launched into Dylan's Larry Normanesque song of waiting for the last days. ("I Will Love Him," another song Dylan sang in Toronto, includes the prophecy-laden lines: "He said when the fig tree was blooming He will be at the gate / He was talking about the state of Israel in 1948.")

With the fervent conviction of a new Christian, Dylan took his Gospel message to the temple of worldly irreverence: *Saturday Night Live*. Four impassioned backup singers helped compensate for his own tense and washed-out appearance on the October 1979 show. Dylan brought three hard-edged songs from his recently released *Slow Train Coming*: "Gotta Serve Somebody," which won a Grammy that year (and which Dylan performed on the awards show); "I Believe in You," which Dylan bawled out above some formidable organ support; and "When You Gonna Wake Up?," with its scattershot diatribe against Karl Marx, Henry Kissinger, "adulterers in churches and pornography in the schools," crooked lawmakers, shady doctors, and "spiritual advisors and gurus" peddling "counterfeit philosophies." All three songs were marked by Dylan's new faith, although they were equivocal enough to be heard without a Christian message; the unmistakable evangelical songs would come on the next album, *Saved*. But by late 1979, most of the SNL audience would have known about Dylan's conversion, and still the applause was loud and long.

Somewhat unexpected was the positive response of seasoned rock critics to *Slow Train Coming*, at least to the music if not the message. Veteran Dylan critic Paul Williams was so inspired by Dylan's Warfield shows in San Francisco that he attended every concert for a week straight, concluding that by the fifth night, the concert was "the equal of any concert Dylan has ever done. . . . His new songs were unmistakably revealed as among the best he's ever written." Charles Shaar Murray wrote that Dylan "returns to the finest vocal form he's ever had." He continued: "Every singer who has ever copped an inflection from Bob Dylan is hereby politely escorted to the back door and ceremonially thrown down the stairs. Moreover, Dylan is still the chairman of the board of rock composers. . . . Far from having his wits addled by religion, Dylan would seem to have sharpened up his act all round."[45]

Even in hard-to-please *Rolling Stone*, editor Jann Wenner praised the album as being Dylan's finest musically, lauding the "strength and simplicity" of his new songs as "equal [to] his early classics." "Dylan is the greatest singer of our times," Wenner declared. "No one is better. No one, in objective fact, is even very close." And there was that unexpected nod from the musical establishment: Best Male Rock Vocal for "Gotta Serve Somebody," Dylan's first Grammy (along with a Dove Award—gospel music's Grammy equivalent—for Best Inspirational Album).[46]

None of these critics, and relatively few record buyers, cared for Dylan's theology. What they admired was the musical craft embedded in the songs and the manifest passion of the performances. As would be expected, attempts to ferret out the essence of Dylan's theology, and his investment in it, were extensive and long lasting. Those who didn't like the songs, and even some who did, objected to their uncompromising, judgmental tone. "What's new is Dylan's use of religious imagery, not to discover and shape a vision of what's at stake in the world," Greil Marcus pointed out, "but to sell a prepackaged doctrine he's received from someone else."[47] This vision was starkly Manichean: the world was black and white, controlled by Satan or Jesus, and everyone had to choose sides, with their eternal destiny in the balance.

While few rock critics knew enough about Christianity to understand the nuances of Dylan's beliefs, journalist Ron Rosenbaum, who had conducted a lengthy interview with Dylan for *Playboy* not long before his conversion, shrewdly singled out the particular religious milieu that shaped Dylan's gospel music. "The trouble is not the Christianity but the Californian in the conversion," he wrote. "One tell-tale sign that California is the culprit is the logo of Dylan's Vineyard church in Tarzana. There's a picture of Jesus in that logo which makes Him look like a Marin County coke dealer, a late-seventies smoothie, a quintessentially Californian Christ." Rosenbaum urged Dylan not necessarily to forsake Christ for Judaism, but to come home to New York where he belonged.[48]

Missed by critics and journalists, and crucial for grasping Dylan's affinity to the Religious Right, was Christian apocalypticism. It was this thread that linked Dylan's gospel songs both to his earlier folk music material and to the evangelical revival that helped produce the Religious Right. Apocalyptic fears fueled by prophecy belief were crucially different from nonreligious ones, however. If the secular Left read the times as calling for practical policies like the nuclear-freeze campaign, many evangelicals spun the warning signs differently. War meant the beginning of authentic eternal peace. Peacemakers were likely the Antichrist or his minions. The worse things got, the better—if you were saved.

At one of his bumpiest shows—for unruly university students in Tempe, Arizona—Dylan ended up giving an extended gloss on Lindsey's *The Late*

*Great Planet Earth*. He spoke of the book of Revelation, the northern power, Rosh, whose symbol is the bear, and of another country from the east with an army of 200 million. His message bombed. "I shouldn't have been telling it to them," he admitted later at a different concert. "I just got carried away. I mentioned it to them and then I watched. And Russia was going to come down and attack in the Middle East. It says this in the Bible. . . . And all these people—there must've been 50,000. . . . Maybe it wasn't 50,000, 5,000 maybe. . . . I don't know maybe three—3,000—they all booed. Everybody just booed; and it was the whole auditorium of people. I said, Russia's gonna come down and attack the Middle East. And it was Oooh! They couldn't hear that. They didn't believe it. And a month later Russia moved her troops into, I think, Afghanistan."[49]

Beginning in 1979, many of Dylan's song lyrics and public remarks were consistent with the conservative Christian worldview reshaping American politics. One report claimed he had joined the Assemblies of God, a fiercely conservative Pentecostal denomination. At times, Dylan sided with proponents of traditional Christian morality. "There's a form of medium called Zen," he said at an April 1980 concert in Montreal. "They got a way of twisting things all around, make what's good seem bad and what's bad seem good. I was talking to a girl the other day who just lives from orgasm to orgasm. I know that's a strange thing, but that's what she's said to do because of these so-called modern times. But she's not satisfied." He called birth control "another hoax that women shouldn't have bought, but they did. I mean, if a man don't wanna knock up a woman, that's his problem, you know what I mean." He continued: "But the problem is not abortion. The problem is the whole concept behind abortion. Abortion is the end result of going out and screwing somebody to begin with. Casual sex."[50]

At a concert in Hartford, Dylan reminisced about the tour's first shows in San Francisco. "I think it's either one-third or two-thirds of the population that are homosexuals in San Francisco," he mused. "Now, I guess they're working up to a hundred percent. I don't know. But anyway, it's a growing place for homosexuals, and I read they have homosexual politics, and it's a political party. I don't mean it's going on in somebody's closet, I mean it's political! All right, you know what I'm talking about? Anyway, I would just think, well, I guess the iniquity's not yet full. And I don't wanna be around when it is." Dylan conceded in an interview that the Bible labels homosexuality "an abomination." Asked about his old friend Allen Ginsberg, he responded, "Yeah, well, but that's no reason for *me* to condemn somebody, because they drink or they're corrupt in orthodox ways or they wear their shirt inside out. I mean, that's *their* scene. It certainly doesn't matter to *me*. I've got no ax to grind with any of that."[51]

Yet Dylan maintained a degree of separation from family-values evangelicals. When journalist Robert Hilburn asked him about politics in November 1980, he responded: "I think people have to be careful about all that. . . . It's real dangerous. You can find anything you want in the Bible. You can twist it around any way you want and a lot of people do that. I just don't think you can legislate morality. . . . The basic thing, I feel, is to get in touch with Christ yourself." His politics during this period might be described as biblically grounded libertarian populism. "Well, for me, there is no right and there is no left," he told journalist Mikal Gilmore in 1986. "There's truth and there's untruth, y'know? There's honesty and there's hypocrisy. Look in the Bible, you don't see nothing about right or left."[52]

Asked whether being a Christian entailed conservative views, he invoked the parable of the rich man entering heaven being like a camel entering the eye of a needle. "I mean is *that* conservative?" he asked. "I don't know, I've heard a lot of preachers say how God wants everybody to be wealthy and healthy. Well, it doesn't say that in the Bible." Even with his old admirer Carter locked in a tough reelection campaign, Dylan had almost nothing to say about electoral politics. "They're running for president now," he said vaguely in Worcester. "They're gonna save the country. Gonna save the country. But you can't save nothing unless *you're* saved."[53]

Dylan was leery of globalization, both for theological reasons and for its impact on workers. He complained about the line of thinking that "we're not just the United States anymore, we're *global*. We're thinkin' in terms of the whole world because communications come right into your house. Well, that's what the book of Revelation is all *about*. And you can just about *know* that anybody who comes out for peace is *not* for peace." Globalism was shaping the economy in ominous ways: "Right now, it seems like in the States, and most other countries, too, there's a big push on to make a big *global* country — *one big country* — where you can get all the materials from one place and assemble them someplace else and sell 'em in another place, and the whole world is just all one, controlled by the same people, you know?" Computers were an important and threatening part of this new globalist regime. "Everything is computerized now, it's all computers," Dylan insisted. "I see that as the beginning of the end."[54]

End-times prophecy remained his reference point. Even as he revised some of his earlier statements ("I never said I'm born again. That's just a media term."), Dylan reiterated: "I believe in the book of Revelation. The leaders of this world are eventually going to play God, if they're not *already* playing God, and eventually a man will come that everybody will think is God." He added: "The battle of Armageddon is specifically spelled out, where it will be fought, and if you wanna get technical, *when* it will be fought. And the battle of Armageddon definitely will be fought in the Middle East." In his concert homilies, he referred often to events in Iran, where Americans were held hostage at the U.S. embassy. "The situation in Iran, the students rebelling, you know, even over here they're rebelling," Dylan said, referring to anti-Shah demonstrations in the United States. "They don't let the Iranians sneak into the whorehouses. But that don't matter much because we know this world will be destroyed."[55] Still, Dylan balanced his constant warnings of end times and Armageddon with Isaiah's peaceful image of the millennium: the lion lying down with the lamb.

Dylan's hostility toward globalism, economic integration, computer technology, corporate elites, and efforts to achieve world peace ("There is not going to *be* any peace," he declared on more than one occasion); his support for Israel; and his conviction that Armageddon would begin in the Middle East were all echoes of a theology preached by Chuck Smith to the hippie Jesus People, popularized for a wide paperback readership by Hal Lindsey, carried into the L.A. entertainment world by the Calvary Chapel acolytes who founded the Vineyard, and expressed in Christian rock by Larry Norman. His views on traditional morality, tempered somewhat by a libertarian streak (itself a strain in Jesus's Gospel teaching), were part and parcel of this evangelical worldview. Dylan's nationalism never wavered. "God will stay with America as long as America stays with God," he announced a few months before the 1980 election. "A lot of people, maybe even the president, maybe a lot of senators, you hear them speak and they'll speak of the attributes of God. But none of them are speaking about being a disciple of Christ."[56]

## The Perfect Storm

The storming of the U.S. embassy in Tehran on 4 November 1979 and the seizure of sixty-six American hostages by Iranian students was the beginning of the perfect political storm that would bring the Carter presidency to an end in exactly one year. Four months earlier, Carter had delivered his "crisis of confidence" speech bemoaning Americans' loss of a belief in progress. "Our people are losing that faith not only in government itself," he observed, "but in the ability of citizens to serve as the ultimate rulers and shapers of our democracy." Carter went on to propose a detailed energy plan, but the developments in Iran posed an even greater threat to national morale. The hostage crisis, with its stark images of blindfolded American hostages paraded by their captors and furious students burning U.S. flags and chanting anti-American slogans, dominated nightly news through the November 1980 election.

"Never before had a news story so thoroughly captured the imagination of the U.S. public," wrote a Carter administration official. "Never had the nation sat so totally transfixed before its television sets awaiting the latest predictable chants of 'Death to America' alternating with the day's interview with a brave relative of one of the hostages." And it preoccupied the administration during a brutal election year. "There were two White Houses," explained Hamilton Jordan, "one working on the hostages, the other working on everything else."[57]

Everything else included an invasion of Afghanistan by 85,000 Soviet troops, who arrived on Christmas Day to replace the current leader with a pro-Moscow hardliner. In response to these moves by the nation considered Gog by prophecy believers, Carter was forced to make a series of painful decisions: halt U.S. grain sales to the Soviet Union; withdraw U.S. athletes from the Moscow Olympics; and, most disappointing of all, ask the Senate to table the SALT II nuclear-arms treaty, which he had regarded as one of his historic achievements. Then in April came the embarrassing failure of the top-secret Delta Force hostage rescue mission, in which helicopters failed in the Iranian desert before a midair collision between a helicopter and a transport plane killed eight military personnel and badly burned five others.

All of this took place amid an election year backdrop in which Carter was bracing for a Republican challenge from the conservative right while fending off a bruising challenge from Ted Kennedy and the Democratic left. The economy slid from bad to worse in the spring, with a prime rate of 18.5 percent, an inflation rate of 20 percent, unemployment approaching 25 percent in manufacturing centers like Detroit, falling housing starts, and a plunging Dow Jones spooked by inflation. In an effort to curb inflation, Carter proposed slashes in social programs, adding fuel to Kennedy's primary challenge. Vice president Mondale privately bemoaned the fact that his boss was "hurting the poor, raising defense to the roof, dropping SALT, alienating the Jews and even moderate liberals"; longtime advisor Jordan worried about losing key portions of Carter's political base.[58]

Carter narrowly prevailed against Kennedy at the Democratic National Convention in New York, but he was dying from a thousand political cuts. Liberals resented his cuts to education and public works. Despite the apparent success of the Camp David agreement, Jews distrusted Carter and the depth of his support for Israel. The business community was dismayed by interest rates and inflation. Conservatives had numerous grounds for discontent, both domestic and international, including Carter's support for affirmative action for women and blacks, his advocacy for human rights and policies favorable to the Third World, and his perceived lack of support for defense spending and strong displays of U.S. power.

The Religious Right, of course, had its own discontents. The Iran crisis only highlighted what many evangelicals had come to believe: that America was a Christian nation beset by infidels. "Islam was contrasted explicitly with Christianity," Melani McAlister writes, "and perhaps in no other political situation in the 1970s did the mainstream media and politicians so insistently present the United States as a 'Christian' nation. In 1979, after almost two decades of slow secularization of U.S. political life . . . it was relatively uncommon for the mainstream media to evoke Christianity as a public symbol of nationalism. . . . But as 'Islam' emerged as the category for understanding Iran, Christianity became remarkably prominent in the media accounts."[59]

In this climate, leading evangelicals, including Pat Robertson, Bill Bright, and James Robison, organized a day-long "Washington for Jesus" rally on the National Mall in April 1980 to commemorate the anniversary of the Jamestown settlers of 1607, who had erected a cross on the Virginia coast. The crowd was estimated to be as high as half a million, making it larger than any other gathering to that point, including the March on Washington crowd of 1963. Four months later, Robison spearheaded a Religious Roundtable conference that brought some 2,500 pastors from around the country to talk grassroots mobilizing strategies and hear speeches from the A-team of the Religious Right: Jerry Falwell, Robertson, Robison, Paul Weyrich, Phyllis Schlafly, Tim LaHaye, Senator Jessie Helms, and Congressman Phillip Crane, among others. Dr. Bailey Smith, newly elected president of the Southern Baptist Convention, made news by stating that "God Almighty does not hear the prayer of a Jew."[60] But it was Ronald Reagan who captured the hearts and minds of the thousands gathered at Reunion Arena and the millions who followed the conference on television and radio.

Freshly nominated for the Republican ticket a month earlier, Reagan had been fine-tuning his rhetoric for evangelical audiences. Divorced, lackadaisical in his church attendance, and, despite his hard-right image, a surprisingly moderate governor of California when it came to abortion and gay rights, he had some work to do. "One of the real puzzles . . . was how Mr. Reagan could capture the affections of these people," noted Baptist preacher James Dunn. "He was a Hollywood libertine . . . had a child conceived out of wedlock before he and Nancy married, admitted to drug use during his Hollywood years, and according to Henry Steele Commager, was the least religious president in American history." But as *New York Times* reporter Kenneth Briggs observed, Reagan had a deep intuitive feel for what mattered to evangelicals: "There were lots of ways in which, through direct address and perhaps through some code words, he conveyed to them that he was one of them, and that they could count on him to deliver what they were looking for in their national life and in their community life."[61]

Preparing to topple a devout Southern Baptist, Reagan embraced a variety of positions dear to conservative evangelicals: creationism, tuition tax credits, resentment that the Supreme Court had "expelled God from the classroom." He touted "traditional Judeo-Christian values," quipped that everyone who favored abortion had already been born, and claimed that the Bible was the one book he would choose to be shipwrecked with, since "all the complex questions facing us at home and abroad have their answer in that single book." These convictions were of fairly recent vintage, however. Little discussed at the time was the fact that Reagan did have a set of core Christian beliefs of much longer duration: end-times prophecy. An avid reader of *The Late Great Planet Earth*, Governor Reagan had taken the opportunity at a Sacramento dinner party for California legislators in 1971 to insist on the accelerating signs of the Apocalypse, including the founding of Israel and a recent coup in Libya. "Everything is falling into place," he was quoted as saying. "It can't be long now. Ezekiel says that fire and brimstone will be rained upon the enemies of God's people. That must mean that they'll be destroyed by nuclear weapons. . . . For the first time ever, everything is in place for the battle of Armageddon and the second coming of Christ."[62]

As much as Chuck Smith, Lonnie Frisbee, Marsha Stevens, and Keith Green, Reagan was deeply shaped by the milieu of Southern California. Just as the Jesus People had helped create a new image of Jesus as youthful, militant, and engaged in a long-shot battle against the forces that be, so did Reagan and his handlers remake the Republican Party in a way that set it against the Establishment—whether in Washington, D.C., New York City, or Hollywood. The message resonated well with a generation of baby boomers, many of whom had rejected organized religion and were casting off their wayward past and settling into the uneasy consolations of family life and middle age. The Republican Party stood for personal prosperity and traditional values—both of which were highly desirable to young adults concerned about careers, financial stability, and children beginning to reach the temptation-fraught adolescent years. Under Reagan, the GOP now evoked rebellion against the old political Establishment, against both Big Government in the United States and a godless Evil Empire threatening democratic values around the globe.

The 1980 election came down to the wire. As Election Day—and the first anniversary of the Iran hostage seizure—approached on 4 November, voters who had made up their minds were evenly split, and fence-sitters were expected to break roughly down the middle. At 2:00 A.M., Carter campaign manager Jordan got a phone call from White House pollster Pat Caddell. "The sky has fallen in," he told Jordan. "We are getting murdered. All the people that have been waiting and holding out for some reason to vote Democratic have left us. I've never seen anything like it in polling. Here we are neck and neck with Reagan up until the very end and everything breaks against us. It's the hostage thing." Caddell correctly predicted a loss of eight to ten points, a major defeat.[63]

Organizers of the Religious Right had no doubt that their efforts had been decisive. Ed Dobson sat in Jerry Falwell's truck in the parking lot of Thomas Road Baptist Church, both of them basking in news reports that the Moral Majority had influenced the election. Paul Weyrich was ecstatic to see evidence of long-awaited evangelical-Catholic "cobelligerency" that helped elect to the Senate born-again Charles Grassley in Iowa and Catholic Jeremiah Denton in Alabama. James Robison was filmed at home watching the election returns. "I think it was the Harris Poll that said the next day, 'The preachers gave it to Reagan,'" Robison reflected. "There was no question in my mind that we had really contributed. Just like religious leaders delivered in the civil-rights movement, the Religious Right—whatever you want to call them, New Right, Christian people, caring people, family people, people with traditional values, and, yes, outspoken preachers—impacted the direction of this country, and they impacted the election. There is no doubt about it."[64]

Not all evangelicals were equally jubilant, of course. Johnny Cash had been a big admirer of James Robison, but still he was sorry to see Carter go. It wasn't that Cash didn't like the new president; he found him "a genuinely nice man . . . very friendly and down to earth." There was something missing, though. Cash remembered running into Loretta Lynn and her husband at a function in the Reagan White House. "Jimmy Carter and his people were recently gone from office, and we didn't know any of the new crowd," Cash recalled. "Loretta came up to me at one point and said, 'It just don't feel right, does it, Johnny?' 'What doesn't?' I replied. 'Reagan in the White House,' she said. I had to agree. 'Yeah, it felt pretty good with Carter here, didn't it?' 'It sure did,' she said, sadly."[65]

# EPILOGUE

Did Christian rock help usher in the Reagan Revolution? That it changed the way American evangelicals worship and locate themselves socially is indisputable. Worship music is not theologically neutral; the tunes and texts of songs carry powerful messages about belief, both implicit and explicit. Likewise, if the preceding chapters have shown anything it is that theology is not politically neutral. Music shapes how people make sense of themselves, God, and the world, and these beliefs have important consequences for how they live their lives—including which candidates get their votes. Musicians of the Jesus Movement provided the original model for congregational praise music that has revolutionized worship in evangelical churches. And they helped create the basis for a kind of parallel universe of Christian music, so that listeners can surround themselves 24/7 with music that sounds like mainstream pop music but has lyrics with Christian content. Both of these have changed the political valence of evangelicalism. But what larger significance did the musical fruit of the Jesus Movement have?

Despite some extraordinary political swings over the past generation, the historical bloc over which Ronald Reagan presides as symbol and inspiration still exerts a strong hold on American society. Christian popular music has played a part in maintaining this bloc. "The greatest long-term impact of the

[Jesus] movement," Robert Ellwood observed presciently in 1973, "may be in that it held a generation of young people of evangelical background to their churches."[1] To use the language of marketing, it helped rebrand Christianity for baby boomers. By helping make worship more relevant and comfortable for generations of evangelicals born since World War II, Christian rock and CCM have helped spur the rise of what sociologist Donald Miller calls "new paradigm churches."

Miller contends that churches like Calvary and the Vineyard (now generally dubbed "megachurches") extended the therapeutic, individualistic, and antiestablishment ethos of the sixties into new precincts of American society. These rapidly proliferating congregations created a nonjudgmental space for people to be open about themselves without embracing the tendencies toward narcissism and self-fulfillment coursing through secular society. New paradigm churches emphasized a strongly personalized Gospel free of prescribed readings of scripture or liturgy but also stressed personal accountability and commitment to a larger purpose beyond self-actualization. Finally, these institutions rejected religious routines and bureaucratic forms while stressing the vital importance of the church community, not simply on Sunday mornings but throughout the week.[2]

And these churches tended to attract politically conservative members, to encourage their conservative tendencies, or both. This is the moment to turn away from broad cultural conjectures to more empirical reckonings. In a broad survey of members of new paradigm churches, including Calvary and Vineyard, Miller found that only 6 percent identified themselves as slightly liberal, liberal, or extremely liberal; 68 percent considered themselves slightly conservative, conservative, or extremely conservative. In the 1992 presidential election, 70 percent of these Christians voted for George H. W. Bush, while 8 percent supported Bill Clinton. Of the pastors surveyed at Calvary and Vineyard, only 3 percent of Vineyard pastors considered themselves even slightly liberal; 85 percent considered themselves conservative or slightly conservative, as did the Calvary pastors (who supported Bush unanimously in 1992; all of 1 percent of Vineyard pastors voted for Clinton). The ministers affiliated overwhelmingly with the Republican Party.[3]

That the spiritual heirs of the Jesus Movement lean conservative is borne out by other studies. A survey of members at more than 400 megachurches conducted in 2005 found that 83 percent were somewhat or predominantly conservative, while 6 percent were liberal or somewhat liberal. Zeroing in more specifically on the Jesus Movement—the social location on which this book has focused—a survey of more than 800 former Jesus People conducted by Larry Eskridge found that 42 percent identified themselves as liberal before joining the Jesus Movement, 27 percent as moderate, and 22 percent as conservative. By the time they were surveyed between 1997 and 2004, the percentage of moderates remained basically unchanged, while the percentage of conservatives had shot up to 57 percent and only 10 percent identified themselves as liberal.[4]

These findings are underscored by the research of political scientist Jon A. Shields, who argues that conservative evangelicals have become a game-changing political force in recent decades not because of Christian Right leaders like Falwell and Robertson but despite them. "One of the great political ironies of the past few decades is that the Christian Right has been much more successful than its political rivals at fulfilling New Left hopes for American democracy," he asserts. "Far more than any movement since the early campaign for civil rights, the Christian Right has helped revive participatory democracy in America by overcoming citizens' alienation from politics." Highly publicized pressure groups like the Moral Majority that operated through direct mail had little to do with this, according to Shields, who conducted extensive analysis of election survey data along with numerous interviews; what produced electoral success was evangelicals' return to grassroots mobilization through the churches, including the use of voter guides—techniques that had worked for evangelicals in historic campaigns for abolition, temperance, and civil rights.[5]

Looking at the broad links between religious and political behavior since the seventies underscores these findings about the conservative political inclinations of sixties youth. At least as far back as FDR and the New Deal and through the seventies, a significant majority of voters under age forty supported Democratic candidates. This political generation gap peaked in 1972 when George McGovern ran for president; it was the election in which many boomers voted for the first time—and, incidentally, about the time the Jesus Movement peaked. Over the next decade, the generation gap reversed itself, so that by the Reagan era, young voters tended to support Republican candidates.

Concurrently, a worship "attendance gap" emerged for the first time. Beginning in 1972, regular churchgoers started voting predominately Republican, while less-regular attendees or nonattendees tilted Democratic. This attendance gap held steady through the eighties, giving Republicans a narrow advantage; it widened during the nineties, as the country entered the "culture war" era, and it was an important backdrop to the divisive elections of 2000 and 2004 that elevated George W. Bush to the White House. In short, younger voters were becoming more conservative and Republican, as were church-attending voters (including large numbers of boomers).[6]

In an era of electoral combat characterized by competing interest groups coupled with weak party identification on the part of crucial swing voters, these conservative evangelicals have provided a substantial boon to the Republican Party because the churches they attend are such effective institutions at mobilizing voters. And they have been expanding rapidly since the seventies, in contrast to the declining members of labor unions that have long provided institutional support for the Democratic Party. "There are more church attenders than there are union members," points out political scientist Andrea Campbell; "the nature of membership is more intensive; and churches reach down to lower socioeconomic levels. Thus the conservative Christian churches are more of a political boon for the party that attracts most of their votes — the Republicans — than are the declining unions for the Democratic Party."[7]

The political sea change that began in the seventies had a regional dimension as well. Just as evangelical churches gained strength at the expense of labor unions, so the South gained political clout at the expense of the industrial North. Beginning in the late sixties, a profound regional realignment of American culture took place. "American culture acquired a southern accent," Michael Denning writes. "Southern religions — the black and white Baptist, Pentecostal, and Holiness churches — grew rapidly: Jimmy Carter became the first Southern Baptist to be elected president. Southern musics — 'race' and 'hillbilly' — were renamed rhythm and blues and country and western and dominated postwar vernacular music."[8] Elvis Presley replaced Frank Sinatra as an icon of the working class.

"By the 1980s," Denning observes, "the 'Southernization' of American culture — and of American working-class culture — could be glimpsed when Jesse Jackson, in his rainbow coalition, was seen flanked by Stevie Wonder and Willie Nelson."[9] But it could also be glimpsed when GOP campaign mastermind Lee Atwater could jam with blues great B. B. King and exploit the cultural cachet of being a white bluesman while conjuring up the Willie Horton campaign commercial for George H. W. Bush, which helped extend the Reagan-Bush era by another four years. Atwater was rewarded by being tapped to chair the Republican National Committee.

The emergence of contemporary Christian music as a distinct genre reflects the tail end of this process. The relocation of the fledgling CCM industry from California to rural Texas and, more important, Nashville was part of this larger trend. Bernie Sheahan recalled the politics of Christian rock changing about 1980, roughly the time she moved to Nashville. "I don't remember discussing politics or lining up on sides before Reagan," she said. But soon the assumption became rooted that all evangelicals, even the rockers, are Republicans. "The tie-in between Christian music and evangelical right-wing politics is so close now that to find a Christian musician who is a lefty is pretty hard. . . . I don't know what it would do to somebody's fan base if they were playing for a Hillary Clinton fund-raiser. It wouldn't be a good move."[10]

Born in 1960, Amy Grant was too young to be a Jesus Freak, but she was influenced by "a remnant hippie group" she met at a Nashville inner-city church where she joined a Bible study in high school. She began writing songs at fifteen and recorded her first record for Myrrh a year later, selling 50,000 copies in its first year. During the eighties, her career exploded, and from then to the present, she became unquestionably the dominant figure in contemporary Christian music. Rick Tarrant remembered hearing Grant on the radio at the beginning of her career.

> I was traveling from Memphis to Dallas, and I picked up a little radio station out of Little Rock. And they were playing some Amy Grant music. Amy Grant was probably eighteen at the time, if that, and I believe they had Amy on the telephone. This guy would come on and say, *Wall, frainds and neighbors, that was Amy Grant. And we got lovely Miss Amy on the telephone rawt now. Amy, what kin the good folks expect to hear from you tonight? Yeah, an' ya goin' a sing that purty number for 'em agin?* And I just remember thinking, this is *so* hokey! I thought Amy was a bright upcoming young star and that she needed to be showcased a whole lot better than that. So that was part of the impetus for me wanting to get involved, to showcase some of these artists like Amy Grant.[11]

Tarrant began creating hour-long radio specials on Christian artists and selling them to companies in Nashville, who realized there was a niche market for this sort of programming. "I can remember some people listening to my stuff and saying it sounded too worldly," Tarrant said. "Well, finally I deduced that that meant it sounded professional. If they called me worldly, I just assumed that was a compliment."

These were the years when Christian pop music was becoming more political. As Tarrant explained:

> At the same time when you saw a lot of young people and contemporary artists coming along and people embracing this music, singing

about Jesus, it seems that it also coincided with people like Jerry Falwell and Pat Robertson bringing Christians into the political realm. Most of us go through life and we don't understand the political process, we don't understand about caucuses and all that kind of stuff. They don't teach us that in civics class. You have to learn that being a Washington insider or somehow getting involved in the political process. I can remember when Pat Robertson and Jerry Falwell began to seemingly systematically teach people about causes and how you got involved in your local structure.

I don't think the music had anything to do with that. I think [music and politics] crossed paths, maybe merged, and saw some synergy and synchronicity perhaps. . . . And maybe one became a vehicle for the other. And maybe one became used by the other. Politics learned a long time ago how to use the church, and how to use church members, whether it was the black church or the white church. Politicians were always welcome, at least down South here in black churches, to use the pulpit as a place for political speeches. And I think in the eighties we began to see more of that with the Moral Majority or whatever you want to call it. I'm sure they used the church and used Christian music to help propagate more of a social agenda.

Thinking about the long-term fallout of the Jesus Movement, Sheahan identified some more subtle effects on how younger Americans experience their faith. "I think American religion has always been individualistic, of course," she said. "But the Jesus Movement brought it into a language that was very individualistic. You know, Jesus and me. So it made Jesus my own. And the church was not the institution in between."

"The personalization of Jesus and me was so baby boomerish," Sheahan added. "The world revolves around me, therefore Christianity revolves around me. And my relationship to Jesus is now personal rather than in community." This Jesus Movement–shaped spirituality affected the way many evangelicals defined themselves politically. "It empowered people in kind of a strange way," she noted. "Even though I've said that it's individualistic, it's the power of a lot of individuals that makes a group that has political power." Characteristically, Larry Norman put it more bluntly: "I think that we defined ourselves as Christians who took moral positions on abortion—we were against it; homosexuality—we were against it; drugs—we were against it. So we've got a whole curriculum of no-no's."[12]

For evangelicals, this curriculum continues to change. Abortion and homosexuality have been joined and, in some sectors, overshadowed by other issues of concern: environmental stewardship, health care, AIDS, human trafficking, and poverty in the developing world. What role music will play in those campaigns—what songs will arise to focus attention and mobilize prayer and action—remains to be seen. Considering the last several decades, it doesn't seem far-fetched to expect that these songs will play an appreciable role in reshaping the social and political landscape of evangelicals and hence of the United States.

In other words: sex, drugs, and rock 'n' roll appear to be with us for the foreseeable future. But the Father, the Son, and the Holy Ghost show no sign of withering away. The dance continues.

## ACKNOWLEDGMENTS

Born at the tail end of the baby boom, I experienced firsthand much of the music and social change described in this narrative, but as a child observing older siblings and their friends. Powerful music came early into my life this way (thanks, sibs!). I remember poring over the stiff, brown-covered libretto while listening obsessively to my sister's copy of *Jesus Christ Superstar*. The outskirts of New York City were far removed from the Pacific spawning grounds of Jesus People. But at the Presbyterian church across the street, a newly minted youth pastor from Iowa with an early-Beatles haircut was attracting a hippielike cast of characters to the youth group. Not yet a teenager, I could only walk through their funky lounge, painted bright yellow with Peter Max–style murals on the walls.

What I knew of the youth counterculture, as well as the Jesus Movement, came mostly through the vividly photographed issues of *Life* and *Look* that piled up on our coffee table before being relegated to the basement. But there were worse ways to gain some knowledge about the wider world, and those magazines seemed to love the counterculture. Somehow, the idea of Jesus and his disciples as a band of protean hippies never seemed far-fetched to me.

My musical tastes took a very different turn from *Jesus Christ Superstar* or any of the Christian rock that emerged from the Jesus Movement. Not until more than twenty years later, in Japan of all places, did I learn that a genre called contemporary Christian music even existed. A Japanese colleague lectured on this genre he called "CCM" and even brought in copies of a magazine I'd never heard of, simply titled CCM. He was especially taken with an attractive singer — new to me — named Amy Grant.

In short, I come to this study as someone influenced by the spiritual and musical currents of the Jesus Movement but not as a product of the movement or particular fan of its music. While I count a number of evangelicals as friends, family, and colleagues — enough to know that my media-cast assumptions are usually upended by face-to-face encounters with actual evangelicals — I don't number myself among them. A church community has long been vital to my spiritual sense, however. Whatever insight or blindness this vantage point contributes to this study will be up to readers to decide.

In real time, producing a work of history can feel interminably, sometimes intolerably solitary. (Try to say that last part five times fast.) But in retrospect, what stands out are memories of the relationships and connections that made the book possible. More than previous projects, this book has brought me in contact with not just imaginary readers, colleagues, and students but with living, breathing historical subjects — how refreshing!

I first want to thank those who read the manuscript, in whole or in part, at various stages of production and offered commentary and encouragement: Jim Jabara, Mary Griffith, Malcolm Magee, Shawn Young, Christopher Chase, Sarah Lazin, Chris Mills, and Larry Eskridge (who knows more about the Jesus Movement than anybody). Others provided opportunities to present my research at several forums, including Amy DeRogatis, Hal Bush, Arthur Versluis, Eric Weisbard for the Experience Music Project, and the "Cool U" lecture at Michigan State University (MSU). For help with illustrations, thanks to David Di Sabatino, Marsha Stevens-Pino, and Peter Berg, the head of Special Collections at the MSU library. Though we've not met, Mark Powell and his encyclopedic knowledge of CCM has been invaluable for my own work. At UNC Press, Elaine Maisner patiently steered my manuscript through editorial shoals, and Jay Mazzocchi provided eagle-eyed copyediting.

Filmmaker Jim Jabara and fellow researcher Shawn Young joined me in entering a kind of Jesus Movement time machine, with visits to films and interviews at the Cornerstone Music Festival in Illinois and the thriving Jesus People USA community in Chicago; I benefited greatly from their companionship and know-how. I appreciate the great candor and hospitality of the JPUSA people, especially Glenn Kaiser and John Herren. Thanks also to Bud and Joan, whose Topanga Canyon home provided a launching pad for pilgrimages to historic sites in Orange County and up the coast to Oregon. Brother-in-law Charlie (who just missed being a Jesus Freak) has schooled me in rock 'n' roll, U.S. history, and all things evangelical for nearly four decades.

The creation of a book concerned with turbulent years and personal lives happened to coincide with a less-than-tranquil interlude in my own life, one that gave new meaning to John Lennon's aphorism: life is what happens to you while you're busy making other plans. I'm thankful to many people who extended encouragement, no one more than multitalented historian Malcolm Magee. In appreciation for his generous enthusiasm, both personal and historiographical, I dedicate this book.

As for Henry and Carolina—thanks for hanging in there and growing up so well.

# NOTES

## Introduction

1 Miller, *Reinventing American Protestantism*, 209, 210, 223; Thumma, Travis, and Bird, "Megachurches Today 2005," 7; Eskridge, "God's Forever Family," 394; John Clifford Green, *Faith Factor*, 64–66, 99–102; Shields, *Democratic Virtues of the Christian Right*, 50–54, 119–40.

2 The "new music studies" have generated a large body of scholarship. For starters, see Attali, *Noise*; McClary, *Feminine Endings*; and Small, *Musicking*.

3 Denning, *Cultural Front*.

## Chapter 1

1 Vachon, "Jesus Movement Is Upon Us," 19.

2 Interview with Thom Granger, 7 June 2007.

3 "New Rebel Cry," 59.

4 Streiker, *Jesus Trip*, 79.

5 Interview with Marsha Stevens, 9 December 2007.

6 Ibid.

7 Vachon, "Jesus Movement Is Upon Us," 16.

8 Harvey Cox, "Religion in the Age of Aquarius," in Heenan, ed., *Mystery, Magic, and Miracle*, 25.

9 Hiley H. Ward, *Far-Out Saints*; Kittler, *Jesus Kids and Their Leaders*.

10 Interview with Jerry Bryant, 7 June 2007.

11 Palosaari quoted in Kittler, *Jesus Kids and Their Leaders*, 199.

12 Interview with John Kaiser, 2 July 2008; interview with Wendy Kaiser, 2 July 2008; interview with John Herren, 2 July 2008; Powell, *Encyclopedia of Contemporary Christian Music* (hereafter abbreviated as *ECCM*), 753, 819.

13 Ellwood, *One Way*, 63–64.

14 Streiker, *Jesus Trip*, 21–22.

15 Enroth, Ericson, and Peters, *The Jesus People*, 58.

16 Quoted in Miriam Williams, *Heaven's Harlots*, 39–40; Enroth, Ericson, and Peters, *The Jesus People*, 40.

17 Interview with Thom Granger, 7 June 2007; Williams quoted in Eskridge, "God's Forever Family," 115, and Kittler, *Jesus Kids and Their Leaders*, 121.

18 Interview with John Styll, 7 June 2007.

19 Interviews with Ted Wise and Steve Heefner, in *Frisbee*.

20 Vachon, *Time to Be Born*, 5–6; Eskridge, "God's Forever Family," 95.

21 Eskridge, "God's Forever Family," 82–99.

22 Details on Frisbee's life from *Frisbee*.

23 Fromm, "Textual Communities and New Song," 172.

24 Eskridge, "God's Forever Family," 111–17 (quotation on 116).

25 Fromm, "Textual Communities and New Song," 174–75.

26 *Frisbee*.

27 Kittler, *Jesus Kids and Their Leaders*, 101–2.

28 Fromm, "Textual Communities and New Song," 177.

29 Baker, *Contemporary Christian Music*, 37.

30 Interview with Chuck Girard, in *First Love*.

31 Baker, *Contemporary Christian Music*, 37.

32 Interview with Tommy Coomes, in *First Love*.

33 Baker, *Contemporary Christian Music*, 27; interview with Tommy Coomes, in *First Love*.

34 Interview with Chuck Girard, in *First Love*; Baker, *Contemporary Christian Music*, 38.

35 In a survey of 812 former Jesus People conducted between 1997 and 2004, Love Song was voted the most influential/favorite Jesus music group, and *Love Song* was voted the most influential album by a margin of nearly four to one. Eskridge, "God's Forever Family," 401–2; Smith quoted in Fromm, "Textual Communities and New Song," 194–95.

36 Interview with Thom Granger, 7 June 2007.

37 Ibid.

38 Baker, *Contemporary Christian Music*, 58–59.

39 Fromm, "Textual Communities and New Song," 204–5.

40 Ibid., 197–98.

41 Ibid., 219.

42 Baker, *Contemporary Christian Music*, 83.

43 McGirr, *Suburban Warriors*.

44 Ibid., 240–61.

45 Denning, *Cultural Front*, 26; Ellwood, *One Way*, 11–20.

46 Shires, *Hippies of the Religious Right*, 196.

47 Tipton, *Getting Saved from the Sixties*; Kent, *From Slogans to Mantras*.


## Chapter 2

1 Interview with Larry Norman, 9 July 2007.

2 *The Best of People! Vol. 2.*

3 Ibid.

4 Cash and Mason, "Is Larry Norman Through?"; interview with Larry Norman, 9 July 2007.

5 This and succeeding paragraphs based on an interview with Larry Norman, 9 July 2007.

6 Interview with Geoff Levin and Denny Fridkin in *Fallen Angel*. Based on interviews with many former friends and associates, *Fallen Angel* makes it clear that Norman was always willing and capable of spinning self-serving yarns; his anecdotes and claims need to be regarded with vigilant skepticism.

7 Carmichael quoted in Baker, *Contemporary Christian Music*, 15; interview with John Styll, 7 June 2007.

8 Nassour and Broderick, *Rock Opera*, 39, 38.

9 Prothero, *American Jesus*, 37.

10 Heenan, *Mystery, Magic, and Miracle*, 28; Schaeffer, *Crazy for God*, 211–12; Shires, *Hippies of the Religious Right*, 89–90.

11 Lennon quoted in Seay with Neely, *Stairway to Heaven*, 129.

12 Nassour and Broderick, *Rock Opera*, 22–23.

13 Richards, *Great Rock Musicals*, 381–478; Patrick Morrow, "Sgt. Pepper, Hair, and Tommy," in Heenan, *Mystery, Magic, and Miracle*, 155–67.

14 Richards, *Great Rock Musicals*, 381.

15 Nassour and Broderick, *Rock Opera*, 21.

16 Interview with Larry Norman, 9 July 2007.

17 Barton, "Godspell Story"; Leach, "Interview with Stephen Schwartz."

18 Barton, "Godspell Story"; Leach, "Interview with Stephen Schwartz."

19 Baker, *Contemporary Christian Music*, 51–52.

20 Nassour and Broderick, *Rock Opera*, 96.

21 Groocock, "A 'Superstar' Reunion of Sorts."

22 Nassour and Broderick, *Rock Opera*, 98–99.

23 Ibid., 25.

24 Ibid., 33.

25 Ibid., 185; Sternfeld, "The Megamusical," 49–50.

26 Nassour and Broderick, *Rock Opera*, 41.

27 Ibid., 38–39; Dylan, "With God on Our Side."

28 Nassour and Broderick, *Rock Opera*, 154, 177.

29 Interview with Bernie Sheahan, 8 June 2007.

30 Interview with Larry Norman, 9 July 2007.

31 Baker, *Contemporary Christian Music*, 45–46.

32 Interview with Jerry Bryant, 7 June 2007.

33 Interview with John Styll, 7 June 2007.

34 Eskridge, "God's Forever Family," 304, Powell, *ECCM*, 819.

35 *Concert for Bangladesh.*

36 Gambaccini, "Will It Go Round in Circles," 16; Harrington, "'Fifth Beatle' Billy Preston."

37 Prothero, *American Jesus*, 229–90.

## Chapter 3

1 Details from Eshleman with Rohrer, *Explo Story*; and *Jesus Sound Explosion*.

2 Eshleman with Rohrer, *Explo Story*, 90, 92–93.

3 Interview with Larry Norman, 9 July 2007.

4 Plowman, "Explo '72," 31–32.

5 Eshleman with Rohrer, *Explo Story*, 8, 36.

6 Ibid., 5–6.

7 Plowman, "Explo '72," 31.

8 Eshleman with Rohrer, *Explo Story*, 55–56.

9 Plowman, "Explo '72," 32. Members of the People's Christian Coalition would go on to found Sojourners, the Christian intentional community based in Washington, D.C.

10 Eshleman with Rohrer, *Explo Story*, 10.

11 Ibid., 74, 76.

12 Ibid., 44.

13 Eskridge, "'One Way,'" 86.

14 Ibid., 84.

15 "New Rebel Cry," 56.

16 Quebedeaux, *I Found It!*, 188–89.

17 John G. Turner, *Bill Bright*, 119–26.

18 Quebedeaux, *I Found It!*, 32.

19 Ibid., 32.

20 Vachon, *A Time to Be Born*, 17–18; Streiker, *Jesus Trip*, 92.

21 Kittler, *Jesus Kids and Their Leaders*, 135.

22　Interview with Jerry Bryant, 7 June 2007.

23　Balmer, *Mine Eyes Have Seen the Glory*, 31–47.

24　Quebedeaux, *I Found It!*, 25.

25　Streiker, *Jesus Trip*, 73.

26　McAlister, *Epic Encounters*, 165.

27　Lindsey and Carlson, *Late Great Planet Earth*, 13, 124, 125–26.

28　Boyer, *When Time Shall Be No More*, 128.

29　Interview with Rick Tarrant, 9 June 2007.

30　Larry Norman, *Upon This Rock*. The song was voted the top "Jesus music" song in the Eskridge–Di Sabatino survey of more than 800 former Jesus People. Eskridge, "God's Forever Family," 402.

31　Interview with Larry Norman, 9 July 2007.

32　*The Best of People! Vol. 2.*

33　Larry Norman, *Only Visiting This Planet*. The album is tied for second on the Eskridge–Di Sabatino survey; *Upon This Rock* is ranked next. Eskridge, "God's Forever Family," 402.

34　Dylan, "A Hard Rain's A-Gonna Fall."

35　Cash, "Matthew 24 (Is Knocking at the Door)."

36　Baker, *Contemporary Christian Music*, 72; Gitlin, *The Sixties*, 195–97.

37　Unterberger, "Barry McGuire."

38　Interview with Barry McGuire, in *First Love*.

39　Shires, *Hippies of the Religious Right*, 150. John G. Turner notes the Explo '72–Watergate coincidence in *Bill Bright*, 144.

40　Martin, *With God on Our Side*, 97, 98.

41　John G. Turner, *Bill Bright*, 144; Ellwood, *One Way*, 91; Streiker, *Jesus Trip*, 115.

42　Streiker, *Jesus Trip*, 117.

43　Denning, *Cultural Front*; 67–77; John G. Turner, *Bill Bright*, 145–46.

## Chapter 4

1　Franklin with Ritz, *Aretha*, 151; liner notes, *Aretha Franklin Amazing Grace*. Unless otherwise identified, quotations are transcribed from the sound recording.

2　Bego, *Aretha Franklin*, 153.

3　Franklin with Ritz, *Aretha*, 151; Bego, *Aretha Franklin*, 149.

4　Bego, *Aretha Franklin*, 152, 149.

5　Franklin with Ritz, *Aretha*, 152.

6　Powell, *ECCM*, 342.

7　Franklin with Ritz, *Aretha*, 40. Wigger, *Taking Heaven by Storm*; Cox, *Fire from Heaven*.

8　Interview with Simon (last name unknown), "NBC First Tuesday: The Ultimate Trip."

9   Hiley H. Ward, *Far-Out Saints*, 84.

10  Ibid., 88.

11  Ibid., 91.

12  Ross with Sherrill, *Scott Free*; Robertson with Buckingham, *Shout It from the Housetops*, 310, 311.

13  Graham, *Jesus Generation*, 28.

14  Eshleman with Rohrer, *Explo Story*, 56.

15  Ibid., 46.

16  Powell, *ECCM*, 210; interview with Rick Tarrant, 9 June 2007.

17  Crouch with Bell, *Through It All*, 20.

18  Ibid., 39.

19  Ibid., 45.

20  Ibid., 49.

21  Ibid., 59.

22  Ibid., 65.

23  Powell, *ECCM*, 211.

24  Crouch with Bell, *Through It All*, 105; "Andraé Crouch," 43.

25  Vachon, *Time to Be Born*, 117, 119.

26  Andraé Crouch and the Disciples, *Live at Carnegie Hall*.

27  Crouch with Bell, *Through It All*, 107, 110, 112.

28  Ibid., 113, 135.

29  Ibid., 130–31.

30  Ibid., 136.

31  Ibid., 120, 125.

32  Ibid., 122.

33  Ibid., 123, 124.

34  Ross with Sherrill, *Scott Free*, 73–156; Eskridge, "God's Forever Family," 131–39.

35  Ritz, *Divided Soul*, 149.

36  Gaye, liner notes, *What's Going On*.

37  Ritz, *Divided Soul*, 5.

38  Powell, *ECCM*, 357; Ritz, *Divided Soul*, 148.

39  Ritz, *Divided Soul*, 267.

40  Ibid., 119.

41  Ibid., 151.

42  Ibid., 151; Steve Turner, *Trouble Man*, 112.

43  Ritz, *Divided Soul*, 131–32.

44  Werner, *Higher Ground*, 48.

45  Ibid., 169, 199.

46  Wonder, *Music of My Mind*; Wonder, *Talking Book*.

47  Wonder, *Innervisions*.

48  Werner, *Higher Ground*, 197.

49  Earth, Wind & Fire, *Last Days and Time*.

50 Gibbs, "Sonic Elements," 15; Gibbs, "Earth Wind & Fire," 26.

51 Ellwood, *One Way*, 54.


## Chapter 5

1 Cash, *Man in Black*, 211–12.

2 Cash, in *Gospel Road*.

3 Cash with Carr, *Cash: The Autobiography*, 221–22.

4 Cash, *Man in Black*, 200–201.

5 Cash with Carr, *Cash: The Autobiography*, 228.

6 Ibid., 229.

7 Cash, *Man in Black*, 219–20.

8 Streissguth, *Johnny Cash*, 183.

9 Cash with Carr, *Cash: The Autobiography*, 228; Streissguth, *Johnny Cash*, 184.

10 Cash, *Man in Black*, 25.

11 Ibid., 36–38.

12 Ibid., 113.

13 Black, "Man in Black"; Cash, *Man in Black*, 87.

14 Streissguth, *Johnny Cash*, 106.

15 Cash with Carr, *Cash: The Autobiography*, 170, 176.

16 Cash, *Man in Black*, 208–10.

17 Ibid., 208.

18 Cash with Carr, *Cash: The Autobiography*, 208.

19 Cash, "What Is Truth?"

20 Cash, *Man in Black*, 197.

21 Cash with Carr, *Cash: The Autobiography*, 203.

22 Cash, *Man in Black*, 197.

23 Streissguth, *Johnny Cash*, 170, 171.

24 Cash, *Man in Black*, 201.

25 Ibid., 194; Cash with Carr, *Cash: The Autobiography*, 212.

26 Ritz, *Divided Soul*, 197; Flanagan, "Johnny Cash."

27 Interview with Bernie Sheahan, 8 June 2007. For a provocative book-length meditation on this watershed year, see Killen, *1973 Nervous Breakdown*, which includes a section on the panic over religious cults but only one paragraph on the Jesus Movement.

28 *Godspell*.

29 Nassour and Broderick, *Rock Opera*, 226.

30 *Jesus Christ Superstar*.

31 Sternfeld, "The Megamusical," 63–64.

32 Neeley quoted in Nassour and Broderick, *Rock Opera*, 240–41.

33 Fox, "Jesus as a Celebrity," 6; Fox, *Jesus in America*, 379.

34 Fox, *Jesus in America*, 377–80 (quotation on 380).

35  Kernochan and Smith, *Marjoe.*

36  Canby, "Marjoe."

37  Kernochan, "Resurrecting 'Marjoe.'"


## Chapter 6

1   Green with Seay, *Take Me to the River*, 314.

2   Ibid., 314.

3   Ibid., 315–16.

4   Ibid., 240.

5   Ibid., 275, 217.

6   Ibid., 277, 279, 280.

7   *Gospel According to Al Green.*

8   Green with Seay, *Take Me to the River*, 289, 304, 305.

9   *Gospel According to Al Green.*

10  Green with Seay, *Take Me to the River*, 300, 313.

11  King, "Love and Unhappiness," 191.

12  Green with Seay, *Take Me to the River*, 290–91.

13  Seay with Neely, *Stairway to Heaven*, 97.

14  Walker, *Laurel Canyon*, 203.

15  Green with Seay, *Take Me to the River*, 163–64, 275.

16  Matthew Ward, *My 2nd Chapter*, 124–25.

17  Crouch with Bell, *Through It All*, 123–24.

18  Ross with Sherrill, *Scott Free*, 31.

19  Ibid., 122.

20  Ibid., 122–23.

21  Ibid., 150–53.

22  Interview with Jerry Bryant, 7 June 2007; Green and Hazard, *No Compromise*, 113.

23  "New Rebel Cry," 61.

24  McFadden, *Jesus Revolution*, 189–90.

25  Graham, *Jesus Generation*, 71.

26  Ibid., 80, 86.

27  Hiley H. Ward, *Far-Out Saints*, 98, 93, 95; Enroth, Ericson, and Peters, *The Jesus People*, 219.

28  Hiley H. Ward, *Far-Out Saints*, 94; Streiker, *Jesus Trip*, 109–11.

29  "NBC First Tuesday: The Ultimate Trip"; McFadden, *Jesus Revolution*, 106.

30  Bailey, *Sex in the Heartland*, 10.

31  Ritz, *Divided Soul*, 178, 175.

32  Steve Turner, *Trouble Man*, 135, 136.

33  Cahill, "The Spirit, the Flesh, and Marvin Gaye," 42–43.

34  Douglas, "Marvin Gaye," 54.

35 Steve Turner, *Trouble Man*, 144.

36 Tweed, *Crossing and Dwelling*, 54, 158.


## Chapter 7

1 Baker, *Contemporary Christian Music*, 86–95.

2 Davis with Gallagher, *Letting down My Hair*, 116–17, 222–23.

3 Unterberger, "Barry McGuire."

4 Ibid.

5 Green and Hazard, *No Compromise*, 75.

6 McGuire, "Dolphins," *To the Bride*.

7 McGuire, "Shock Absorbers," *To the Bride*.

8 McGuire, "Jesus People," *To the Bride*.

9 Interview with Annie Herring, in *First Love*.

10 Matthew Ward, *My 2nd Chapter*, 6, 45.

11 Ibid., 122, 77.

12 Ibid., 7–8.

13 Ibid., 109.

14 Biographical details on Green's life are drawn from Green and Hazard, *No Compromise*.

15 Ibid., 72, 73.

16 Ibid., 79.

17 Ibid., 83.

18 Ibid., 126.

19 Ibid., 99–100, 113.

20 Ibid., 90.

21 E-mail from Bill Dwyer, 24 September 2007.

22 Interview with Larry Norman, 9 July 2007.

23 Green and Hazard, *No Compromise*, 134.

24 Ibid., 75–76.

25 Ibid., 131, 142.

26 Ibid., 144.

27 Ibid., 94.

28 Ellwood, *One Way*, 54.

29 McGuire, "Anyone but Jesus," *To the Bride*.

30 "Edited IRC Interview."

31 Prothero, *American Jesus*, 125; Kent, *From Slogans to Mantras*.

32 Earth, Wind & Fire, "They Don't See," *Last Days and Times*; Earth, Wind & Fire, "Keep Your Head to the Sky," *Head to the Sky*; Earth, Wind & Fire, "Devotion" and "Open Our Eyes," *Open Our Eyes*.

33 Earth, Wind & Fire, "All about Love" and "See the Light," *That's the Way of the World*.

34 Gibbs, "Sonic Elements," 15.

35 Willman, "Leon Patillo and Philip Bailey," 27.

36 Gilmore, "Baptism by Earth, Wind and Fire," 14.

37 Ibid., 14.

38 Gibbs, "Sonic Elements," 15; Rensin, "Earth, Wind & Fire," 16.

39 Berg, "John McLaughlin"; Primack, "Herbie Hancock"; Stryker, "An Hour with Herbie Hancock"; Berg, "Professor C. C."

40 Townley, "Santana's White Hope," 16; Fraim, *Spirit Catcher*, 181–82.

41 Willman, "Leon Patillo and Philip Bailey," 24. Never a Buddhist, Santana invited Patillo back a couple of years later, but the singer decided to stick with Christian music instead.

42 Ibid., 27, 28.

43 Matthew Ward, *My 2nd Chapter*, 84.

44 Baker, *Contemporary Christian Music*, 84.

45 Rabey, "Remembering the Jesus Movement," 100.

46 Baker, *Contemporary Christian Music*, 13; Rabey, "Remembering the Jesus Movement," 100.

47 Bivins, *Religion of Fear*, 89–128; Luhr, *Witnessing Suburbia*; Larson quoted in Baker, *Contemporary Christian Music*, 78–79.

48 Powell, *ECCM*, 568.


## Chapter 8

1 "Born Again!," 75; John G. Turner, *Bill Bright*, 147.

2 "Whatever Happened to . . . Young 'Jesus People,'" 49.

3 Eskridge, "God's Forever Family," 303–38 (quotation on 320).

4 "Whatever Happened to . . . Young 'Jesus People,'" 49.

5 "Born Again!"; interview with John Styll, 7 June 2007.

6 "Born Again!," 76, 75.

7 Ibid., 68; Sharlet, *The Family*, 246.

8 Scheer, "Playboy Interview: Jimmy Carter," 165.

9 Ibid., 164.

10 Bourne, *Jimmy Carter*, 273.

11 Carter, *Presidential Campaign 1976*, 24; Bourne, *Jimmy Carter*, 242.

12 Scheer, "Playboy Interview: Jimmy Carter," 165.

13 Sloman, *On the Road with Bob Dylan*, 107; Scheer, "Playboy Interview: Jimmy Carter," 165; Carter, *Presidential Campaign 1976*, 352.

14 Scheer, "Playboy Interview: Jimmy Carter," 167.

15 Ibid., 167.

16 Ibid., 166, 161.

17 Ibid., 161.

18  Ibid.

19  Bourne, *Jimmy Carter*, 348; Ribuffo, "Family Policy Past as Prologue," 9.

20  Martin, *With God on Our Side*, 148.

21  Cash with Carr, *Cash: The Autobiography*, 214–25.

22  Streissguth, *Johnny Cash*, 246.

23  Cash, *Man in Black*, 213, 242, 243.

24  Thomas with Jenkins, *Home Where I Belong*, 121.

25  Ibid., 80.

26  Ibid., 117, 91.

27  Ibid., 89.

28  Ibid., 116.

29  Ibid., 130, 131.

30  Interview with John Styll, 7 June 2007; Powell, *ECCM*, 947.

31  Interview with John Styll, 7 June 2007.

32  Powell, *ECCM*, 648–51; e-mail from Larry Eskridge, 15 January 2010.

33  Donaldson, "Billy Ray Hearn," 46.

34  Ross with Sherrill, *Scott Free*, 67; Robertson with Buckingham, *Shout It from the Housetops*, 309. (Robertson places the year as 1968.)

35  Ross with Sherrill, *Scott Free*, 74.

36  Ibid., 88.

37  Interview with Rick Tarrant, 9 June 2007.

38  Werner, *Higher Ground*, 228, 203.

39  Wonder, "Heaven Is 10 Zillion Light Years Away," *Fulfillingness' First Finale*.

40  Wonder, "Have a Talk with God," *Songs in the Key of Life*.

41  Green with Seay, *Take Me to the River*, 301–2, 327.

42  Ibid., 331–32.

43  *Gospel According to Al Green.*

44  Less, "Al Green," 19. For more than thirty years, Green has continued to preach from that pulpit, making his church a leading Memphis tourist attraction.

45  Steve Turner, *Trouble Man*, 144.

46  Ritz, *Divided Soul*, 213.

47  Steve Turner, *Trouble Man*, 144; Ritz, *Divided Soul*, 216, 217.

48  Steve Turner, *Trouble Man*, 146; Ritz, *Divided Soul*, 208–9.

49  Robert Lindsey, "Many Rebels of the 1960's Depressed," 1, 40.

## Chapter 9

1  Bourne, *Jimmy Carter*, 365–66, 368.

2  Baker, *Contemporary Christian Music*, 97–98.

3  Ibid., 102–3, 110, 129.

4  Carter, "Gospel Music Association," 1614–15.

5 Interview with Larry Norman, 7 July 2007.

6 Larry Norman, *Something New under the Son*.

7 Pam Norman, "Sweet Song of Salvation," 13.

8 Newcomb, "Larry Norman," 24; Goddard and Green, "Buzz Interview"; Larry Norman, "On Being Interview": Pamela Newman and Randy Stonehill interviewed by David Di Sabatino in *Fallen Angel*.

9 Balmer, *Thy Kingdom Come*, 9–10.

10 Interview with Larry Norman, 7 July 2009; Newcomb, "Larry Norman," 24. As with many of Norman's claims, his account of the accident has been questioned; see *Fallen Angel*.

11 Newcomb, "Larry Norman," 24.

12 Gillespie, "New Music Interview."

13 O'Neill, *Troubadour for the Lord*, 32–92 (quotation on 59); Powell, *ECCM*, 919–21.

14 Powell, *ECCM*, 166.

15 Powell, "Marsha's Tears"; Powell, *ECCM*, 165.

16 Powell, *ECCM*, 871; Hamilton, "Triumph of the Praise Songs."

17 Interview with Marsha Stevens, 9 December 2007.

18 Powell, *ECCM*, 871.

19 Powell, "Marsha's Tears."

20 Interview with Marsha Stevens, 9 December 2007.

21 *Frisbee*.

22 Ibid.

23 Miriam Williams, *Heaven's Harlots*, 40.

24 Ibid., 96.

25 Ibid., 144. After years of struggle and four more children with an Italian husband, Williams finally broke with the Children of God (by then renamed the Family) in 1988. See also Lattin, *Jesus Freaks*.

26 Martin, *With God on Our Side*, 154–55.

27 Flint and Porter, "Jimmy Carter," 31, 32.

28 Ribuffo, "Family Policy Past as Prologue," 11; Bourne, *Jimmy Carter*, 467.

29 Bourne, *Jimmy Carter*, 467; Martin, *With God on Our Side*, 207.

30 Martin, *With God on Our Side*, 189; Flint and Porter, "Jimmy Carter," 44–45; Foege, *The Empire God Built*, 101.

31 Martin, *With God on Our Side*, 200.

32 Ibid., 206.

33 Friedman, "Cat Stevens Returns."

34 McAlister, *Epic Encounters*, 20.

35 LaHaye quoted in Boyer, *When Time Shall Be No More*, 188.

36 Interview with Marsha Stevens, 9 December 2007.

37 Robertson with Buckingham, *Shout It from the Housetops*, 291; Boyer, *When Time Shall Be No More*, 138.

38  Boyer, *When Time Shall Be No More*, 203, 189, 208; McAlister, *Epic Encounters*, 194.

39  Boyer, *When Time Shall Be No More*, 265–66.

40  Ibid., 207–8, 275–76.

41  Bourne, *Jimmy Carter*, 444–46.

42  Flint and Porter, "Jimmy Carter," 34–35.

## Chapter 10

1  Green and Hazard, *No Compromise*, 197–98.

2  Boyer, *When Time Shall Be No More*, 135–36, 234.

3  Green and Hazard, *No Compromise*, 198.

4  Ibid., 214, 215–16.

5  Interview with Jerry Bryant, 7 June 2007.

6  Ibid.

7  Robertson with Buckingham, *Shout It from the Housetops*, 63–64.

8  Interview with Jerry Bryant, 7 June 2007.

9  Green and Hazard, *No Compromise*, 162–63.

10  Ibid., 182–83.

11  Ibid., 190–91, 195.

12  Ibid., 233.

13  Ibid., 222.

14  Cott, *Bob Dylan: The Essential Interviews*, 234; Marshall with Ford, *Restless Pilgrim*, 5.

15  Stookey, "Bob Dylan Finds His Source"; Marshall with Ford, *Restless Pilgrim*, 10.

16  Cott, *Bob Dylan: The Essential Interviews*, 230.

17  Dylan, *Chronicles*, 124.

18  Prothero, *American Jesus*, 229–66.

19  Marshall with Ford, *Restless Pilgrim*, 95–96.

20  Cott, *Bob Dylan: The Essential Interviews*, 301.

21  Miller, *Reinventing American Protestantism*, 47; Wimber, *John Wimber*, 151.

22  Interview with Mitch Glaser, in *Bob Dylan 1975–1981*.

23  E-mail from Bill Dwyer, 24 September 2007.

24  Ibid.

25  Cott, *Bob Dylan: The Essential Interviews*, 184.

26  Marshall with Ford, *Restless Pilgrim*, 21–30 (quotation on 24).

27  Heylin, *Bob Dylan*, 316.

28  Interview with Bill Dwyer, 3 July 2007; interview with Jerry Bryant, 7 June 2007.

29  Interview with Bill Dwyer, 3 July 2007.

30  Wooding, "'Please Pray for Bob Dylan'"; Heylin, *Bob Dylan*, 323.

31  Wooding, "'Please Pray for Bob Dylan'"; Marshall with Ford, *Restless Pilgrim*, 31.

32 Interview with Jerry Bryant, 7 June 2007.

33 Wooding, "'Please Pray for Bob Dylan.'"

34 Interview with Jerry Bryant, 7 June 2007.

35 Don Williams, *Bob Dylan*, 17; Marshall with Ford, *Restless Pilgrim*, 41–42.

36 Interview with Joel Selvin, in *Bob Dylan 1975–1981*.

37 Marshall with Ford, *Restless Pilgrim*, 148.

38 Interview with Larry Norman, 9 July 2007.

39 Heylin, *Saved!*, 12–13.

40 Ibid., 107.

41 Ibid., 84, 102.

42 Ibid., 65, 98–99.

43 Ibid., 100, 39–41.

44 *The Gospel Years, 1979–1980.*

45 Paul Williams, *Dylan—What Happened?*, 8. Williams was inspired to bang out his book explaining the born-again Dylan in a couple of weeks after seeing the shows. Benson, *Bob Dylan Companion*, 157–58.

46 Don Williams, *Bob Dylan*, 15, 147. Against all odds, *Slow Training Coming* became Dylan's second-best-selling album to date, surpassing two earlier masterpieces, *Blonde on Blonde* and *Blood on the Tracks.*

47 Thomson and Gutman, *The Dylan Companion*, 238.

48 Ibid., 236, 237.

49 Heylin, *Saved!*, 17–18.

50 Ibid., 57–58; Cott, *Bob Dylan: The Essential Interviews*, 305, 306.

51 Heylin, *Saved!*, 78–79; Cott, *Bob Dylan: The Essential Interviews*, 305, 306.

52 Cott, *Bob Dylan: The Essential Interviews*, 280, 344.

53 Ibid., 344; Heylin, *Saved!*, 81. Much later, Dylan would confide in a memoir that his "favorite politician was Senator Barry Goldwater, who reminded me of Tom Mix, and there wasn't any way to explain that to anybody." Dylan, *Chronicles*, 283.

54 Cott, *Bob Dylan: The Essential Interviews*, 292–93.

55 Ibid., 288, 291; Heylin, *Saved!*, 21.

56 Cott, *Bob Dylan: The Essential Interviews*, 291, 276.

57 McAlister, *Epic Encounters*, 207; Jordan, *Crisis*, 459.

58 Bourne, *Jimmy Carter*, 458.

59 McAlister, *Epic Encounters*, 211.

60 Martin, *With God on Our Side*, 212, 214–15.

61 Bourne, *Jimmy Carter*, 468; Martin, *With God on Our Side*, 208–9.

62 Martin, *With God on Our Side*, 217–18; Boyer, *When Time Shall Be No More*, 142, 162.

63 Jordan, *Crisis*, 365–66.

64 Martin, *With God On Our Side*, 220.

65 Cash with Carr, *Cash: The Autobiography*, 214.

## Epilogue

1 Ellwood, *One Way*, 135.

2 Miller, *Reinventing American Protestantism*, 21–22.

3 Ibid., 209, 210, 223. Miller's results were based on more than 3,500 responses by church attenders and nearly 400 responses by senior pastors.

4 Thumma, Travis, and Bird, "Megachurches Today 2005," 7; Eskridge, "God's Forever Family," 394.

5 Shields, *Democratic Virtues of the Christian Right*, 153, 50–54, 119–40.

6 John Clifford Green, *Faith Factor*, 64–66, 99–102.

7 Andrea Louise Campbell, "Parties, Electoral Participation, and Shifting Voting Blocks," 93–94.

8 Denning, *Cultural Front*, 467.

9 Denning, *Culture in the Age of Three Worlds*, 230.

10 Interview with Bernie Sheahan, June 2007.

11 Interview with Rick Tarrant, June 2007.

12 Interview with Bernie Sheahan, June 2007; interview with Larry Norman, 9 July 2007.

# BIBLIOGRAPHY

## Interviews

"Brother Ray," Bushnell, Ill., 1 July 2008

Jerry Bryant, Nashville, 7 June 2007

Tom Cameron, Bushnell, Ill., 1 July 2008

Bill Dwyer, telephone, 3 July 2007; e-mail, 24 September 2007

Charles Fromm, telephone, 30 May 2007

Thom Granger, Nashville, 7 June 2007

John Herren, Bushnell, Ill., 2 July 2008; Chicago, 23 February 2009

Glenn Kaiser, Bushnell, Ill., 2 July 2008; Chicago, 23 February 2009

Wendy Kaiser, Bushnell, Ill., 2 July 2008

Larry Norman, Salem, Ore., 9 July 2007

Bernie Sheahan, Nashville, 8 June 2007; San Jose, 7 July 2007

Marsha Stevens, Vincennes, Ind., 9 December 2007

John Styll, Nashville, 7 June 2007

Rick Tarrant, Memphis, 9 June 2007

Larry Taylor, Vincennes, Ind., 9 December 2007

John Trott, Bushnell, Ill., 2 July 2008

## Books and Articles

"Andraé Crouch" (interview). *Contemporary Christian Music*, June 1988, 43, 71–72.

Attali, Jacques. *Noise: The Political Economy of Music*. Minneapolis: University of Minnesota Press, 1985.

Bailey, Beth L. *Sex in the Heartland*. Cambridge, Mass.: Harvard University Press, 1999.

Baker, Paul. *Contemporary Christian Music: Where It Came from, What It Is, Where It's Going*. Westchester, Ill.: Crossway Books, 1985.

———. "Whatever Happened to . . . ? Randy Matthews." *Contemporary Christian Music*, December 1986, 13.

Balmer, Randall. *Mine Eyes Have Seen the Glory: A Journey into the Evangelical Subculture in America*. 3rd ed. New York: Oxford University Press, 2000.

———. *Thy Kingdom Come: An Evangelical's Lament: How the Religious Right Distorts the Faith and Threatens America*. New York: Basic Books, 2006.

Barton, Joseph. "The Godspell Story." *America*, 11 December 1971, ⟨http://www .geocities.com/Broadway/Lobby/4209/index.html⟩. 15 June 2006.

Beaujon, Andrew. *Body Piercing Saved My Life: Inside the Phenomenon of Christian Rock*. Cambridge, Mass.: Da Capo, 2006.

Beck, Hubert. *Why Can't the Church Be Like This?* St. Louis: Concordia Publishing House, 1973.

Bego, Mark. *Aretha Franklin: The Queen of Soul*. New York: St. Martin's Press, 1989.

Benson, Carl, ed. *The Bob Dylan Companion: Four Decades of Commentary*. New York: Schirmer Books, 1998.

Berg, Chuck. "John McLaughlin: Evolution of a Master." *Down Beat*, 15 June 1978, 14–16, 47–48.

———. "Professor C. C. and His Amazing Perpetual Communication Company." *Down Beat*, 25 March 1976, 12–14.

Bivins, Jason C. *Religion of Fear: The Politics of Horror in Conservative Evangelicalism*. New York: Oxford University Press, 2008.

Black, C. Clifton. "The Man in Black: Johnny Cash—1932–2003." *Christian Century*, 4 October 2003, ⟨www.findarticles.com/p/articles/mi/m1058/is_20_120/ai_ 109132328/print⟩. 23 October 2006.

"Born Again! The Year of the Evangelicals." *Newsweek*, 25 October 1976, 68–70, 75–76, 78.

Bourne, Peter G. *Jimmy Carter: A Comprehensive Biography from Plains to Post-Presidency*. New York: Scribner, 1997.

Boyer, Paul S. *When Time Shall Be No More: Prophecy Belief in Modern American Culture*. Cambridge, Mass.: Harvard University Press, 1992.

Bryant, Jerry. "Remembering Keith Green." Article in author's possession.

Burns, Carolyn A. "Settling in with Leon Patillo." *Contemporary Christian Music*, June 1982, 12–14.

Cahill, Tim. "The Spirit, the Flesh and Marvin Gaye." *Rolling Stone*, 11 April 1974, 40, 42–44.

Campbell, Andrea Louise. "Parties, Electoral Participation, and Shifting Voting Blocks." In *The Transformation of American Politics: Activist Government and the Rise of Conservatism*, edited by Paul Pierson and Theda Skocpol. Princeton: Princeton University Press, 2007.

Campbell, Glen, with Tom Carter. *Rhinestone Cowboy: An Autobiography*. New York: St. Martins Press, 1995.

Canby, Vincent. "'Marjoe,' Documentary about Evangelist, Arrives." *New York Times*, 25 July 1972, ⟨http://movies.nytimes.com/movie/review?res=9F05E3D6123DE53B BC4D51DFB1668389669EDE⟩. 17 September 2009.

Carter, Jimmy. "Gospel Music Association. Remarks at a White House Performance. September 9, 1979." 1614–15.

———. *The Presidential Campaign 1976*, vol. 1, pts. 1 and 2. Washington, D.C.: U.S. Government Printing Office, 1978.

Cash, Johnny. *Man in Black*. Grand Rapids, Mich.: Zondervan, 1975.

———. "Matthew 24 (Is Knocking at the Door)." ⟨http://www.mtv.com/lyrics/cash_ johnny/matthew_24_is_knocking_at_the_door/3463644/lyrics.jhtml⟩. 15 July 2007.

———. "What Is Truth?" ⟨http://www.lyricsdepot.com/johnny-cash/what-is-truth .html⟩. 10 August 2007.

Cash, Johnny, with Patrick Carr. *Cash: The Autobiography*. San Francisco: HarperSanFrancisco, 1997.

Cash, Michael, and Steve Mason. "Is Larry Norman Through?," ⟨http://www.only visiting.com/larry/interviews/VOG/larry.html⟩. 25 July 2006.

Cott, Jonathan. *Bob Dylan: The Essential Interviews*. New York: Wenner Books, 2006.

Cox, Harvey. *Fire from Heaven: The Rise of Pentecostal Spirituality and the Reshaping of Religion in the Twenty-First Century*. New York: Da Capo, 2001. First published 1996 by Cassell and Company.

Crouch, Andraé, with Nina Bell. *Through It All*. Waco, Tex.: Word Books, 1974.

Cusick, Don. "Johnny Cash." *Contemporary Christian Music*, April 1981, 8–9, 46.

Dart, John. "'Godspell' Anniversary." *Christian Century*, 20 January 1982, ⟨http:// www.geocities.com/cugodspell/⟩. 15 June 2006.

Davis, Lorrie, with Rachel Gallagher. *Letting down My Hair: Two Years with the Love Rock Tribe—From Dawning to Downing of Aquarius*. New York: A. Fields Books, 1973.

"The Deluge of Disastermania." *Time*, 5 March 1979, 84.

Denning, Michael. *The Cultural Front: The Laboring of American Culture in the Twentieth Century*. New York: Verso, 1996.

———. *Culture in the Age of Three Worlds*. New York: Verso, 2004.

Di Sabatino, David. *The Jesus People Movement: An Annotated Bibliography and General Resource*. Westport, Conn.: Greenwood Press, 1999.

Donaldson, Devlin. "Barry McGuire." *Contemporary Christian Music*, June 1988, 35, 73–74.

———. "Billy Ray Hearn." *Contemporary Christian Music*, June 1988, 46–47.

"Donna Summer Announces New Album, U.S. Tour." *Contemporary Christian Music*, June 1981, 10, 12.

Douglas, Carlyle C. "Marvin Gaye." *Ebony*, November 1974, 51, 54, 56, 58, 60, 62.

Drane, James F. *A New American Reformation: A Study of Youth Culture and Religion*. New York: Philosophical Library, 1973.

Dylan, Bob. *Chronicles: Volume 1*. New York: Simon & Schuster, 2004.

———. "A Hard Rain's A-Gonna Fall." ⟨http://www.bobdylan.com/#/songs/hard-rains-gonna-fall⟩. 13 August 2007.

———. "With God on Our Side." ⟨http://www.bobdylan.com/#/songs/god-our-side⟩. 11 July 2007.

"The Edited IRC Interview" (with Larry Norman). April 1997, ⟨www.onlyvisiting .com/larry/interviews/internet2/questions.html⟩. 24 October 2006.

Ellingson, Stephen. *The Megachurch and the Mainline: Remaking Religious Tradition in the Twenty-First Century*. Chicago: University of Chicago Press, 2007.

Ellwood, Robert S. *One Way: The Jesus Movement and Its Meaning*. Englewood Cliffs, N.J.: Prentice-Hall, 1973.

Enroth, Ronald M., Edward E. Ericson Jr., and C. Breckinridge Peters. *The Jesus People: Old-Time Religion in the Age of Aquarius*. Grand Rapids: Eerdmans, 1972.

Eshleman, Paul, with Norman Rohrer. *The Explo Story: A Plan to Change the World*. Glendale, Calif.: G/L Publications, 1972.

Eskridge, Larry. "God's Forever Family: The Jesus People Movement in America, 1966–1977." Ph.D. diss., University of Stirling, 2005.

———. "'One Way': Billy Graham, the Jesus Generation, and the Idea of an Evangelical Youth Culture." *Church History* 67, no. 1 (March 1998): 83–106.

Finke, Roger, and Rodney Stark. *The Churching of America, 1776–2005: Winners and Losers in Our Religious Economy*. New Brunswick: Rutgers University Press, 2005.

Flanagan, Bill. "Johnny Cash: A Musician for All." CBS News, 14 September 2003, ⟨http://www.cbsnews.com/stories/2003/09/15/sunday/main573336.shtml?source =search_story⟩. 12 September 2007.

Flint, Andrew R., and Joy Porter. "Jimmy Carter: The Re-emergence of Faith-Based Politics and the Abortion Rights Issue." *Presidential Studies Quarterly* 35, no. 1 (March 2005): 28–51.

Foege, Alec. *The Empire God Built: Inside Pat Robertson's Media Machine*. New York: John Wiley, 1996.

Fox, Richard W. "Jesus as a Celebrity." *Journal of American and Canadian Studies* 24 (2006): 3–16.

————. *Jesus in America: Personal Savior, Cultural Hero, National Obsession*. New York: HarperCollins, 2004.

Fraim, John. *Spirit Catcher: The Life and Art of John Coltrane*. West Liberty, Ohio: GreatHouse, 1996.

Franklin, Aretha, with David Ritz. *Aretha: From These Roots*. New York: Villard, 1999.

Friedman, Roger. "Cat Stevens Returns, Explains Himself." Fox News, 20 December 2006, ⟨http://www.foxnews.com/story/0,2933,237698,00.html⟩. 12 September 2007.

Fromm, Charles. "Textual Communities and New Song in the Multimedia Age: The Routinization of Charisma in the Jesus Movement." Ph.D. diss., Fuller Theological Seminary, 2006.

Frum, David. *How We Got Here: The 70's, the Decade That Brought You Modern Life—for Better or Worse*. New York: Basic Books, 2000.

Gaines, Steven S. *Marjoe: The Life of Marjoe Gortner*. New York: Harper & Row, 1973.

Gambaccini, Paul. "Will It Go Round in Circles." *Rolling Stone*, 2 August 1973, 16.

Garber, Marjorie, and Rebecca L. Walkowitz. *One Nation under God? Religion and American Culture*. New York: Routledge, 1999.

Gibbs, Vernon. "Earth Wind & Fire: Memories of Trane & Motown." *Rolling Stone*, 6 December 1973, 26.

————. "Sonic Elements: Earth, Wind & Fire." *Down Beat*, 19 June 1975, 13–15.

Gillespie, Don. "New Music Interview (1980)." ⟨http://www.onlyvisiting.com/larry/interviews/interview4.html⟩. 24 October 2006.

Gilmore, Mikal. "Baptism by Earth, Wind & Fire." *Rolling Stone*, 26 January 1978, 14–15.

Gilmour, Michael J. *Tangled up in the Bible: Bob Dylan and Scripture*. New York: Continuum, 2004.

Gitlin, Todd. *The Sixties: Years of Hope, Days of Rage*. New York: Bantam Books, 1987.

Goddard, Steve, and Roger Green. "Buzz Interview (1981)." ⟨http://www.onlyvisiting.com/larry/interviews/interview3.html⟩. 24 October 2006.

Graham, Billy. *The Jesus Generation*. Grand Rapids, Mich.: Zondervan, 1971.

Green, Al, with Davin Seay. *Take Me to the River*. New York: HarperEntertainment, 2000.

Green, John Clifford. *The Faith Factor: How Religion Influences American Elections*. Westport, Conn.: Praeger, 2007.

Green, Melody, and David Hazard. *No Compromise: The Life Story of Keith Green*. Chatsworth, Calif.: Sparrow Press, 1989.

Groocock, Gwendolen. "A 'Superstar' Reunion of Sorts." *Suffolk Times Online*, 16 March 2000, ⟨http://web.archive.org/web/20070310203500/http://www.timesreview.com/st03-16-00/stories/news2.htm⟩

Hamilton, Michael S. "The Triumph of the Praise Songs." *Christianity Today*, 14 July

2009, ⟨http://www.christianitytoday.com/ct/1999/july12/9t8028.html⟩. 14 July
2009.

Harrington, Richard. "'Fifth Beatle' Billy Preston Made the Greats Even Greater."
*Washington Post*, 8 June 2006, C-5.

"Has Born-Again Bob Dylan Returned to Judaism?" *Christianity Today*, 13 January
1984, ⟨www.christianitytoday.com/ct/2001/121/45.0.html⟩.

Heenan, Edward F., ed. *Mystery, Magic, and Miracle: Religion in a Post-Aquarian Age*.
Englewood Cliffs, N.J.: Prentice-Hall, 1973.

Hendershot, Heather. *Shaking the World for Jesus: Media and Conservative Evangelical
Culture*. Chicago: University of Chicago Press, 2004.

Heylin, Clinton. *Bob Dylan: Behind the Shades*. New York: Summit Books, 1991.

———, ed. *Saved! The Gospel Speeches of Bob Dylan*. Madras: Hanuman Books, 1990.

Howard, Jay R., and John M. Streck. *Apostles of Rock: The Splintered World of
Contemporary Christian Music*. Lexington: University Press of Kentucky, 1999.

Jacob, Michael. *Pop Goes Jesus: An Investigation of Pop Religion in Britain and America*.
Oxford: Mowbrays, 1972.

Jordan, Hamilton. *Crisis: The Last Year of the Carter Presidency*. New York: Putnam,
1982.

Kent, Stephen A. *From Slogans to Mantras: Social Protest and Religious Conversion in
the Late Vietnam War Era*. Syracuse, N.Y.: Syracuse University Press, 2001.

Kernochan, Sarah. "Resurrecting 'Marjoe.'" ⟨http://www.sarahkernochan.com/
documentaries/index.html⟩. 18 September 2009.

Killen, Andreas. *1973 Nervous Breakdown: Watergate, Warhol, and the Birth of Post-
Sixties America*. New York: Bloomsbury, 2007.

King, Aliya S. "Love and Unhappiness." *Vibe*, December 2004, 186–91.

Kittler, Glenn D. *The Jesus Kids and Their Leaders*. New York: Warner Paperback, 1972.

"Larry Norman: The Original Christian Street Rocker." *Contemporary Christian Music*,
March 1981, 8–11, 25.

Lattin, Don. *Jesus Freaks: A True Story of Murder and Madness on the Evangelical Edge*.
New York: HarperCollins, 2007.

Leach, Ashley. "An Interview with Stephen Schwartz." ⟨http://www.geocities.com/
cugodspell/interview.html⟩. 15 June 2006.

Less, David. "Al Green: Soul Reborn but Sales Waste Away." *Down Beat*, 5 April 1979,
19–20.

Lindsey, Brink. "The Aquarians and the Evangelicals: How Left-Wing Hippies and
Right-Wing Fundamentalists Created a Libertarian America." ⟨www.reasoncom/
news/show/120265.html⟩. 10 August 2007.

Lindsey, Hal, and C. C. Carlson. *The Late Great Planet Earth*. Grand Rapids, Mich.:
Zondervan, 1970.

Lindsey, Robert. "Many Rebels of the 1960's Depressed as They Near 30." *New York
Times*, 29 February 1976, 1, 40.

Luhr, Eileen. *Witnessing Suburbia: Conservatives and Christian Youth Culture.* Berkeley: University of California Press, 2009.

Marley, David John. "Ronald Reagan and the Splintering of the Religious Right." *Journal of Church and State* 48 (Autumn 2006): 851–68.

Marshall, Scott M., with Marcia Ford. *Restless Pilgrim: The Spiritual Journey of Bob Dylan.* Orlando: Relevant Books, 2004.

Martin, William C. *With God on Our Side: The Rise of the Religious Right in America.* New York: Broadway Books, 1996.

McAlister, Melani. *Epic Encounters: Culture, Media, and U.S. Interests in the Middle East, 1945–2000.* Berkeley: University of California Press, 2001.

McClary, Susan. *Feminine Endings: Music, Gender, and Sexuality.* Minneapolis: University of Minnesota Press, 2002.

McFadden, Michael. *The Jesus Revolution.* New York: Harper & Row, 1972.

McGirr, Lisa. *Suburban Warriors: The Origins of the New American Right.* Princeton, N.J.: Princeton University Press, 2001.

Menand, Louis. "The Seventies Show: What Did the Decade Mean?" *New Yorker*, 28 May 2001, 128–33.

Miller, Donald E. *Reinventing American Protestantism: Christianity in the New Millennium.* Berkeley: University of California Press, 1997.

Morgenstern, Dan. "Superstar: Beyond Redemption." *Down Beat*, 9 December 1971, 13.

Nassour, Ellis, and Richard Broderick. *Rock Opera: The Creation of Jesus Christ Superstar, from Record Album to Broadway Show and Motion Picture.* New York: Hawthorn Books, 1973.

Newcomb, Brian Quincy. "Larry Norman: The Long Journey Home." *Contemporary Christian Music*, June 1989, 22–25, 30.

"The New Rebel Cry: Jesus Is Coming!" *Time*, 21 June 1971, 56–63.

"A Non-Profit Prophet? Keith Green: An Exclusive Interview." *Contemporary Christian Music*, March 1980, 6–7.

Norman, Larry. "The Growth of the Christian Music Industry." Cross Rhythms, 11 October 2006, ⟨http://www.crossrhythms.co.uk/articles/music/Larry_Norman_The_Growth_Of_The_Christian_Music_Industry/24341/p1/⟩. 24 October 2006.

———. "On Being Interview (1985–1986)." ⟨http://www.onlyvisiting.com/larry/interviews/onbeing.html⟩. 25 July 2006.

Norman, Pam. "Sweet Song of Salvation." *Decision*, September 1972, 3, 13.

O'Neill, Dan. *Troubadour for the Lord: The Story of John Michael Talbot.* New York: Bantam Books, 1987.

"Only Visiting This Planet." Cross Rhythms, December 1993, ⟨http://www.onlyvisiting.com/larry/interviews/crossrhythms.html⟩. 25 July 2006.

Oppenheimer, Mark. *Knocking on Heaven's Door: American Religion in the Age of Counterculture.* New Haven: Yale University Press, 2003.

*People! Vol. II Songbook with Lyrics and Notes.* N.d. In author's possession.

Platt, Karen Marie. "B. J. Thomas's View from the Stage: He's Fed up with Hecklers," *CCM*, March 1982, 11–13.

Plowman, Edward E. "Explo '72: 'Godstock' in Big D." *Christianity Today*, 7 July 1972, 31–32.

Powell, Mark Allan. *Encyclopedia of Contemporary Christian Music.* Peabody, Mass.: Hendrickson Publishers, 2002.

———. "Marsha's Tears: An Orphan of the Church." *Christian Century*, 17 March 1999, ⟨http://findarticles.com/p/articles/mi_m1058/is_9_116/ai_54216308/?tag =content;col1⟩. 21 October 2007.

Primack, Bret. "Herbie Hancock: Chameleon in His Disco Phase." *Down Beat*, 17 May 1979, 12–13, 42.

Prothero, Stephen. *American Jesus: How the Son of God Became a National Icon.* New York: Farrar, Straus and Giroux, 2003.

Quebedeaux, Richard. *I Found It! The Story of Bill Bright and Campus Crusade.* San Francisco: Harper & Row, 1979.

Rabey, Steve. "The Profits of Praise: The Praise and Worship Music Has Changed the Way the Church Sings." *Christianity Today*, 12 July 1999, ⟨http://www.christianity today.com/ct/1999/july12/9t8032.html⟩. 14 July 2009.

———. "Randy Matthews . . . The Long Road to Now." *Contemporary Christian Music*, December 1980, 14.

———. "Randy Matthews: Unplugged, but Still Rockin'." *CCM*, May 1997, 100.

———. "Remembering the Jesus Movement." *Christianity Today*, 22 November 1985, 53, 55.

Radosh, Daniel. *Rapture Ready! Adventures in the Parallel Universe of Christian Pop Culture.* New York: Scribner, 2008.

Rensin, David. "Earth, Wind & Fire: Signs Rise for Shining Stars." *Rolling Stone*, 29 January 1976, 16.

Ribuffo, Leo P. "Family Policy Past as Prologue: Jimmy Carter, the White House Conference on Families, and the Mobilization of the New Christian Right." *Review of Policy Research* 23, no. 2 (March 2006): 311–38.

Richards, Stanley, ed. *Great Rock Musicals.* New York: Stein and Day, 1979.

Ritz, David. *Divided Soul: The Life of Marvin Gaye.* New York: McGraw-Hill, 1985.

Robertson, Pat, with Jamie Buckingham. *Shout It from the Housetops: The Autobiography of Pat Robertson.* Alachua, Fla.: Bridge-Logos, 1976.

Ross, Scott, with John and Elizabeth Sherrill. *Scott Free.* Old Tappan, N.J.: Chosen Books, 1976.

Schaeffer, Frank. *Crazy for God: How I Grew Up as One of the Elect, Helped Found the Religious Right, and Lived to Take All (or Almost All) of It Back.* New York: Carroll & Graf, 2007.

Schaffer, James P. "An Innermost Vision." *Down Beat*, 26 April 1973, 11–14.

Scheer, Robert. "Playboy Interview: Jimmy Carter." *The Playboy Interview: The Best of Three Decades, 1962–1992*. Chicago, 1992.

Schulman, Bruce J. *The Seventies: The Great Shift in American Culture, Society, and Politics*. New York: Free Press, 2001.

Schulman, Bruce J., and Julian E. Zelizer, eds. *Rightward Bound: Making American Conservative in the 1970s*. Cambridge, Mass.: Harvard University Press, 2008.

Seay, Davin. "Andraé Crouch: Stepping Out in Faith." *Contemporary Christian Music*, November 1979, 6–7, 38–39.

———. "Faith and (Body) Works." *Contemporary Christian Music*, December 1985, 26–30.

Seay, Davin, with Mary Neely. *Stairway to Heaven: The Spiritual Roots of Rock 'n' Roll*. New York: Ballantine Books, 1987.

Shapiro, Peter. *Turn the Beat Around: The Secret History of Disco*. New York: Faber and Faber, 2005.

Sharlet, Jeff. *The Family: The Secret Fundamentalism at the Heart of American Power*. New York: Harper Perennial, 2008.

Shields, Jon A. *The Democratic Virtues of the Christian Right*. Princeton: Princeton University Press, 2009.

Shires, Preston. *Hippies of the Religious Right*. Waco, Tex.: Baylor University Press, 2007.

Silk, Mark. *Spiritual Politics: Religion and America since World War II*. New York: Simon & Schuster, 1989.

Sloman, Larry. *On the Road with Bob Dylan: Rolling with the Thunder*. New York: Bantam Books, 1978.

Small, Christopher. *Musicking: The Meanings of Performing and Listening*. Hanover, N.H.: University Press of New England, 1998.

*Spiritual Journeys: How Faith Has Influenced Twelve Music Icons*. Lake Mary, Fla.: Relevant Books, 2003.

Sternfeld, Jessica. "The Megamusical: Revolution on Broadway in the 1970s and '80s." Vol. 1. Ph.D. diss., Princeton University, November 2002.

Stookey, Noel Paul. "Bob Dylan Finds His Source." *Christianity Today*, 4 January 1980, ⟨www.christianitytoday.com/ct/2001/121/43.0.html⟩. 6 May 2003.

*The Street People; Selections from "Right On," Berkeley's Christian Underground Student Newspaper*. Valley Forge, Pa.: Judson Press, 1971.

Streiker, Lowell D. *The Jesus Trip: Advent of the Jesus Freaks*. Nashville: Abingdon Press, 1971.

Streissguth, Michael. *Johnny Cash: The Biography*. New York: Da Capo, 2006.

Stryker, Mark. "An Hour with Herbie Hancock." *Detroit Free Press*, 2 March 2005, ⟨www.freep.com/entertainment/music/handock2e_20050302.htm⟩. 15 March 2005.

Styll, John. "Historymakers: A New Song in Music City." *CCM*, March 2006, 54.

———. "Historymakers: The Spirit of '76." *CCM*, June 2006, 66.

———. "Historymakers: Turn Your Radio On." *CCM*. Photocopy in author's possession.

Sullivan, James. "Eclectic Talent Billy Preston Dead at 59." Rollingstone.com, 6 June 2006, ⟨http://www.rollingstone.com/news/story/10503919/eclectic_talent_billy_preston_dead_at_59⟩.

Summer, Donna, with Marc Eliot. *Ordinary Girl: The Journey*. New York: Villard, 2003.

Thomas, B. J., and Gloria Thomas. *In Tune: Finding How Good Life Can Be*. Old Tappan, N.J.: Fleming H. Revell Company, 1983.

Thomas, B. J., with Jerry B. Jenkins. *Home Where I Belong*. Waco, Tex.: Word Books, 1978.

Thompson, John J. *Raised by Wolves: The Story of Christian Rock and Roll*. Toronto: ECW Press, 2000.

Thomson, Elizabeth, and David Gutman, eds. *The Dylan Companion*. London: Macmillan, 1990.

Thumma, Scott, Dave Travis, and Warren Bird. "Megachurches Today 2005: Summary of Research Findings." Hartford, Conn.: Hartford Institute for Religion Research, 2005, ⟨http://hirr.hartsem.edu/megachurch/megachurches.html⟩. 27 July 2009.

Tipton, Steven M. *Getting Saved from the Sixties: Moral Meaning in Conversion and Cultural Change*. Berkeley: University of California Press, 1981.

Townley, Ray. "Santana's White Hope." *Down Beat*, 6 June 1974, 16–17.

Turner, John G. *Bill Bright and Campus Crusade for Christ: The Renewal of Evangelicalism in Postwar America*. Chapel Hill: University of North Carolina Press, 2008.

Turner, Steve. *Trouble Man: The Life and Death of Marvin Gaye*. New York: Ecco Press, 2000.

Tweed, Thomas A. *Crossing and Dwelling: A Theory of Religion*. Cambridge, Mass.: Harvard University Press, 2006.

Underwood, Lee. "Boy Wonder Grows Up." *Down Beat*, 12 September 1974, 14–15, 42.

Unterberger, Richie. "Barry McGuire." ⟨www.richieunterberger.com/mcguire.html⟩. 5 June 2006.

Urbansky, Dave. "The Preacher's Life: Andraé Crouch, Gospel's Reigning King, Adjusts to the Role of Pastor Rather than Performer." *Contemporary Christian Music*, February 1997, 25, 27–29.

Vachon, Brian. "The Jesus Movement Is Upon Us." *Look*, 9 February 1971, 15–22.

———. *A Time to Be Born*. Englewood Cliffs, N.J.: Prentice-Hall, 1972.

Walker, Michael. *Laurel Canyon: The Inside Story of Rock and Roll's Legendary Neighborhood*. New York: Faber and Faber, 2006.

Ward, Hiley H. *The Far-Out Saints of the Jesus Communes: A Firsthand Report and Interpretation of the Jesus People Movement*. New York: Association Press, 1972.

Ward, Matthew. *My 2nd Chapter: The Matthew Ward Story*. Colorado Springs: Waterbrook Press, 2006.

Webb, Stephen H. *Dylan Redeemed: From Highway 61 to Saved*. New York: Continuum, 2006.

Werner, Craig Hansen. *Higher Ground: Stevie Wonder, Aretha Franklin, Curtis Mayfield, and the Rise and Fall of American Soul*. New York: Crown Publishers, 2004.

"Whatever Happened to . . . Young 'Jesus People' — Coming of Age." *U.S. News & World Report*, 29 March 1976, 49.

Wigger, John H. *Taking Heaven by Storm: Methodism and the Rise of Popular Christianity in America*. New York: Oxford University Press, 1998.

Williams, Don. *Bob Dylan: The Man, the Music, the Message*. Old Tappan, N.J.: Fleming H. Revell Company, 1985.

Williams, Miriam. *Heaven's Harlots: My Fifteen Years as a Sacred Prostitute in the Children of God Cult*. New York: Eagle Brook, 1998.

Williams, Paul. *Dylan — What Happened?* South Bend, Ind.: Glen Ellen and books/ Entwhistle Books, 1980.

Willman, Chris. "Leon Patillo and Philip Bailey: Counting the High Cost of Music Ministry." *Contemporary Christian Music*, October 1985, 24, 27–28.

Wimber, Carol. *John Wimber: The Way It Was*. London: Hodder and Stoughton, 1999.

Wooding, Dan. "'Please Pray for Bob Dylan' Asks His Former Pastor." 25 April 1999. ⟨http://expectingrain.com/dok/who/g/gulliksenken.html⟩. 28 June 2007.

## Films

*Bob Dylan 1975–1981: Rolling Thunder and the Gospel Years*. Directed by Joel Gilbert. Highway 61 Entertainment Production, 2006.

*The Concert for Bangladesh: George Harrison and Friends*. Directed by Saul Swimmer. Apple R2 970480, 1972, 2005.

*Fallen Angel: The Outlaw Larry Norman*. Directed by David Di Sabatino, 2009.

*First Love: A Historic Meeting of Jesus Music Pioneers*. Directed by Steve Greisen. Reel Productions, 2006.

*Frisbee: The Life and Death of a Hippie Preacher*. Directed by David Di Sabatino, 2005.

*Godspell: A Musical Based on the Gospel According to St. Matthew*. Directed by David Greene. Columbia Pictures, 1973.

*Gospel According to Al Green*. Directed by Robert Mugge, 1984.

*Gospel Road*. Directed by Robert Elfstrom, 1973.

*The Gospel Years, 1979–1980*. Watchdog, n.d.

*Gotta Serve Somebody: The Gospel Songs of Bob Dylan*. Directed by Michael B. Borofsky, 2006.

*His Land: A Musical Journey into the Soul of a Nation*. Directed by James F. Collier, 1970.

*Jesus Christ Superstar*. Directed by Norman Jewison. Universal Pictures, 1973.

The Late Great Planet Earth. Directed by Robert Amram and Rolf Forsberg, 1979.

Marjoe. Directed by Sarah Kernochan and Howard Smith, 1972. ⟨http://video.google
.com/videoplay?docid=-178629120699935619#⟩.

"NBC First Tuesday: The Ultimate Trip." 1971. ⟨http://www.xfamily.org/index.php/
NBC_First_Tuesday:_The_Ultimate_Trip⟩.

The Son Worshippers. ⟨http://www.youtube.com/watch?v=CvHSP3kT16A⟩.

Why Should the Devil Have All the Good Music? Directed by Heather Whinna and
Vickie Hunter, 2004.

## Recordings

Andraé Crouch and the Disciples. The Best of Andraé. Light Records 4874, 2005.

———. Live at Carnegie Hall. Light Records 4876, 2003.

———. Live in London. Light Records 51416 1036 2, 1978.

Dylan, Bob. Saved. Columbia CK-36553, 1980.

———. Shot of Love. Columbia CK-37496, 1981.

———. Slow Train Coming. Columbia CK-36120, 1979.

Earth, Wind & Fire. Head to the Sky. Columbia CK-32194, 1989. Originally released in
1973.

———. Last Days and Time. Columbia CK-31702, 1972.

———. Open Our Eyes. Columbia 61615, 2001. Originally released in 1974.

———. That's the Way of the World. Columbia CK-33280, 1999. Originally released in
1975.

Franklin, Aretha. Aretha Franklin Amazing Grace: The Complete Recordings. Atlantic
75627, 1999. Originally released in 1972.

Frisbee: The Life and Death of a Hippie Preacher (official soundtrack). Jester Media,
2007.

Gaye, Marvin. What's Going On. Motown 95027, 2005. Originally released in 1971.

Green, Al. Greatest Hits. Hi Records T2-30800, 1973, 1975, 1995. Originally released
in 1972.

Green, Keith. The Ultimate Collection. Sparrow Records SPD 42440, 2002.

Jesus Sound Explosion. Recorded Live at Explo '72. Campus Crusade for Christ, 1972.

McGuire, Barry, 2nd Chapter of Acts, and a Band Called David. To the Bride. Word
Entertainment WD2-886415, 2006. Originally released in 1975.

Norman, Larry. Only Visiting This Planet. Solid Rock SRD 005, 2004. Originally
released in 1972.

———. Something New under the Son. Solid Rock SRD 008, 2003. Originally
released in 1977.

———. Upon This Rock. Solid Rock SRD 969, 2002. Originally released in 1969.

———. The Very Best of Larry Norman, Vol. 1. Solid Rock SRD 904, 2003.

People! The Best of People! Vol. 1. 40-Year Anniversary. People! Records SRP 001, 1966.

———. *The Best of People! Vol. 2. 40-Year Anniversary*. People! Records SRP 002, 1966.

Stonehill, Randy. *Welcome to Paradise*. Sold Rock SRD 002, 2003. Originally released in 1976.

Thomas, B. J. *Classics*. Masters 1096, n.d.

Wonder, Stevie. *Fulfillingness' First Finale*. Motown B00004S35Z, 1974.

———. *Innervisions*. Motown B00004S363, 1973.

———. *Music on My Mind*. Motown 012157353-2, 2000. Originally released in 1972.

———. *Songs in the Key of Life*. Motown B00004SZWD, 1976.

———. *Talking Book*. Motown T6-31951, 1972.

*WOW Gold: 30 Landmark Christian Songs of the 70's, 80's, and 90's*. Provident Music Group 83061-0533-2, n.d.

# INDEX